Zanskar

The Hidden Kingdom

Zanskar

The Hidden Kingdom

MICHEL PEISSEL

COLLINS and HARVILL PRESS

London, 1979

ISBN 0 00 262998 4

Set in Bembo

Made and printed in Great Britain by
William Collins Sons & Co Ltd, Glasgow
for Collins, St James's Place and
Harvill Press, 30A Pavilion Road,
London SW1

To
Nordrup of Thunri
monk of Karsha

Contents

Illustrations

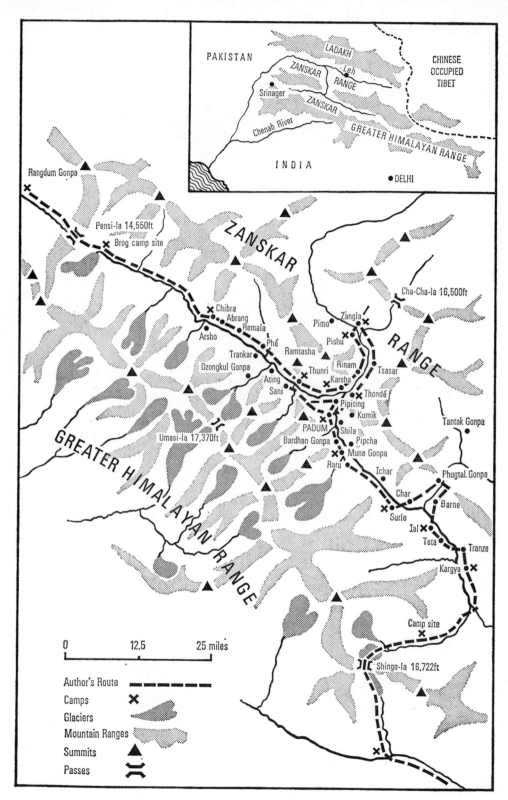

Author's route

I

Beyond Paradise

Zanskar, the 'Land of White Copper', is a land where fairies congregate. A land of black wolves and blue poppies, ibex and snow leopards, glaciers and tundra, of howling winds and freezing cold. A land populated by spirits and monks, maidens and archers, a land with cave monasteries and fast streams in which gold is found, along with that famous white copper which gave the place its name. Zanskar is a land with two kings who still lord over a feudal peasantry, the highest inhabitants of our planet. This land truly exists, yet one could search a long time to find its name on a map. At best one might find a mountain range in the western Himalayas marked 'Zaskar' – the spelling mistake being the repetition of an error made over a hundred years ago by the native secret agents whom the British sent in disguise to map the more remote corners of the Himalayas. Since their visit few outsiders have strayed there; even the hardy sportsmen who combed the Himalayas for the rare *Ovis ammon* and ibex passed by Zanskar 'because one cannot find guides'. 'Unexplored', mentioned the *Indian Gazetteer* at the beginning of the century, and strangely enough in 1976 one could have written nearly the same thing, for no one has studied the area, which at best gets a passing mention in the work of the few travellers to other Himalayan districts such as Ladakh. Yet the Kingdom of Zanskar was founded in the year AD 930, a hundred and thirty-six years before William conquered England, all this being well recorded in Tibetan texts, as I was to discover.

One of the reasons why Zanskar has escaped investigation, study, or exploration is that it is surely one of the most inaccessible and highest valleys of our planet. Two hundred miles long, the valley floor is at a staggering mean altitude of 13,150 feet, but stranger still, the valley has no entrance. The two rivers that flow in it meet to dig a canyon a hundred and fifty miles long and so deep that one cannot travel down it to enter or leave the land. Therefore the only way into Zanskar is either over the Great Himalayan Range, across passes the lowest of which is 16,720 feet, or over the barren and ill-known, difficult Zanskar Range that closes Zanskar to the north. Yet even these passes are closed eight months a year, thus completely isolating the local population.

My journey across this valley kingdom was undertaken appropriately in the year man sent a capsule to Mars in order to find out if that distant planet was inhabited by life. If that journey was one into the future, mine was truly a journey into the past. A strange past which is, I discovered, still very present in our own minds. I went to Zanskar to discover how its population survived an altitude and climate that seemed beyond the limits of human endurance, intent also to be the first to record what I felt must be a unique culture as yet unspoilt and unchanged. I knew no one had studied the region, while my special asset for such a task is that I speak colloquial Tibetan and could thus converse freely with the local population.

More important perhaps than places are people, and so I have tried to record here above all the long chain of friends and acquaintances who made my journey possible. A journey that proved to be an arduous adventure as I ended up walking about three hundred and forty miles across the most rugged of Himalayan trails to traverse, in the company of two monks, what is considered the highest land mass of our planet.

To reach Zanskar from Europe I flew first to India. At New Delhi I took another plane to Srinagar, the capital of Kashmir, set in a 5,000-foot-high valley in the foothills of the western Himalayas. From there I planned to travel by bus along the strategic military road which today crosses the Himalayas, linking Srinagar to Leh, the ancient residence of the Tibetan-speaking Kings of Ladakh, cousins to the Kings of Zanskar and their northern neighbours. Halfway to Leh I planned to stop at an ancient trading village called Kargil; from there on I was uncertain of how to travel. Such was all I knew of my route when, landing in Srinagar, I set out to meet Sonam, my only friend in that town.

I had met Sonam, a Tibetan refugee, the preceding year while travelling to Ladakh. He lives in a rather run-down brick house standing beside Dal Lake, where many of the famous houseboats of Kashmir are anchored. These houseboats are luxurious barges of elaborately panelled Himalayan cedar to which Indian merchants retire in the peak of summer in quest of mountain coolness, so also do blue-haired ladies who, with other tourists, creep out of charter planes on never-ending flights around the world. Sonam survived by selling Tibetan objects to these tourists. I needed his help in planning my journey and lost no time looking him up. I wanted his advice on securing a travelling companion whom I could trust and who might know Zanskar.

Sonam was pleased to see me and after proudly showing me his new shop, invited me to have tea in his one-room flat. There I found his plump wife perspiring on one of the two beds. At the foot of the other bed sat an elegant woman plaiting her hair.

'I've never been to Zanskar,' was Sonam's comment, 'but I have read about it. I understand it is a very beautiful and happy land, in fact in the Tibetan book I read it says it is one of the "Revealed Lands".'

'What do you mean?' I asked.

'Well, it did not exist but was found,' explained Sonam. 'The gods opened up the earth, discovered the valley beneath it and thus revealed it to existence. Because of this it is a very sacred place.'

I wondered in what book or manuscript Sonam had gathered this information, while I recalled the opening phrases of what are known as the 'Zanskar Chronicles'. 'It is a land where fairies congregate.' How beautiful it all sounded and how contrary to the visions I had had on examining my map. Leaving the subject of fairies, I enquired about finding a companion for my trip. Sonam was thoughtful.

'I don't advise you to take a Tibetan refugee,' he said. 'Few speak good Ladakhi and fewer Zanskari, and they will not know the area. I suggest you find someone in Kargil.'

'You can ask the owner of the Tibetan restaurant there,' volunteered the beautiful woman at the end of the bed. 'He is a friend of mine and will certainly find a reliable person from Zanskar for you in the bazaar, where they occasionally come to trade.'

By now I was quite seduced by this woman who had that proud and unforgettable charm of Tibetan aristocrats. Tibetan women, especially educated ones, have a rare distinction and their poise is a little unnerving for Europeans. I was delighted to learn that the beautiful woman and I might be travelling together by bus to Kargil as she was leaving the same day as I for Ladakh.

'Anyway,' she added as I left, 'the owner of the Tibetan hotel in Kargil will help you.'

For three days after this interview I rushed around Srinagar shopping for food. Experience had taught me that I would find little or nothing on the Central Asian highlands: no meat, no eggs, no chicken, as to kill is frowned upon by Buddhists. Yet, as Kashmir is Moslem, I could not find in Srinagar pork or beef either, for Kashmir is part of Hindu India. It was fortunate that I had brought a few cans of meat with me from Europe; eventually these cans, along with lentils and peanut butter, were to be my only source of protein. In Srinagar I purchased rice and curry powder along with sugar, staple commodities unknown in the mountains.

As I gathered my last-minute supplies and packed them into wicker baskets, I began seriously to wonder what on earth I was doing setting out for a place 'where fairies congregate'.

How was it that at thirty-nine I was still playing boy scout and believed in fairies? Was it that I would never grow up? I was getting to be an old child, for if I had fewer hairs on my head, my heart still thumped for the same things that had enthused me as a boy. I still dreamt of adventure, danger and excitement. My heroes were also still the same, the travellers and explorers of days gone by. I had always wanted to be an explorer, treading over virgin horizons, establishing good relations with the local people, peering into forgotten valleys in worlds I could call my own. I was and remain a dreamer, in a world of beeping satellites, fast planes, plastic spoons, aluminium airports, cafeterias, time-clocks, bargain basements, artificial sunlight and little or no mystery.

Very early I had tried to ignore the harsh realities of our modern world to search out the last places on our globe where one could still live romantic adventures worthy of my heroes. Thus it was that for eighteen years I had spent my life in lost and lonely places, either pacing the jungles of Central America or climbing the lesser-known trails of the Himalayas in quest of my dreams, of those values lost to our modern world. I had been lucky to be able to devote nearly all my time to the satisfaction of my curiosity in adventurous journeys to remote regions. Lucky also to have stumbled upon yet unrecorded ancient Mayan ruins in Central America, lucky to have been allowed to travel to the forbidden and unexplored strategic border areas of Nepal where I became the first European to study the Kingdom of Mustang, a land that had escaped observation from the West. Lucky again to receive one of the very first permissions to travel and study the remote mountain regions of eastern Bhutan. But strangely, as I grew older, I found I did not grow up: I still dreamt of my heroes, I still yearned for new horizons, yet all around me horizons were closing under the double impact of modern politics and technology. There were now no more remote areas, what with jet travel, helicopters and the immense international tourist industry. Foreigners had invaded every place of charm and beauty so that a travel agent could send anyone to Everest base camp, or to Bhutan, or to visit the temples I had found in the then uncharted jungles of Quintana Roo.

Where could I go? I who was committed to exploration and haunted by the memory of those times I had been allowed to live the thrills of discovery. Haunted by my memories of dawns in strange places without names. Had the time come for me to grow up now that I was growing old?

Such were the questions that were worrying me when I heard that at last the Indian Government was allowing foreigners into the long forbidden, strategic regions of the western Himalayas. For ten years I had been trying to go there, having even had a personal interview on the subject with Mrs Gandhi. My request had been turned down, the reasons for this refusal being that Ladakh was indeed the most strategic of all India's frontiers, what with the armies of China on one of its borders, and those of Pakistan on the other. These three nations claimed the great expanse of the western Himalayas as theirs. As a result, India had thousands of troops sent to its north-western frontier and banned all travel to that region by foreigners.

I have always been fascinated by what is forbidden, and knew that the only truly unexplored places in the world were those that were inaccessible for political reasons.

The western Himalayas had a long tradition of seclusion. Even before Maoist China, the British had considered this frontier as strategic.

Since I had such a stake in the Himalayas, I could not be indifferent to the news that I heard in 1975 on my return from a journey to Central America: 'Ladakh has been opened to foreigners'. My first reaction was one of scepticism. Why would India suddenly throw open her most sensitive frontier? Then, when the news was confirmed, I immediately made arrangements to go there. I did not even ask myself why I had been yearning for so long to reach the land of the famous Ladakhi Kings. I knew Ladakh to be as close as I could ever get to the old Tibet that no more existed. A land of monks and monasteries, of great parched deserts and craggy mountains.

I had found Ladakh fascinating, yet its charm was marred for me by the never-distant roar of trucks, and the less obvious but all-pervading presence of Indian troops. Ladakh had become one vast military depot

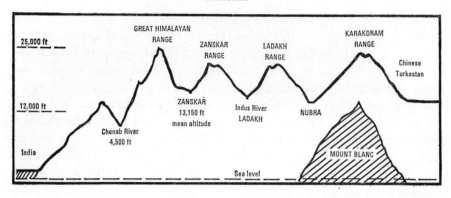

Cross-section of the Western Himalayas
illustrating that the Zanskar Valley is the highest
valley set in the heart of
the world's highest land mass

and, as such, had lost that aura of magic charm common to other Himalayan regions.

It was when in Ladakh that I had heard Zanskar mentioned for the first time. Lost, secluded and inaccessible, I knew immediately that it was there I should go.

Back in Europe, the more I had peered at my maps, the more Zanskar seemed mysterious and alluring. The high mountains that enclosed the valley were themselves isolated from any centres of habitation. I could well imagine Zanskar as a high-altitude, mountainous desert of the most rugged kind, a land of canyons and gullies given over to lonely eagles and sandstorms. I made up my mind to explore every corner of the land as I had once done in Mustang. I knew this would be an arduous task for I had never been to such a high and inaccessible place in all my Himalayan wanderings. Secretly I wished that this journey should be more than just an investigation of the area's customs, but also a pilgrimage right across the Himalayas. I wanted to cross not only the Zanskar Range but the Great Himalayan Range itself, planning to travel out to the southern face of the great mountains after having entirely traversed the highest land mass in the world. Would I succeed? I could not tell.

At dawn Srinagar seemed like a ghost town, as a rickety taxi took me down empty streets to the B-class bus station. Here was a sinister cemetery of immobile monsters on wheels populated by hawkers and beggars. I had to wait for three hours, a conspicuous figure: tall, white, prosperous-looking I was the sure aim of all the local beggars. But stations are hardly gay affairs and here at Srinagar it seemed a sadder place than most: it was a sort of purgatory to elusive destinations.

I sighed with relief when at last my bus rumbled off on what was to be a twelve-hour ride. My fellow passengers were for the most part Dards, members of a little-known race who are believed to have been the aboriginal population of the western Himalayas. An Aryan tribe, the Dards have overlong, thin noses, pointed, rounded heads and light-coloured eyes making them seem like a caricature of the European type, especially in contrast to the broad-faced Mongolian Ladakhis, some of whom had also boarded the bus. All were dressed in dirty homespun gowns, making the bus seem a den of beggars on wheels.

Behind me an old lady coughed into my neck, while before me a child stared at me while drooling over my knee. I smiled to all concerned, including a Dard beauty whose forehead disappeared under the weight of silver pendants falling from a tiara of small turquoise stones. As potholes rattled us into place smiles began to circulate.

This could have appeared a normal bus ride to the casual observer familiar with the dusty roads of India. Yet it was no ordinary ride, as this bus is the only public transport to daily cross (in summer only) the world's most formidable mountain range, the 3,200-mile-long Himalayas.

For such a rare and intrepid journey one would have dreamt of a modern machine with special gears and super brakes. Alas, our vehicle appeared sick and seemed terribly prone to flying off hairpin bends or losing its brakes; it certainly looked incapable of rising to 11,531 feet over the Zoji-la, the lowest, yet not inconsiderable, pass across the entire Himalayan chain.

The road, which followed the ancient caravan route, had been hastily built in 1963 by the Indian Army when suddenly they realised that Ladakh, a Tibetan-speaking territory they had claimed for their own, had been in part seized by the Chinese. In fact the Chinese had not invaded Ladakh, they had simply walked into its remote eastern province in 1959 and secretly built there a major road which was only detected two years later by an Indian border patrol. This is an indication of how untravelled and vast are the western Himalayas.

Leaving the 'Vale of Kashmir' as it is called, the old bus began to climb along a roaring torrent flowing between willow and poplar trees. Rising ever upwards through pine trees it eventually reached Sonamarg, the 'Golden Field', a British colonial resort for those who enjoy walks and pony rides. The first mountain ranges that had seemed distant from Srinagar were now close and clear, as alpine pastures bordered with forest slowly rose towards eternal snows. They looked more like the Alps than any Himalayan region I had yet seen.

We stopped here to drink some tea and eat rice and curry in a wayside shack before setting off again in convoy, as from now on the military road was a 'one way street': open in the morning to traffic down the mountain and in the afternoon to vehicles going up. The bus began to climb in earnest, giving heart-rending screeches of strain as in low gear it struggled up a scree slope in a series of hairpin bends. How the road could hang to the loose and damp gravel I did not know, and preferred at times to close my eyes. The fact that others had met with violent death here was soon brought home by little monuments inscribed with the names of Indian military personnel who had fallen over the cliff. I recalled the Bhutanese peasant who had once remarked to me, 'On mountain roads we have no wounded – only dead.'

I now also remembered the story I had heard the year before about how thirty-two trucks of a convoy had gone over a precipice around a bend before the thirty-third was lucky enough to stop in time and give the alarm.

The last hairpin bend led to a muddy suicidal causeway that cut right through a glacier, whose melting ice flowed under the bus. Skidding to within inches of a 4,000-foot vertical dive the bus pulled on up to the Zoji-la just as the old lady behind me was sick on her dress, while the young man before me leant out of the window in convulsions. Such are the romantic delights of modern travel, making one wonder whether the wheel was such a good invention after all.

In one last bend the road turned into the mountain and we crossed the pass. Gone in a flash was the green alpine scenery of the Sonamarg valley, gone were the trees and forests of the southern slopes: in an instant I had passed from the humid flanks of the Himalayas to the desert-like, dry tundra of its northern face. Now we drove through broad valleys hemmed in by rocky and treeless peaks stacked one behind the other.

I had at last reached the barren world I so loved. In an instant the freezing air and the crystal-clear light brought back the memories of past journeys, of those many months I had spent on the trails of Nepal, Bhutan and Mustang. I wondered whether this journey would not prove an anticlimax after the many marvellous experiences I had already encountered in the Himalayas. Could there be anything left really worth exploring, I wondered, what with buses crossing the Himalayas, a pressurised hotel near Everest base camp and tourists invading Bhutan? I knew Mustang had held out as forbidden territory, yet had not the Nepalese just rounded up the last Tibetan freedom-fighters with the intention of opening up 'my Kingdom' to hordes of visitors who alas would only too soon disrupt the harmony of this little Shangri-la?

There are few regions whose sheer physical beauty is as great as the Himalayas'. If Kashmir with its shaded lakes reflecting the snow-covered peaks is close to everyone's image of paradise, on the other hand the high Himalayas with its stark and crystal-clear light illuminating peaks hundreds of miles away is a true vision for the soul. It is all a matter of degree, and beyond doubt there is a special intensity of things at 12,000 feet in the Himalayas that brings out the gods within us.

As we rumbled on I thought of those first Europeans who had crossed the Zoji-la and reached Ladakh. The first on record was a Portuguese merchant, an illiterate man by the name of Diogo d'Almeida. He came (apparently alone) in 1600 or 1602 and was amazed by what he believed he had discovered: it was a land run by 'strange Christians whose monks recalled those of Portugal'. He reported his discoveries to the Bishop of Goa, who thought at first that Diogo had been to the frontiers of China where Nestorian Christians were known to be established. It took some time to discover that in fact Diogo was referring to a land yet unexplored called Ladakh.

The next European travellers to visit Ladakh some thirty years later were Jesuit missionaries. They passed several times through the land en route to their Tibetan missions established in Tsaparang, Lhasa and Shigatse. These various Christian missions flourished for one hundred and fifteen years until 1745. After that no European is known to have travelled through this part of the Himalayas until the arrival of William Moorcroft, one of England's most enlightened gentlemen explorers, who entered Ladakh by the Zoji-la pass in 1820.

As the bus stopped at Dras – now a checkpost – and the first town after the pass, I recalled how it was near here that Moorcroft had been given a bible dated 1586. Had this been left, or lost by Diogo or by one of the missionaries? (No doubt it had originally belonged to some missionary since Diogo was illiterate.)

Moorcroft was a medical doctor who had surprisingly specialised in veterinary sciences. His observations on Ladakh are most enlightening concerning the fauna and flora. All this we know from his diaries and papers brought over to India after his death by his native servant. Indeed, like Scott, Moorcroft and his companion Trebeck died on his one and only great journey. Moorcroft never lived to tell his tale, but it fortunately has reached us through his ample and amazingly detailed notes. From these notes written between 1820 and 1825 we learn also of his encounter in Ladakh, not far from Dras, with a man who looked like a tramp. He was in fact a young Hungarian scholar, Csoma de Körös, heading east in quest of the origins of his race. Körös was a solemn and studious young man with a bent for adventure. Although on a private mission, Moorcroft acted as an official envoy of British India and encouraged the young man, telling him not to roam around pointlessly but to study the local language. Moorcroft even gave the young Körös some money and introduced him to the King of Ladakh's secretary, a man from Zanskar. Csoma de Körös eventually went with him to Zanskar to learn Tibetan. Thus it is to Moorcroft that we owe the birth of Tibetan studies, for Körös became one of the first European Tibetan scholars (second after the Jesuit, Ippolito Desideri), and was later considered to be the pioneer of modern Tibetan studies.

Csoma de Körös was the first European to visit Zanskar. He arrived in June 1823, stayed for nearly a year and returned the following winter. Here was born his true vocation as a Tibetan scholar. Yet though we have dozens of works by Körös, nowhere in his books does he mention Zanskar, except to complain of how terribly cold his stay there was, and how he had to barricade himself all winter in a room to learn the language and the script.

I find it very strange that I have been unable to locate any manuscripts by Körös referring to his long stay in the 'Land of White Copper'.

All this made me even more curious to visit the area. It seems ironical that a hundred and fifty years after Körös' visit I had been unable to find anything more than a few fleeting references to Zanskar. Somehow all travellers and explorers seemed to have passed Zanskar by, visiting instead Ladakh and other adjoining regions. The second European on record to have been to Zanskar was Dr Thomas Thomson, who went there in 1848 but left no detailed account of his brief visit; he did not speak the language and besides, as a botanist, was more interested in plants than people. As I recalled the sparse literature on the area I was worried by the possibility that if so little had been written about Zanskar it was because there was little or nothing worth saying about the land. Could it be that Zanskar was utterly uninteresting?

pay for his horses and for his services. I was too tired to discuss details that night so I asked the young monks to return early the next morning.

At last I lay down to what I thought was well-earned sleep only to appreciate I had overlooked the fleas for which Kargil is famous. As I sat scratching myself I thought of all those travellers who had passed sleepless nights at this ancient crossroads of caravans heading for Tibet, Afghanistan, China and Sinkiang.

Protected by the mountains and set on the edge of the Suru river, an affluent of the Indus, Kargil has remained the distant and elusive goal of many a conqueror, not the least of whom was Alexander the Great. All through his troops' long marches from Greece across Asia his men were spurred on by the story of the wealth to be found in the land of the 'gold-searching ants', which many thought to be a legendary land. Eventually his armies reached the lower Indus, but they were unable or afraid to follow its course into the terrible mountains. Had they done so they could have reached Kargil, at the junction of the Indus with the Suru river, which scholars have recently identified as the land of the gold-digging ants.

The following morning Nordrup appeared, a wide grin too charming to inspire confidence illuminating his freshly scrubbed face. We discussed his wages, and when I explained that he would have to cook for me and take charge and supervise my belongings, he simply stated:

'I'm not much of a cook, as you will see.' Then he explained that there might be a truck in a day's time leaving for Pakarachic, a village along the road under construction up the Suru valley, a day's walk from the monastery of Rangdum where Nordrup's horses were waiting.

Experience has taught me to distrust trucks and be very wary of Oriental departure times and dates. Having nothing to do but purchase kerosene and a kettle in the bazaar, I set off to pay a call on the local police officer and the district magistrate to whom I had letters of recommendation. One never knows what help one may need. The region I planned to visit had been closed to foreigners for nearly thirty years, and anyway to stray off beaten paths in India, as in most of Asia, is to ask for trouble, particularly in the sensitive Himalayan border areas. The hundreds of army trucks and the several camps I had passed on the way up reminded me that the cease-fire line of the war with Pakistan ran barely three miles from Kargil, while to the east Chinese troops were entrenched on Ladakhi soil face to face with Indian soldiers. It did not seem to bother either the Indians or the Chinese that Ladakh, which they both claimed, had belonged to the Tibetan-speaking Himalayans, who for a thousand years had been the subjects of the Kings of Leh. These Kings had ruled Ladakh since the year AD 930 when it broke away from Tibet.

The police superintendent was very polite, though as a Moslem he could not understand why I should be interested in primitive Buddhist Zanskar, yet he gave me a letter of recommendation to a police officer he had despatched to Padum, the capital.

The next day I was up at dawn, afraid of missing my truck, but I waited in vain all morning for it to arrive until the rumour that a landslide had cut the road up the Suru valley was confirmed. That meant it might be days before any truck could come or go. Meanwhile Nordrup had disappeared. Angry at the delay, and my guide's disappearance, I paced the bazaar looking for him and possibly a jeep that I could hire to travel at least up to the landslide.

I soon learned that no jeeps were available and to my humiliation that the three jeeps of Kargil had all been hired in advance by a group of Swiss climbers going to Zanskar. I made my informant repeat this news to make certain I had not misunderstood him – it was true. It was bitter to discover that I had arrived too late, that Zanskar was already written on the world's tourist map. Over the years I had always prided myself on being amongst the first, if not the very first, to penetrate the remote regions I wished to study. Could it really be that Zanskar was already written up in brochures, a land ready for organised tours? Fortunately this proved not to be the case and anyway the tour did not make it. But I could not know this at the time and my bad mood was not improved with further assaults by Kargil fleas. Eventually Nordrup turned up all smiles, still persuaded the truck would arrive the very next day at dawn. He then started telling me a complicated story about his maybe not being able to accompany me all the way. I was upset, by the delay and the prospect of losing Nordrup. I appreciated that Nordrup was a little too clever, funny and fickle, so I told him point blank I wanted no monkey business, that the whole idea of my hiring him was that we should become friends and he should introduce me to his country. He replied that he was not for hire and had never worked for money but he would come out of friendship; nevertheless he had a serious problem as some of the horses now at the Rangdum monastery were not his but belonged to his fellow villagers, and others were owned by the monastery of Karsha to which he belonged. I began to wonder if my journey was not a terrible mistake. Zanskar might very well prove to be but a barren valley invaded by tourists and I a fool to go there.

It seemed a miracle that the next morning at six o'clock there was a truck in the main street of Kargil; on its blue flank was written 'P.W.D. J & K' (Public Works Department, Jammu and Kashmir).

The truck was already overloaded when my things were hurled on its back. I climbed aboard with a young Frenchman and his Belgian friend who had bumped into me the day before. The young men professed to be fans of mine and so, much as I preferred to travel alone, I could hardly refuse to give them the information they wanted as to the departure of a truck for Zanskar. It was in the company of two Europeans that I left Kargil.

I was given the honour of 'front seat', as they say in India, next to two other 'front seat' passengers in the crammed cabin with the burly driver. The co-driver rode on the sideboard as we roared out of Kargil, abandoned the major road and began slowly to head up the Suru valley. The famous valley of the 'gold-searching ants', a valley inhabited by Baltis, an ethnic group hailing from the far western region of the upper Indus known as Baltistan. The Baltis have a language of their own and appear to be a racial mixture of Dards and Mongols. Converted recently to Islam they originally were Buddhists. With their change of faith had come a change of customs, and their villages – for all the natural beauty of their valley with its many willow trees and oasis-like clusters of apricot trees around green fields – lacked the beauty of those I had seen in Ladakh. Dirty and run-down, the villages were without great interest, occasionally sporting little mosques whose small domes painted in bright, gaudy flowered designs seemed like toy structures with tiny minarets striking an incongruous note in a scenery of insolent and grandiose beauty.

The Suru valley is like a desert; not a blade of grass grows upon its stony flanks which rise majestically up to glaciers that issue from lofty snow-covered peaks. In this lunar landscape the villages seemed like green pools of vegetation and shade, delineated on the barren valley floor as great green patches on a grey tapestry.

At one of the countless halts, during which the truck's engine was watered down by the assistant driver, I clambered on top of the vehicle to join Nordrup. Covered in yellow dust he looked like a blond Mongol with dark eyes. On seeing him my heart warmed – I had really begun to like him.

At midday we stopped by a little brook which emerged from a glacier above our heads. I ate a small packet of biscuits and joined Nordrup and two other Zanskaris, for some Tibetan tea. They then demonstrated how to make toy Tibetan trumpets from a weed growing by the river. These were made by cutting the damp hollow stems of a celery-like plant; when one blew into them they gave out the exact sound of the giant, long Tibetan horns – a deep guttural noise reminiscent of a foghorn. Having finished playing a mock religious concert, amid hilarious laughter we struggled back on top of the truck. The Suru valley soon narrowed and the road which until now had been fair, became worse. On two occasions we were obliged to push and as a result my heart began to pound, for we had reached the altitude of 11,000 feet.

By three o'clock we had covered only forty miles, not much for seven hours' driving. The valley was extremely narrow and the road zigzagged dangerously along the sheer shoulders of steep mountains. All around rose great peaks whose names I tried in vain to elicit from Nordrup. Our driver eventually stopped his vehicle and explained that he could go no further and that his was surely the first truck to have come this far on such a terrible road, still in the process of being built. Large rocks had blocked our progress in several places. I did not know where we were as the map I had been able to acquire was of such a small scale that it was useless. The only accurate maps of the area are classified and although I had been allowed to look at one at the Royal Geographical Society in London and later at the Office of Tourism in Srinagar, I had but memory by which to guide me to and across Zanskar.

We did go on but the truck became stuck more and more frequently as we progressed through sand and gravel, around hairpin bends so tight that we could hardly extricate ourselves as we proceeded. Finally we became totally stuck in a bog at the head of a narrow gorge. Good luck had it that, as if by magic, from a tent nearby emerged the driver of a bulldozer working on the road. When his machine had pulled us out of the mud our exhausted truck driver declared that this time he really would go no further. Indignant, I protested, asking that at least he haul us to the next village. Reluctantly the Indian got back behind the wheel, visibly upset by the altitude, the sight of snow all around and the terrible state of the track. His apprehension was justified when a mile further up, rounding a bend, smoke began to pour out of the engine which finally broke down.

We all disembarked near the miserable village of Pakarachic. It was surrounded by glaciers which glowed in the evening sun. To the east above us rose the majestic twin peaks of Nun and Kun, 23,400 and 23,250 feet high respectively. These two peaks, the highest of the entire region, mark the north-west entrance into Zanskar. Filled with excitement I looked upon their formidable mass. All day we had travelled between rows of snow-capped mountains; now looking south at what was the north face of some of these peaks we could see ice and snow beneath us.

'What are the chances of repair?' I asked the driver's assistant whose head was in the engine.

'A couple of days,' came the answer. 'We need a spare part.'

'How far are we from Rangdum and your ponies?' I asked Nordrup.

'A day and a half away,' was the bleak reply.

'Try to hire some ponies from the village,' I suggested, and sent Nordrup down to the little, flat-roofed, earthen houses nestling at the foot of what seemed to be the ruins of a fort.

While Nordrup looked around for horses I walked half a mile up the road and came upon three jeeps neatly parked at the end of a field where a group of eighteen sturdy young men and women were busy setting up tents. This was the group from Zurich on their organised trek to Zanskar. I tried to hire one of their jeeps but I learned that the vehicles could travel no further as the road was too terrible from here on to Rangdum Gompa.

I came back to the truck from which the bundles, barrels, parcels and sacks that had composed its odd cargo had been unloaded. In the mean-time Nordrup returned with the news that there were no ponies available: they were all away grazing upon distant pastures at over a day's walk in the mountains.

In despair I pitched my tent while Nordrup sorted out those bundles of merchandise he was bringing into Zanskar.

There are two things I loathe: one is to walk along a motor road; the other is to camp beside one. I was now about to do both and this seriously offended my pride as a would-be explorer.

A first night in a tent after months of warm beds in houses is always an ordeal and the following day I was in a rather unhappy mood. The truck looked completely broken-down while an eerie dawn light struck Nun and Kun high above. How many days we would be stuck I could not tell. No one, it seemed, was prepared to carry our bags on their backs, human coolies being unknown in this part of the world where rightly beasts of burden are always beasts.

Towards eleven o'clock, six hours after rising, I heard the rumble of a distant truck which soon roared into sight. This overloaded vehicle was actually planning to go to Rangdum along the incomplete track to deliver food and fuel to the various road-building camps on the way. A little pleading and a large amount of rupees got Nordrup, the two young men and myself aboard. Seated on top of bags already perched over wobbly oil drums we set out as soon as the obstructing broken-down truck had been eased off the road.

Then there began a hair-raising ride as the driver showed off his suicidal talents, rushing rocks and dangling an odd wheel over the edge of great cliffs. I admired his skill while clinging on for life, peering over precipices that fell to freezing torrents which seemed to beckon us. At the very foot of Nun and Kun we drove level with a great glacier which fell right down to the roaring river we had been following. At one moment we stopped as we crossed a small caravan led by a handsome man of about thirty years old. He exchanged a few words with Nordrup and then rode on.

'That was Nyima Norbu, the son of the rGyalpo of Zangla.'

'The King of Zangla!' I had hardly time to look back before the truck lunged forward again. Soon we were coursing amongst the rubble of small moraines between a hedge of alternating glaciers and peaks. I had trouble in believing that so many mountains could exist. Elsewhere in the Himalayas I had seen many a lofty peak but never such a systematic series of independent ones as now arose separate and distinct on either side of us, one to every three miles, ten in thirty miles or perhaps fifteen! Exhausted and covered in dust, very bold after many a near accident, we rumbled on to a vast stone-covered dry riverbed several miles wide and as many long. We had reached a high open plain composed of marshes and gravel-covered flood land surrounded on all sides by great peaks topped in snow. In the centre of this vast plain – no doubt an ancient lake – a solitary hill rose unexpectedly, topped by the impressive red buildings of Rangdum monastery, a powerful beacon in a landscape truly fit for the gods. A cairn planted with prayer flags fluttering in the wind announced a small village of half a dozen earth-coloured, large, rectangular houses with flat roofs sporting white prayer flags at each corner.

Little children rushed out at the sound of the truck while, in fear, yaks pulled at their ropes tied to wooden rings in their noses. Monks in red robes walked among superbly attired women wearing great red, home-spun woollen gowns and amazing head-dresses of turquoises and fur.

In an instant I felt again the heartbeat of the continent of snows. I had arrived. Leaving this first village, the truck skirted the large monastery and carried on a mile and a half to a small rectangular chapel where it came to a stop. We had reached the road's end. From now on I knew my trail would be one of sweat and joy. Here the wheel lost all its rights and I parted from it without regret.

3

Blue Stones

When I awoke the next morning a thin sheet of ice covered my tent. It was the 26th of July. The sun had not yet risen as I stood stunned by the cold, listening to the eerie silence that flooded the vast panorama before me. Slowly, one by one, rays of golden light picked out the white summits deepening, in contrast, the shade which engulfed the valley floor. In the foreground rose the small rectangular monastery near which I had camped. In the distance a pony's bell tinkled beside a marsh whose pools of water reflected the light on the summits like cold steel. A beam then streaked between two peaks to spotlight the impressive red mass of the Rangdum monastery on its hill. Occasionally the air was rent by the distant bellowing of a yak, the bark of a watchdog. That morning, like all mornings, this lonely valley was awakening to life. Few places could have been more isolated than the valley of Rangdum before the road was built: a sort of desolate no man's land between Zanskar and the Suru valley, a lonely pasture for robust yaks. What with ice in July I imagined the winters here must last eleven months.

When at last the sun struck my tent, melting the ice and warming the air, several figures emerged from the nearby chapel, of whom Nordrup was one. He came forward with his jolly smile to explain that he was off to collect his horses grazing in the mountains. We would only be able to leave tomorrow. I accepted this delay with few regrets as it would give me a little time to get acclimatised. We were at 12,000 feet and to rush out immediately over a 14,500-foot pass could, I knew, have the most unpleasant effects. Modern transport, such as buses and trucks and even worse, planes and helicopters, do not give one's system time to get used to high altitudes. At Rangdum atmospheric pressure was close to half that at sea-level and the air was extremely poor in oxygen. To compensate for this one has to breathe twice as fast until, to make up for the lack of oxygen, one's body produces three times as many red blood cells as one had before. These extra red blood cells will soak in more oxygen at each breath. It takes approximately one full month to produce these cells and until this process is completed one is always short of breath, and one's heart thumps. Considerable exertion, like climbing, can be fatal and at best is very exhausting. Many people react to the lack of oxygen by getting headaches and having buzzing sounds in the ear, others have a sensation of airy lightness very close to drunkenness, a feeling that often lasts for several days. This was the feeling I now had, one of being purified by the high thin air, a certain spiritual lightness which matched my euphoric state of mind at having at last reached the fringes of the world to which I had dedicated most of my life. I now recaptured a feeling of continuity with my past journeys to the point that I wondered if I had ever lived anywhere else.

As a rule mountains are constricting, blocking out the sun and limiting the horizon; but this is quite untrue of the Himalayan highlands because the air there is so dry and clear that mountains can be clearly seen, even a hundred miles away. Because the earth is round, the most remote peaks barely show their crests. As a result one gets the impression that the world falls down below one, the feeling of being on top or on the roof of the world. Standing at 12,000 feet at Rangdum the highest peaks appeared beneath me, thus giving the mountains a vastness unknown in other regions of the globe.

The total lack of trees or bushes at Rangdum made it hard to judge distances, and from where I had pitched my small tent I could not tell whether the large monastery was one, two, or ten miles away. I could see quite distinctly people and caravans making their way across the marshy plains. The air was so limpid that I could distinguish not only a human figure many miles distant but also the colour of their robes. Light on the Himalayan northern face is not far from being akin to that on the moon, creating pitch-black shadows. This phenomenon is not so much due to the ultraviolet rays as to the total absence of water vapour in the air. The air is so dry that when on rare occasions it rains, the rain has been known to evaporate before touching the ground. In Ladakh it sometimes does not rain for several years. I wondered whether Zanskar was more humid since it was further south.

Before we left, Nordrup told me that a religious ceremony of some importance was to be held that day at the Rangdum monastery. I decided to attend, and realised that the people I had been watching out on the plain were all converging on the sanctuary.

Along with the two villages near it, the Rangdum monastery has a special status: it is outside the dominions of Zanskar and Ladakh, and belongs to a sort of religious republic affiliated to the famous Lamayuru monastery of Ladakh, the oldest in the region, situated halfway between Kargil and Leh. In spite of this independence, certain villages in Zanskar traditionally send young boys to the Rangdum monastery, and it was from these villages that most of the pilgrims to the festival had come.

Unaware that the green patches of grass I was heading for were bogs, I decided to take a short cut to the monastery. Ankle-deep in mud, I had to backtrack to the trail which circled the plain on high ground. On my way I was overtaken by a long line of Moslem traders, recognisable because of their tattered and nondescript garments. Later I was passed by a smaller caravan led by a smart red-robed Zanskari peasant with his wife, who bore a shining display of turquoise and silver charm boxes, silver bracelets and rings on every finger.

I was exhausted on reaching the foot of the monastery, where I forded a river on a fellow pilgrim's pony. The cruel, high-altitude sun was already burning deep into my skin with little respect for thick applications of sun cream. I then climbed a steep track leading to several steps and a large portal with a heavy wooden door. At its side another door led to a small outhouse which would play, I was soon to discover, a crucial though hardly religious role in the festivities. Passing through the main door I found myself in a paved courtyard crowded with children playing with two donkeys so small as to seem like large dogs. The children wore saffron wool caps, some with turquoises sewn on the front, others decorated with wild flowers. Little girls, like their mothers, wore wine-coloured homespun woollen garments hanging to the ground over loose-sleeved silk blouses of brilliant colours. The little boys were decked in replicas of their fathers' gowns, which were either natural wool or the colour of wine, with red waistbands. These gowns hang practically to the ground and have a high collar. The wool is brushed and gives their cloaks a warm and fluffy appearance.

Going through a second doorway I entered a larger courtyard, in the centre of which stood a chorten and a tall flagpole draped in prayer flags. Chortens are the characteristic Buddhist domed monuments found in a great variety of shapes all over the Himalayas and Tibet. Their shape recalls the ancient tombs of India, but chortens are not necessarily tombs, although relics or ashes of saintly monks are often incorporated in these structures. The rectangular base of the monuments is supposed to represent the earth, the rounded central section or dome represents water, and the spire – fire, while the crowning parasol represents wind. These are the four elements Buddhists believe to be the components of the universe and the elements from which man is made.

The large courtyard was jammed with pilgrims. The women were especially impressive, wearing flamboyant blue and silver brocade capes over their gowns, and leather headbands studded with hundreds of turquoise stones. I noted several the size of the palm of a hand. Such an abundance of precious stones made me wonder whether they might be mined in the area, but this was not the case as I was told they were all imported from Tibet. These turquoise-like pebbles are not cut to any particular size or shape. Although less prized than the smooth and rather lighter-coloured turquoise of Afghanistan, the rough-veined turquoise of Tibet has a particularly appealing shade and natural look about it. The head-dresses of the women were similar to some I had seen in Ladakh, yet deserve a special description for their originality and splendour.

The women plait their hair in many braids (sometimes up to one hundred and eight, a sacred number). These are then parted on either side of the head; under four plaits at the height of each temple are placed two pieces of black astrakhan fur, like dog's ears of curly sheep's wool. These elfin-like ears give the women a strange shaggy appearance, while the strands of the many plaits are made to shine neatly by applications of butter. To crown all this, on top of the head and falling to the middle of the women's backs is placed an eight-inch-wide leather strap covered with bright red material. On this strap are attached turquoises, the largest ones over the forehead, then in decreasing sizes all the way down the strip. If a woman is very rich the turquoises will all be large and their numbers considerable. Poorer women will have smaller stones and complete the head-dress with beads of rock coral (fossilised sea coral) and even turquoise-coloured porcelain beads. Sometimes a few small silver charm boxes are added to the strap. This elaborate head-dress is further highlighted by other jewellery: heavy silver and turquoise earrings, and massive necklaces, while over the woman's chest gold and silver reliquaries are carried, these being round or rectangular boxes containing sacred statues, printed prayers and blessed silk cordons collected from famous monks. The mosaics of turquoise on the head-dresses give the women a certain reptilian look, and a legend in fact claims that the head-dresses are supposed to represent a sacred snake.

I had seen many a festival in the Himalayas but never a crowd so richly attired and in such contrast to the bleak poverty and barren ruggedness of the region.

My ability to speak Tibetan soon got me invited into a dark kitchen. There I was asked to sit next to the Abbot, who was refreshing himself with countless cups of Tibetan tea. I was begged to drink and so presented my *phor-pa*, a little wooden bowl the like of which all Himalayans carry around with them everywhere. My bowl was filled three times by a young attendant, for such is the custom. The Abbot was a huge bony character in a red sleeveless gown of doubtful cleanliness, and although his tea was wretched his kindness was great. In great detail he told me all about his monastery. The monks he said were drawn from various villages tucked away in the mountains, explaining that they lived at Rangdum for one month in the year. He added that the monastery owned the grazing rights to the marshy plains around it and possessed a sizeable herd of yaks. I could hardly have guessed this by the poor quality of the butter in the tea.

The ceremony was the third day of the local *Newne* ritual, a lay observance which would end that evening with the hanging of new prayer flags on to the mast in the monastery courtyard. A special blessing would also be given with the distribution of sacred, roasted barley cakes painted red with coloured melted butter.

As we talked an odd-looking crowd poked their heads into the dimly lit kitchen to catch sight of the Tibetan-speaking foreigner. Looking outside through the door I could see the bustle around the chorten, the women in their flamboyant capes and the fluttering prayer flags. I rejoiced at having once again found that strange and charming Himalayan world so alien to the one I had left behind.

With my belly full of the Abbot's dubious tea I returned to the court-yard where the women were now all crouched in a corner eating. The men stood around looking on as children ran about playing and shrieking, some carrying minute brothers or sisters on their backs while doing all the dangerous things children do without ever killing themselves. Some were leaning over the edge of the high roof terraces, others climbing up the holy chorten or pushing each other down stairs in a Breughelian chaos. The scene was only marred by the arrival of the Swiss party who had walked up all the way from where their luxurious jeeps had left them at

Pakarachic. The local people were not impressed by this horde of oddly dressed Europeans who photographed everyone point blank, unaware as they clicked their cameras of the joking and sometimes rude remarks made about them by charming, angry young girls.

It was ironical to think that these privileged citizens of a rich society could not have afforded as many jewels as the peasants wore on this occasion. It was a reminder that our society is rich only in credit and perishable goods, and that even the richest have trouble in supporting more than two children.

Knowing the 'secrets' of such Buddhist ceremonies I quietly left the central yard to the tourists and went outside to the little outhouse where already a group of men were well advanced on the happy road to intoxication. In a low room *chang* was being generously poured out of a huge copper pot into dozens of outstretched bowls.

'The Tartars are given to drinking,' wrote Moorcroft, underlining one of the most pleasant traits of Himalayan life. Chang, called 'barley beer' by Westerners, is a brew on its own. It is in fact probably the ideal drink as it is also very nourishing. Mildly intoxicating, it rarely gives a hangover whatever the quantities drunk, and it induces a light happiness that I have never seen lead to drunken brawls. It is a congenial drink and after passing through abstinent India and the dry Arab world it was a delight to meet people with at least some avowed weakness, while friendships nurtured on the fringes of intoxication are always enchanting.

Victorians may well have been shocked but even the greatest lama in the Himalayas knows a good drink from a bad one and no religious ceremony, indeed no festival, would be complete without its floods of chang served outside the monastery gates. In certain communities special holy fields are set apart for the growing of barley to make beer for religious festivals: these are called *Newne* fields. The taste of good chang bears a small resemblance to orange juice and is pleasant to the Western palate. It is an art to discover in each village the household that makes really good chang. The best is found only in the heart of the Himalayas and even there the brews vary from house to house and from valley to valley. At Rangdum I appreciated that maybe I had struck the Burgundy of chang and more than ever I yearned to reach Zanskar.

Feeling very light and happy I witnessed amidst the cheers of the crowd the felling and raising of the giant flagpole in the courtyard, and the blessing of the pilgrims who were given little strips of cloth to tie around their necks. I had made several friends and it was in the highest possible mood that I bade farewell to the monastery, its Abbot and the crowd, to wade across the freezing stream and make my way through the yak herds towards the small chapel by which my tent was pitched. My stop at Rangdum had been the best possible acclimatisation to the new world into which I was about to plunge.

Back at camp I found Nordrup sitting in front of my tent, he seemed a bit vague about his plans and worried about retrieving the loads he had left by the broken-down truck. To make matters worse he had *not* found his ponies but had secured three others to carry me and my bags the following day. I was not very happy with Nordrup's arrangements and began to fear that he might leave me, as I could not obtain a clear declaration of his exact intentions.

The following morning I was awake at dawn, surprised at how easy it was to rise with the sun. The Swiss group, I noticed, had pitched their tents near the village of Tashi Tanje half a mile away, and I decided to visit them, chiefly because my air-mattress had sprung a leak. The idea of sleeping on the ground or of having to pump it up every three hours during the night was too much to bear. I hoped that one of them might have a repair kit.

It was freezing cold when I reached their camp which was in chaos: during the night a little irrigation canal had jumped its banks and flooded their tents. I found everyone sorting their soggy sleeping bags in the cold morning air with a look of discontent on their faces and I could illicit no sympathy for my punctured air-mattress. They had no kits and I returned empty handed. That was the last I saw of this intrepid tour: the group never made it to the capital as delays with ponies obliged them to turn back to meet their rather tight schedule.

My speaking Tibetan did little to hasten the arrival of the horses promised by Nordrup; his plans, it seemed, once again had fallen through, but I now discovered with pleasure that he was no person to accept defeat. Latching on to a passing caravan he found four ponies and a five-day-old foal. It was ten o'clock when my new friends and I turned our backs upon Rangdum, bade goodbye to the road and stepped on to the dotted line that was to lead us into the 'Land of White Copper'.

Saddle sores and blisters do not make very good reading but they cannot be entirely omitted. The same applies to the individual character of every pony one rides, as they inevitably leave a tooth mark or a kick somewhere in one's anatomy. Such are the preoccupations attendant on travelling at speeds calculated in perspiration per hour, falls off animals, the stubbing of one's toes, the wetting of one's boots and the twisting of one's ankles.

The first mile or two were bliss as I walked behind my pony whose minute foal skipped along beside it. The horses were not very robust compared to the rugged Himalayan ponies of Bhutan.

'We did not use to have many horses in Zanskar,' explained Nordrup. 'We used donkeys and dzos (cross breed between cow and yak). Only the rGyalpos (the Kings) had horses. But over the years, with a road up to Kargil, we travel more frequently to the interior and bought these horses there.'

Talking to Nordrup as we walked side by side I learnt that the inhabitants of Zanskar rarely went to Kargil before the road to Rangdum was built. I also found out that they hardly ever travelled out of the valley and that the little trade there, was generally carried on with Lahaul and Kulu over the Great Himalayan Chain along a trail hardly fit for horses.

'Have you been over the Shingo pass to India?' I asked.

'Oh yes, several times,' Nordrup answered.

I was enquiring because I was anxious about my plan to leave, not by the way I had come but by crossing over the entire Great Himalayan Range to the distant southern foothills.

Such a journey seemed ambitious, representing a distance of practically two hundred miles as the crow flies across the highest and whitest stretch on my atlas, at altitudes never below 12,000 feet and rising to 16,722 feet on the Shingo-la. Yet only this journey could acquaint me with the far-flung territories and accesses to the ancient Kingdom of Zanskar.

'I don't advise you to travel over the Great Range,' Nordrup commented. 'It is a long and dangerous journey, far easier for you to return by the same route.'

How easy was the trail we were on, I was not yet certain as I felt the first ill effects of exertion at high altitude. I always wonder how it is that I find myself so often pacing up mountain trails when in fact I dislike climbing. At least that is how I feel at first when my system is still geared to travelling seated in a chair. I was lucky to have a horse to ride although the beast was quite unused to carrying a human load, while its wooden saddle, in spite of carpets, was most uncomfortable. We were now rising up the shoulder of a mountain overlooking a barren, gravel-lined valley down which meandered a white stream that collected the waters from two glaciers falling from two magnificent peaks.

I was wearing powerful sunglasses to ward off the sunlight whose ultraviolet rays at such altitudes (we were nearing 14,000 feet) took on a lethal intensity. Through the thin air I could see every detail of the mountains as if they were but a few yards away: every stone, rock and icefall stood out clearly. The absence of any haze made distant peaks appear exactly like near ones. On all sides high summits lay hidden beneath the horizon, and as we advanced some disappeared while others bobbed up like ships at sea, or rather slow-moving waves.

One of the two young owners of the ponies had a small dog who ran around hunting, on either side of the trail. It was he who was the cause of all the whistling that echoed along our path. It took me some time to appreciate that this was the shrill cry of dozens of marmots, disturbed more by the presence of the dog than by our passage. As we progressed these animals were ever more numerous. The colour of a red fox, they sat on their tails staring at us before popping down into their burrows. It was in vain that I tried to approach one to take a photograph. I had not encountered marmots in the Himalayas before and I wondered why. They were large animals, about the size of a fox, while their burrows were visible from afar because of the pile of earth they had excavated. Marmots are appropriately called *phyi* in Tibetan, a name resembling their whistle. I presumed them to be of the Central Asian variety which has the rather less poetical name of *Marmota bobak*. Giant rodents, they live off the many Himalayan plants and their roots during the brief season in which their habitat is clear of snow. I thought they must store food in their burrows for winter for I doubted if they could hibernate for the full ten months in which this area is under snow. From now on their constant whistling was the background music to our progress, as we slowly rose amid glittering peaks towards a pass that it seemed must dominate the entire world.

Wild flowers grew in abundance by the trail, particularly edelweiss: slightly larger than the European variety. Their petals, when dried, are used by the inhabitants as tinder, which is also made from dried and shredded thistle leaves. The Himalayans today still make fire with a flint or a rock crystal which they strike against a steel blade, the resulting sparks being made to fall on tinder. One can also use as tinder, pieces of Tibetan paper fluff, obtained by ruffling small scraps of paper. I am always amazed by the ease with which fire can be obtained with a flint, that is to say by others; for whenever I tried, the result was my bashing my fingers with the striker and achieving little else than a blister.

Towards midday we stopped for a hasty meal by the wayside. Several lumps of dry horse manure provided a smoky fire which Nordrup and the two other men stoked with enthusiasm. After a considerable time water was heated and tea leaves thrown in, and then a little butter and salt. Later into this brew the three men each threw a handful of barley flour (*tsampa*), from their private store. The resulting mash was eaten with apparent delight and washed down with some tea they had drawn from the pot before putting the tsampa in it.

I have rarely seen a native drink cold water, for they consider it harmful, but a 'good glass of hot water' is frequently asked for by Tibetans. Parched by the dry air and weary from walking, I for one preferred the cold and crystal-clear mountain water. Having eaten (some biscuits and the first of my tins of meat) I fell asleep, exhausted, in the warm sun. Nordrup soon awakened me and together we saddled the ponies, loaded the baskets and kitbags. Saddle sores and a desire to spare the pony induced me to use my feet though they groaned for lower lands, while my heart, feeling the effects of the altitude, pumped away madly; my breath was short and my head full of a weariness that was only chased away by the ever more magnificent sight of the peaks around me. To the south stretched the continuous chain of the Great Himalayan Range, dozens of Matterhorn summits linked by saddle-like passes 19,000 feet high, thus beyond the reach of normal travellers. Behind these passes lay the Chenab valley and then another lesser range leading eventually to the Sutlej river. Beyond that were the low Indian plains, a world of heat and torrential monsoon rains, another universe – that of the tropics walled off from us by the formidable mountain chain. Looking east I tried to guess where the Pensi-la summit lay, towards which we were climbing. The slope so far had been very gradual, nearly flat compared to most Himalayan tracks of the eroded southern foothills.

Most impressive was the solitary bareness of the pass extending over an undulating glacial tundra. It would be two full days before we should encounter a village: this alone spoke more than anything else for the extreme isolation of Zanskar. Yet this was the easiest of all accesses to Zanskar and the lowest; even so it is closed by snow for nine months a year.

As we rose ever up I caught sight of a large herd of horned sheep and goats grazing skimpy pastures growing on soil wetted by melting snow. It was hard to believe that these scraggy-coated goats produced that rare wool, better known as Cashmere. This, in fact, is made from a very fine inner layer of wool which has to be specially plucked and sorted out from the long coarse hairs.

It seems ironical that this wool, much of which comes from the Himalayan goats of Ladakh, Tibet and Zanskar should be known by the name of the region where it is woven, for there are very few sheep and goat in the Vale of Kashmir. The shepherd tending the flock we encountered was a Balti from the Suru valley. To look after sheep in Europe is a profession generally associated with quiet rural romanticism: not so here, as to watch over sheep is constantly to protect them from the jaws of hungry wolves and snow leopards.

Having passed the flock we reached a little cairn of stones. In it were planted sticks to which were attached clusters of yellow, blue and white rectangles of cloth printed with the figures of a horse and with prayers in Tibetan script. These were prayer banners or flags offered up to the 'horses of the wind' for good luck by passing travellers. We had reached the top of the Pensi-la. Yet this was not very evident as we came upon a sort of plateau which stretched for miles before us on the same level as the cairn.

Nordrup informed me that the pass marked the beginning of Zanskar's grazing rights, and so it was that I had at last entered the 'Land of White Copper'. My joy was not reflected in the scenery, one of bleak grandeur that would hardly have warmed anyone's soul but mine. Even my love for barren solitudes waned a little as I peered at the rocky mountains of the Zanskar Range stretching to the left, while to the right the formidable barrier of the Great Himalayan Range with its snow slopes falling into large glaciers continued unbroken. For several miles the terrain was flat so that it was impossible to determine the watershed; confirming this we passed three lakes of different coloured water with no outlets. The sun by now was slowly dropping in the sky, its rays turning to a yellow gold yet they were still so powerful that my calves were actually painfully burnt in a few minutes by the setting sun when my socks had slipped to my ankles.

It was nearly dark when I noticed that we were walking far above a glacier whose green ice flowed in crackled waves beneath us. It was a strange impression to be so high above snow and yet still on dry land. The main reason for this was that being behind the main Himalayan Range we were in its 'rain shadow', a region where little water or even snow fell. In fact the Zanskar Range is the range where the snow line is the highest in the world, as it rises in summer up to 19,700 feet!

Having stayed on level land for several hours the trail suddenly plunged down a cliff, along a steep and near vertical path which led to the first moraine at the foot of the glacier we had been overlooking. Here we decided to camp next to another caravan. It was freezing cold and I hurriedly erected my tent while Nordrup went to collect fuel (dung and brushwood) for his fire. He planned to sleep in the open and, with the other two men, had arranged our pack saddles, luggage and boxes one on top of the other so as to form a semi-circular barricade against the wind. Behind this the three would sleep huddled together without any overhead shelter but with one rough blanket.

Thanks to my Primus stove I soon produced a cup of hot chocolate then I ate a few more biscuits, but was too exhausted to cook anything. Before my tent I could see the sunburnt faces of the men sitting around their small fires, their voices drifted towards me against the distant roar of a torrent. I had difficulty in understanding what they were saying, being unfamiliar with the Zanskari dialect which, although more like Tibetan than Ladakhi, has many archaic expressions unknown in Tibet.

Someone then began to sing, in the halting yet not unmelodious falsetto common to Tibetan love songs, tales about the sky, about the stars and about fair maidens living by distant lakes. Outside, the glacier glowed green and the sky twinkled with the clearest stars I had ever seen.

More than ever I was intrigued to know what might lie ahead. I had gathered from Nordrup that by hurrying we would reach the village of Thunri, where his brother lived, in two days. Beyond there I preferred not to make any definite plans. It was my intention to leave my two companions at this village and proceed on my own. Having heard of the two Kings of Zanskar I was interested in meeting both of them, and to discover who exactly they were. But would they be interested in me? This was another matter and I wondered how I might gain their favour and so be able to do some useful research into the land's history.

The following morning I got up chattering from the cold and prepared myself some tea which I shared with Nordrup and the two pony men. It took some time before the pony and its foal could be found as they had strayed during the night. When they were recovered the tedious chore of saddling and loading them followed, an operation which had to be repeated at the midday stop. As pack animals horses are slower than mules and mules slower than camels, and yaks the slowest of all. The greatest problem when travelling with horses and mules is their need to graze for hours which means that the availability of pastures dictates progress.

On the other hand yaks, being ruminants, can eat up their day's ration in under an hour and then spend the rest of the day munching as they go. I was told there were no mules in Zanskar although they are faster and more sure-footed than ponies. Certainly Zanskar donkeys are so very very small that to cross them with even a small pony would be well nigh impossible.

To a tinkle of bells our bags and provisions stumbled off down the trail and soon we found ourselves fording a rushing torrent that emerged from the Zanskar Range. To my amazement the foal managed to cross it without help. We were now engaged upon the bed of a very high and practically flat valley, a giant causeway between two rows of lofty peaks leading to a blue horizon. This patch of blue sky I guessed to be over the uppermost portion of the Vale of Zanskar, the north-western extremity of the 200-mile-long 'Valley of White Copper'.

Nordrup told me that we were now in the province of Stod, one of the four districts into which Zanskar is divided. Three of these provinces radiate like the spokes of a wheel from the central province of Jung (meaning centre or government), which encompassed the flat plain where the river we were following met the one coming from the opposite direction. These two rivers, after uniting, turn north forming the main Zanskar river which disappears into a canyon. Nordrup told me about the various provinces, and how each of these had their noble families sub-servient to the King of Padum with the exception of the northern provinces where families were dependent on the King of Zangla.

I could not make out the relationship of the two Kings; were they rivals or friends? What was evident was that they both still held consider-able sway in the land, as their names cropped up in most conversations.

I was hoping to get more details from Nordrup when, after fording another freezing river, a caravan approached us from the opposite direc-tion. This caravan was led by a young monk, and a youth dressed in a dark-red homespun cloak.

As both caravans stopped I sat down to rest. Only when I got up did I realise that our ponies had been unloaded: Nordrup then explained that he was going back to Rangdum with the horses I had been using and that I should carry on with his friend's horses. His friend was a young monk he introduced to me as Lobsang.

'Wait a minute!' I protested, sensing some sort of trick. 'Have we not agreed on wages between us? What is this sudden about-turn?' I was upset because I had been counting on Nordrup's good understanding of Tibetan to help me communicate with the inhabitants. I also knew he was educated and could read and write and would thus prove invaluable in studying the land's history. I now found myself in the company of a total stranger, and was about to refuse to go on with him when Nordrup using his boyish charm and smooth talk promised that he would be back in three days, and that I should wait for him at his brother's house at Thunri. He would be there, he said, a day after my arrival, adding that a festival including an archery contest was being held in his village and this certainly I would not want to miss. He also explained that Lobsang and he were just like brothers, that Lobsang had been several times to Tibet and had studied there, so he was even better educated than himself. At such compliments Lobsang smiled politely. Still furious with Nordrup I had to agree as my bags were being placed upon the backs of the new ponies. Before I had time to say anything more Nordrup was off, waving goodbye without so much as having been paid for his services. Was that, I wondered, the last I should see of him?

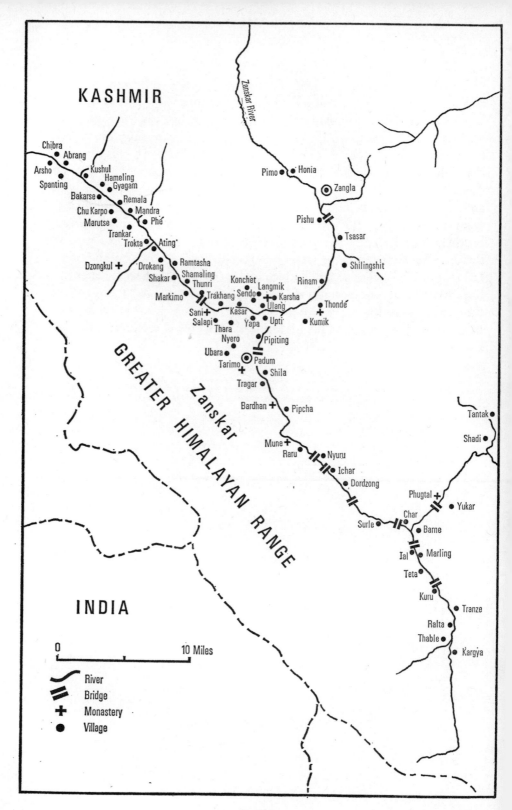

Zanskar

4

Red Hats, Yellow Hats

If Nordrup had been brash, outspoken and fickle, yet he had also been efficient; Lobsang, I soon found, was his opposite: he was discreet, a little slow, terribly straightforward but fortunately equally good-humoured and funny.

From him I gathered how Nordrup and he came to be in business together for their monastery, and how they really were like brothers, travelling and working together. Amazingly, for several years every winter before snow had blocked the passes, Nordrup and Lobsang went down to India where they found employment teaching Tibetan in the school of a large Tibetan refugee settlement in Mysore. Since Mysore is some fourteen hundred miles away from Zanskar I could not help but be surprised by their enterprising spirit. Little did I yet appreciate that even this was not the longest journey these two friends had undertaken together. I later discovered how famous they had become in Zanskar for their travels. As wandering monks they had explored the vast Himalayan world, going to Bhutan, to Lhasa, to Calcutta and Nepal on errands and trading missions, supplying their monastery with gold ink to write holy scriptures and dyes for paint, along with a host of other goods such as holy bells and drums. In these activities, surprisingly enough, Lobsang was only emulating the incredible journeys of his great-uncle, an amazing old man whom I was soon to meet.

Lobsang's stories of these journeys were enough to restore my confidence and by now I was rather happy to have such an enlightened companion.

All day we walked amidst desolation, across the scree slopes of tumbled moraines which in places blocked the valley, passing on one occasion a herd of yaks standing beside a shepherd's miserable shelter.

Towards evening we began to climb above the river on to what seemed to be a moor. Looking at a little flower by the side of the track I recognised a poppy and was soon holding a flower I had long searched for, yet never encountered in my eighteen years of travel in the Himalayas; a blue poppy. It was one of the several species of rare Tibetan blue poppy, which had in the past been the quest of so many botanists.

In all respects the flower and its leaves are similar to the European red wild poppy (at least they seem so to an amateur) with the startling difference that the four flimsy petals are of a magnificent blue that varies from light to dark with a tinge of purple. The very delicacy and flimsiness of the petals gave them subtle variations in tone, while the central seed pod and the pistils are yellow instead of black. Altogether I found the Meconopsis a more graceful flower than our red poppy. Later I identified it as *Meconopsis horridula*, its horrible appellation being unwarranted but for its slightly thorny stem.

The finding of these flowers was like a lucky omen. Shortly after this we reached a pass dominated by a tower and the ruins of a fort whose name was given to me as Ra Dzong. At the foot of this castle that had once guarded the western entrance to the Kingdom, the trail suddenly turned round the shoulder of a mountain and led to the inhabited portion of western Zanskar. I now had before me the province of Stod; while in the foreground stood the little houses of Arsho, the first village of Zanskar.

Arsho stood upon a narrow ledge on the other side of the river, which was now much swollen by melting snows and too wide to be crossed. In this village lived the young man who was accompanying us, yet to reach it he would have to walk all the way down to the only bridge across the stream at Thunri, our destination. From where we were I could just distinguish half a dozen poor-looking rectangular homes of grey earthen bricks with prayer flags on the roofs, which were crumbling under piles of brushwood.

My heart beat with excitement – for what had been for so long only a blur on a map now lay before me. At my feet sprawled a large and practically straight valley bordered by peaks whose glaciers lapped down to narrow plains, set between great scree slopes of ancient avalanches.

Looking for the first time at Zanskar I began to understand why it was called a 'Revealed Land', as indeed its presence is unexpected in such a high and rugged region where it lies as if by a miracle. Looking at the lonely valley set so high above the tree-line and hidden between the wall of the world's most impressive ranges, I began to believe for the first time that Zanskar might very well prove to be the lost valley, the Kingdom of my dreams. As with a blue poppy in my hat I dominated a limitless horizon of virgin peaks somewhere upon the roof of the world, I once again felt that I was about to live an adventure in time. I spurred on my little bay stallion and led my small caravan with its monk and his assistant into a forgotten world.

That night we camped on the edge of the small fields of Chibra, the first village on our side of the upper valley of Zanskar.

Lobsang had collected wild peas which, eaten raw that night, proved to be the only excitement in an otherwise tasteless meal of nondescript packaged soup and biscuits. As I laid out my sleeping bag in my tent it began to rain, after which a howling wind rushed down tugging at the tent pegs. Meanwhile Lobsang and his friend found shelter cowering behind a stone wall, surrounded by the saddles.

The following morning it was cold and dreary: clouds hung like a lid upon the valley. Through the damp grass we plodded past the half-dozen houses of Chibra and the 30-odd houses of the village of Abrang, whose bare facades were occasionally pierced by minute windows hardly large enough for the occupants to stick their heads through to look at the stranger passing by. In this part of the country none of the houses was whitewashed and seemed rather drab, although some were decorated with red swastikas and triangles. Surrounding the houses lay little irrigated fields in which barley stood green and fresh, bordered with wild flowers. Not a tree or a bush was to be found near or around the topmost villages of Stod, for at 13,500 feet they stood far above tree-level. Later in Zanskar I visited villages which were built at an even higher altitude and could contend for the title of the highest villages in the Himalayas, not to say of the globe.

The river known as the 'Stod chu', the upper river, had now grown into a vast, white, roaring torrent fifty feet wide that entirely separated the two sides of the valley. As we progressed we passed five other villages clinging to terraces above the river, then we reached the large settlement of Phe, its entrance marked by a chorten which, like nearly all those in Zanskar, lacked its pointed thirteen-tiered spire.

Tradition has it that the reason for this absence is that these tiers should be carved in wood, which requires a sizeable tree trunk, a commodity so rare that the villages had not been able to find or to purchase any. These truncated chortens soon became the beacons along our trail as it wound its way upon the flanks of the Zanskar Range, contouring great rocky spurs that separated the villages sited on those rare flat platforms which dominate the central river.

In the eleven small villages we crossed that day I did not see one person wearing Western clothes: all the inhabitants were wrapped in thick home-spun cloaks dyed wine-red or left in their natural yellowish colour. On several occasions we passed small caravans of donkeys and yaks going up the valley to graze, they were pushed along by older men or young children, one of whom offered me a little bunch of wild flowers.

At Phe we saw our first monastery, a small building which I did not have the energy to visit as I was still far from accustomed to twelve-hour days walking over rough ground.

I was totally exhausted and miserably wet and cold when Lobsang pointed out the village of Thunri, 'the mountain of the horn', where Nordrup's brother lived and where I hoped to stay the night and possibly remain for a couple of days.

Seeing the village was one thing, but it now took several hours to reach it. On the way I passed the first of the many amazing buildings I was to see in Zanskar. This was Gugutet Gompa, a monastery hanging high up on a cliff above our trail, its rooms dug into the rust-red rock. Below this monastery we came upon the beautiful village of Remala, whose houses, whitewashed and outlined with red-ochre designs, were surrounded by fields alight with a thousand blossoming wild flowers; forget-me-nots, edelweiss and blue primulas.

Lobsang picked a little sprig of minute white flowers for me and asked me to taste the seeds, which turned out to be alpine cumin. In vain I searched for more blue poppies but evidently they grew only at higher altitudes.

Towards evening the valley broadened and trees appeared in the villages, planted alongside little irrigation canals that directed water from roaring streams high in the mountains into the flat lands. The trees were all poplar and willow. The willows were grown for firewood, their tufty branches being cut every three years. The poplars are grown for building houses: when their trunks are thick enough they are cut at about three feet above the ground. One tree furnishes at best two big house posts. On the remaining stump a sod of earth is placed helping further branches to grow, which will eventually be cut and used as crossbeams. House building here, as one can guess, calls for long planning ahead. Just before reaching Thunri I was delighted to see a wood, a pleasure garden a few hundred feet square. Such tree gardens are a great luxury in Zanskar and this one surrounded a fine house that seemed to be that of the local lord. The silver-grey rustle of willow leaves is very similar to that of olive trees and gives a vibrant light whose charm is unequalled. I have always wanted to plant a magic willow wood in Europe to recall those rare oases of shade and colour one occasionally encounters on the barren steppes of the inner Himalayas.

It was nearly dark when I reached Thunri, a village of some thirty-five houses clustered together above fields that fell in terraces down to the central river. Between prayer walls of rounded boulders carved with the invocation '*Om mani padme hum*' I made my way to a large house from which a young man, dressed surprisingly in a Western jacket, emerged.

'Please come stay at my house,' he said in hesitant English.

'No thank you,' I answered. 'But can you tell me where is the home of Nawang Trile?' I enquired in Tibetan.

'You do not want to stay in such a poor and miserable house as that of Nawang,' the young man replied, this time in Tibetan.

'Nawang Trile is the brother of a friend of mine, and even if he lives in a cave, a friend is a friend,' I said.

'How well you speak,' the young man answered, surprised no doubt both by my speaking Tibetan and at my rather moral reply. Several villagers had listened to our exchange and looking at me with respect they now mumbled their approval. One of these men led me to Nordrup's brother's house.

My heart sank when at the far end of the village he pointed to a ruin saying, 'It is here.' Minutes later a tall young monk with a rounded face and tiny eyes and a shy smile appeared. This was Nawang who did look a little like Nordrup. I asked if I could spend the night, explaining that Lobsang would soon be arriving with ponies and my luggage.

'My house is very small and you will not like it,' Nawang said. I would have gladly agreed to this and gone elsewhere but was now publicly committed to staying there. I entered a very low wooden door that led into a dark ground-floor stable, then Nawang, grabbing my arm, directed me up rough stone steps that came out on to a terrace. Another low door led from the terrace to a small, bare, narrow room at one corner of which a little fire smoked in a clay hearth. This was the one and only room left of a house which I gathered had collapsed. Although dark and smoky the room was warm and I asked if I could lay my sleeping bag there. Nawang accepted, apologising for his poverty. I brushed aside his remarks and sat down cross-legged before the hearth where, as in all Himalayan houses, a teapot simmered. Pulling out my wooden bowl I was given a cupful of tea which warmed my spirits and eased the aches I suffered from having walked over twenty-five miles since dawn.

Nawang and I had begun to chat when in came a minute little boy of perhaps six, dressed in a ragged *chuba* made up of odd patches of cloth. The child's shaven head indicated that he was destined to become a monk. I gathered that he was a young nephew of Nawang and Nordrup whose parents lived in Padum and had sent him to his uncle to learn how to read and write and to prepare him for his religious calling.

The child looked miserable in his rags, while his serious and polite speech and reserved manner were sadly touching. Uncle and nephew formed an unusually pleasant pair and we soon became good friends.

I had hardly finished drinking my tea-soup when Lobsang arrived and joined us.

We sat round the fire and joked while the child blew on the flame. I now learnt that here again, as in Rangdum, a festival following the three-day observance of *Newne* was to be held. This observance lasts for several days during which the villagers keep to certain rules of pious conduct; for instance, not to have sexual intercourse, not to eat meat, not to take without giving and not to drink.

On the last day a special blessing was to be given at Thunri by the Abbot of Karsha, the largest monastery of Zanskar – the one to which Nordrup, Nawang and Lobsang belonged. The Lama was to give his blessing on the following day, while the day after an archery contest was to be held between the villagers, followed by a feast and much drinking of chang. This final day of the festivities is called 'Arrow and Beer Drinking', a fearful combination as the two do not seem to mix and might end in a 'drunken shoot-out'. It all sounded rather exciting and after a meal of tinned food I fell asleep to the pleasurable realisation that at long last I had reached the land where the fairies congregate and I hoped soon to discover why.

My journeys to Bhutan, Ladakh, the Everest district of Nepal, to Mustang, and several other Himalayan regions allowed me to appreciate that I had found in Zanskar perhaps the most rugged and unspoiled area of the entire Himalayas. Yet I could not say that so far I had been very enthused by the barren, cold and hostile region I had crossed. For the time being I simply marvelled at the fact that man could survive at such a high altitude in a land that on first sight offered practically nothing but stone, ice and snow all year around.

As on my first setting eyes upon the tormented void of Mustang's high plateau, similarly in Zanskar – looking at the ocean of snow-covered peaks and the cold overhanging glaciers I could not as yet appreciate the hidden charms of what was to prove an amazingly hardy and happy nation. I say nation as no other word is appropriate for Zanskar is not, I soon discovered, a couple of villages or a loose assembly of communities but a true nation, one with its own language, customs, traditions, history and still its own rulers. All these attributes come straight down from the tenth century when, in the year AD 930 Zanskar became a fully independent state, and was to remain so for nine hundred years.

All this I would discover later. My immediate preoccupation was the trivial yet vital problem of how to protect myself from fleas. Discreetly, so as not to offend my host, I sprayed my sleeping bag with insecticide, then, fully dressed, I slipped inside it. Trying to sleep I listened to the hushed voice of Lobsang explaining to Nawang all about the marvels in my kitbags, the cameras and the Primus stove, adding that I was a great man who had been all over the Himalayas but never to Lhasa. At my feet the little boy purred rather than snored.

The houses of the village of Thunri all faced south and backed against a great scree slope of loose stones that rose to an enormous height. Partly buried in rubble along this slope were several large chortens, they marked the steep track that led to the whitewashed buildings of the village monastery. When I emerged from Nawang's smoky den, groups of villagers in their best attire (women covered in jewels like at Rangdum and men in their finest cloaks) were already making their way to the monastery.

Never had I seen a crowd of people so elaborately dressed. I was particularly surprised by the neatness of the children's dresses. The little girls wore saffron bonnets set with turquoises or simply planted with needles (a form of wealth) and wild flowers. They played with each other, joking and laughing as they jumped around their solemn parents. I joined the procession to the monastery, a derelict structure with a small courtyard leading to a little assembly hall, outside which two buildings flanked a stone throne built in the outer wall of the assembly hall.

Entering the assembly hall I found myself before four very ancient monks who begged me to sit down. When they realised I spoke Tibetan one of the monks with a little goatee and thick, round, steel-rimmed glasses explained how he had spent most of his life in Amdo, the eastern district of Tibet, nearly thirty-eight hundred miles away from Zanskar. Later I discovered that a secret link unites Zanskar with that remote north-eastern province of greater Tibet.

It is a general belief in Zanskar that the Amdo region was originally populated by people from Zanskar. As a result many young monks went to study in Amdo. I found this as surprising as if an Irish village priest told of a special link between Ireland and Istanbul. So strong is the belief that Zanskar populated Amdo, which is about twenty times the size and has twenty times the population of Zanskar (in fact the Amdo province is as large as England), that they have a legend about it. This legend relates how a young man from Zanskar went to Amdo and found a huge lake (Lake Kokonor). From this lake emerged a beautiful princess. The two fell in love and had very many children. Thus, they say, the people from Amdo have the same bones (we would say blood) as the inhabitants of Zanskar.

Whatever the truth the connection is remarkable, if not improbable. Because of the very great distance, a journey would be likely to take a year and a half of continual walking day after day. Yet I later met many monks who had spent several years in Amdo and was shown printed banners attesting to the strong link uniting the two regions – the far poles of the Tibetan cultural world.

This of course raised the question as to where did the Zanskaris come from in the first place, one I could not yet answer.

I stayed for half an hour conversing with the monks. I learned that the large monastery of Karsha was of the Yellow Hat sect, that is to say the reformed Gelugpa sect, the one of which the Dalai Lama is the head. In Zanskar all the monasteries belonged either to this sect or to the Drukpa Kargyupa sect, that of Bhutan and one of the older sects known as the Red Hat sect. To which sect the members of any village belonged could be determined by the colour of the little girls' bonnets, these being either saffron-yellow or red.

I was surprised to find here, so far away from Bhutan, such a strong religious influence, even though I already knew that the Bhutanese Church was well implanted in nearby Ladakh.

The difference between the various sects is related to the teachings which they hold as supreme. There are in Tibet and the Himalayas four main sects and fourteen sub-sects. The oldest, called Nyingmapa (which literally means the old ones), believe not only in the classical Buddhist texts but also in the 'revealed' texts found by lamas in certain caves. This sect incorporates many magical practices in its rites which come from the pre-Buddhist magical Bon religion that once dominated all Central Asia.

The Sakyapa sect, which was powerful in the thirteenth century, abandoned these magical practices. Next came the Kargyupa sect which adopted certain Nyingmapa texts. Last, with the saint Tsong Khapa as reformer, came the famous reformed Yellow Hats, the Gelugpa sect whose leaders became the Dalai Lamas, temporal rulers of Tibet and spiritual rulers of Tibet, Mongolia and China.

These sects are not, as one might think, antagonistic, especially not in Zanskar where they share certain assembly halls and chapels. The little monastery of Thunri had only two rather pathetic images of Buddha and some poor religious paintings hanging from the scraggly twisted posts which supported its roof. I was pleased to leave it as I am often ill at ease in the rather eerie atmospheres of some Buddhist chapels.

It is strange that a religion of tolerance, mercy and compassion, as is Tibetan Lamaism, should also have as sub-divinities a horde of hideous and evil-looking demi-gods and spirits. These evil divinities have come from the Hindu pantheon, and worked their way into Tibetan Buddhism along with the countless magical rites and superstitions of the ancient Shamanistic religion of Central Asia, called Bon, to which I have already referred.

Mystery and magic are often, and rightly so, associated with Tibetan Buddhism; yet if this is true at the level of ritual, in general the Buddhists of the Himalayas have mostly retained the better aspects of Buddhist teachings: tolerance, kindness and moderation. Too much is written and said of the world's religions in terms of their dogmas, and rituals, and too little said about what actually filters down to the common man.

Of course there is always a considerable difference between practice and theory, and while Lamaist theory is most complex, in fact shatteringly so with literally one hundred thousand divinities and many magic rituals, tolerance, kindness and compassion are practised by all. On the other hand Moslems and Christians, whose doctrine and rituals concern love and kindness, have produced the intolerance of the Inquisition and the notorious oppressive fanaticism of Islam.

It is a great lesson to see how the naturally turbulent inhabitants of the Himalayas, who are soldiers by nature and have a rugged disposition, moderate their impulses to become tolerant and kind even to the most objectionable people, animal or insect that they encounter. This has always surprised me as I am rather given to showing my aggressive feelings. Many a time I have been reprimanded by Himalayan friends who, quite rightly, made me feel ashamed of my lack of kindness and self-control in cases where in Europe they would be considered a normal reaction.

I must admit I needed self-control not to kill the fleas I caught in the chapel. Instead, with traditional respect for life, I placed the offenders on the ground without squashing them, thus leaving them free to start a new career on someone else.

When thinking of religion, we need in the West to take great pains to appreciate that the word can mean something quite different in other countries. For example, in religion, we Westerners hold an absolute belief, something for which we would be ready to die and it is hard for us to imagine a person who would be both Catholic and Moslem, or even Catholic and Protestant at the same time. Likewise we cannot easily visualise a person who was simultaneously a communist and a conservative. Party cards are we think mutually exclusive. A man is only allowed one religion at a time and this is supposed to have precedence over politics, and nearly everything else. It is not so in Asia, especially in the Himalayas: here I have found that religion is just an explanation and not a law.

Religion in the Buddhist Himalayas is seen not as a belief to which one must adhere but as a normal, integral part of existence. It is accepted somewhat in the way in which we accept driving on the right-hand or left-hand side of the road, knowing that neither side is in any sense absolutely the best. Religion as a normal part of existence involves all life's activities, and as such is never questioned. Yet it is not as demanding or as exclusive as our own creeds. It is taken for granted as custom yet is not taken over-seriously.

When I asked Lobsang and Nawang, and then later Nordrup, whether they liked being monks, or wanted to be monks, it made them laugh; the question of an alternative had never occurred to them.

As a corollary religious laws and beliefs are too numerous and complex not to be transgressed. The complexity of Buddhist rituals breeds a certain casualness which we could never accept in the West. On the other hand, the lack of any truly advanced science to solve some of the mysteries of nature and many of man's problems brings the people of the Himalayas (as it did feudal Christians) to rely on religion and the Church to give an answer to questions that we consider today to be in the field of science.

Religion in simple terms explains all natural phenomena, including disasters, accidents, earthquakes and diseases. This makes life much more bearable since everything has a religious explanation.

Bitterness as the result of rebellion against one's destiny, a strong characteristic of Western man, is unknown in the Himalayas and in much of the East. Believing in statistics can only bring one to rebel against bad luck, rather than accept one's fate and destiny (as a Himalayan would) with a smile as something inevitable. Yet who among us can today dodge statistics?

I explain all this because it helps to understand a certain Asiatic casualness towards death and fate. As Tashi, who had been my companion in Mustang, told me, 'In ninety-nine years all things living today will be dead, so why fear death?' It is the most natural thing and were we to fear it then all humanity should live afraid. The very thought made Tashi laugh yet it had made me tremble, it is sometimes hard to be logical. I now had less fear of death, perhaps because I was older and more relaxed about what might happen and more tolerant of the unexpected.

Climbing down from the monastery I looked over the village of Thunri, not a very charming one and a little run down. Its narrow and badly paved streets wound their way between rows of rather dull clay-coloured houses. It was raining and this little cold drizzle, more characteristic of London, shrouded everything in a frigid melancholy. I accepted the rain.

Back in the house I discussed my plans with Lobsang and Nawang.

'I want to visit all four provinces of Zanskar, I want to see all the villages and all the monasteries and to learn the *lusso* of the land.' (*Lusso* means customs.) Lobsang and Nawang nodded.

'My problem', I went on, 'is that I need horses or men to carry my bags and would like one or both of you to come with me.' I explained that I was a bit disappointed with Nordrup whom I had not been able to trust entirely as he changed plans every day.

The two monks were rather upset, and explained that Nordrup was normally reliable but that he had had problems with all the loads that were left behind when our truck had broken down. I heard the details of the complications of his business deals. Nordrup had commissioned some of the horses of the monastery and had asked some of the various villagers to do business for their owners, and thus became involved in a tangle of debts and obligations whose complexities would have jammed a computer. Sheer courtesy had stopped him from refusing to assist me but his other obligations had won out in the end.

I accepted all this and tried to make a more solid agreement with Lobsang, ensuring that from now on he would accompany me with three ponies all over Zanskar. Lobsang and I then agreed on a price for each horse and a daily fee for himself.

While I ate a small meal of rice cooked by Nawang most of the villagers popped in or sat on the doorstep to see me. Not many foreigners had come this way, judging by the manner in which I was stared at. Little gasps of admiration and lengthy comments were caused by my sleeping bag of 'bird's hair', and the nature of my cooking utensils, my watch, my shirt and other garments. I was equally curious about the possessions and clothes of the Zanskaris and asked the name and varieties of their homespun woollen garments. To weave is a job undertaken only by men in Zanskar, although women spin the wool.

Every day I better appreciated how Zanskar had been uniquely preserved from change. There are many reasons for this, one is that Zanskar is far removed from any trade route or frontier and thus of no strategic interest.

The Kashmiri Government had sent to Padum, the capital, its first permanent administrator only three years before my arrival. This man ran away, unable to bear the climate and the thought of months of isolation. Then, a year ago, another administrator had been sent, a man apparently courageous and sturdy enough to weather the long winter.

I could well imagine what winter might be like for it was freezing cold on the night of 28th July.

In the afternoon a great ceremony of ritual blessing was held in front of the monastery. Seated upon a stone throne against the monastery wall, the Abbot of Karsha, dressed in a yellow pointed cap, bent over to place a sacred vase upon the heads of all the villagers. In turn they approached the Abbot, bowed and then received the blessed touch of the 'benediction of long life'. After this they were given a little sacred chang to drink in the palm of their hand along with a blessed ribbon to be worn around their necks.

All the women sat to the left of the Lama and the men to his right. The crowd of ladies was like an undulating sea of brilliant turquoise. I estimated that there may have been close to half a ton of precious stones on their heads, and this in only one village. A treasure one could hardly expect to find in one of the poorest and most barren valleys of the Himalayas.

With fascinated curiosity I peered at the hundreds of rugged, suntanned, strong and wilful faces. Each weathered by hardships and pleasures was distinctly individual, fashioned by life. I, too, was the subject of much curiosity and many comments. These I overheard: remarks about my strange clothes, my long nose and the light colour of my eyes, and about something rarely found among the Himalayans, my baldness. Few Tibetans are bald. I have always wondered why.

Looking at the crowd I could take good stock of the people's features. At first sight the inhabitants of Zanskar seemed shorter than the inhabitants of Ladakh with broader faces and more Mongolian features, which appeared to indicate a greater influence from central Tibet and a lesser presence of Dardi blood than in Ladakh. This is confirmed by the famous 'Chronicles of Zanskar', a document which is the only historical text specifically related to the history of Zanskar that is known today. It was recorded in 1908 by a native scholar sent to Zanskar by the Moravian missionary, Doctor A. H. Francke, who was one of the first to study the history of Ladakh and the western Himalayas. A two-page incomplete manuscript, the chronicles list mainly the revenues and their origins of the monastery of Phugtal in eastern Zanskar.

After saying that Zanskar was a holy land, and relating a prophecy as to its being a meeting place for fairies, the manuscript says:

At the time of its foundation Zanskar was under Kashmir. When the castle of Drang-tse (in northern Ladakh) was seized by the Kham-pas (Tibetans) a great flight of men and horses took place in all directions; and after that harm was done in various ways (an illustration of the Tibetan expansion in western Himalayas). In retaliation an army was led against the throne of Guge and then the country of Zanskar and all its castles were burnt with fire. Many men were killed. As many men arrived here afterwards from all directions the country rose again.

So it seems that the valley once inhabited by Dards under Kashmiri leadership was devastated and then re-populated by Tibetan immigrants in the wake of the great Tibetan conquest towards the middle of the eighth century. This could explain why the people are so Tibetan-looking as opposed to the other regions such as the Suru valley or the Indus valley.

There are, generally speaking, two types of Tibetans; a short, squat, round-faced type and a tall long-faced type. Although the distinction is open to many intermediate variations it is a fairly good one with which to classify the inhabitants of the innumerable Tibetan ethnic regions. Beyond doubt the Zanskaris were of the short and round-faced type.

How exactly had they come and when, was one of the many questions I hoped my stay in this land might answer. I was intrigued at the thought of perhaps meeting the two Kings, not understanding what role each had played or still played in this unique realm.

At the ceremony I noticed that the nephew of my host walked around in rags while all the other little children had fine warm clothes. I decided to buy him a cloak, or rather to purchase the necessary material for one to be made – there are no ready-made cloaks in Zanskar.

How much material I would need was simple to judge. Instead of having different sizes or set measurements to make a dress, one takes thirty arm's lengths of ten-inch-wide cloth. The cloaks always fit since a tall man has a longer arm than a small boy.

I let it be known that I was ready to purchase material and so several rolls of homespun woollen cloth were brought to Nawang's house by their proud weavers, strong burly farmers showing off their handicraft which one could hardly qualify as masculine. Why men had the exclusivity of weaving I never found out, possibly because of the technical complexity of the looms? However that might be, I appreciated that each man had his different standard and apart from the two types of cloth (close weave and loose weave – the first brushed to fluff), each roll varied considerably in quality. In the end I settled for a roll which was just a little over thirty times the length of the child's arm. His joy was a pleasure to see and I somehow felt that this warm coat would be with him a very long time and might improve what seemed to be rather poor health. Wool cloth in Zanskar, in spite of the great number of goats, is an expensive commodity because of the work involved and there are few people who can afford a change of dress several times in a lifetime. Everyday clothes are endlessly patched but nearly everyone owns a good 'Sunday suit', as I had seen at the festivals. Clothes in Zanskar, like in our own Mediaeval Ages, are a sign of wealth and one is very happy to have were it but one good winter cloak.

My present was appreciated more than any gift of money and Nawang was touched to tears. I must admit I was a little surprised at the price of the material, forgetting that to spin the thread and hand weave the cloth might have taken several months, and this had to be paid for.

I was not so much concerned at the price itself as at the rapid depletion of my reserve of currency. I knew I could find no bank here in which to cash travellers' cheques and so had to make do with the money I had brought along. My fortune consisted of dozens of wads of new one- and two-rupee Indian notes and a few larger bills, as there is very little money in circulation and such a distrust of paper money that dirty or worn-out bills are rarely accepted. Although this change was bulky it was nothing compared to carrying around twenty-four pounds of silver coins, the weight of my cash box during my first expedition to the Himalayas in 1959 when none of the hill people would accept anything except coins.

The subject of money raised the worrying question as to how the inhabitants of Zanskar had acquired their wealth. Cut off from trade routes and living in an enclosed valley which seemed in all appearance stony and poor, how had they succeeded in acquiring such riches I saw worn by the women? Logically they should be among the poorest Himalayans, yet the little I had seen so far pointed to the contrary. Although Nawang lived in the tumbled ruin of what had been his father's house, the other houses of Thunri were large, some with eight to twelve rooms.

That night around a smoky dung fire we all sat huddled together talking about tomorrow's bow and arrow contest. Eventually I fell asleep to the mumble of Lobsang and Nawang reciting prayers.

The next day the weather had still not cleared and the steady drizzle had begun to wreak havoc on the roof of the room in which we were living. The roofs of houses in Zanskar are made of earth laid out over willow branches set down across poplar beams. In the dry air the beaten earth becomes as hard as clay, and this is quite adequate in a land where, in theory, it rarely rained. The lack of rain also explains why the roofs are flat and often with little or no adequate drainage. Now, after two days and nights of spasmodic drizzle the porous clay had in places reverted to mud, and water was seeping through the roof, washing down with it the soot that covered all the beams. As a result I awoke stained in brown ink-like water, wet, cold, and looking ridiculous.

Nawang was more worried than I, fearing that the rain might erode the wall and bring what was left of the house down. Hastily he set about laying more earth on the roof with a shovel in an attempt to block holes and reinforce the rather moth-eaten structure.

It is strange how Himalayan buildings, which often stand for centuries – some for more than six centuries – are vulnerable to one big downpour which can wash many away overnight. The year of my visit, like the preceding year, had had exceptionally wet summers. Anywhere else the drizzle would have gone unnoticed but here in a desert it was judged a great calamity, not only for the houses but because of the swelling of the rivers, already at their peak due to the melting snow from the summits. This meant that many trails to distant pastures would be cut off and possibly also the routes in or out of Zanskar.

Having repaired the house and had morning tea, I with sugar, and my friends with salt, we set out to watch the preparations for the day's festival.

Children were running all over the place in their best dresses but today their hats were entirely covered with flowers; around their faces blue and red blossoms hung in clusters giving a hundred small smiling faces the appearance of little angels.

I have always loved children but in particular Himalayan children, who are outrageously naughty, rowdy and undisciplined. None of these brats bore the sad and solemn look of Indian infants and of so many other Asiatic children. On the contrary, the children here are always rushing around, pushing each other over, laughing and screaming, climbing up and down houses, playing around doors, leaning out of windows, or engaged in a hundred different games. Among their games I recognised touch and go, jumping out of bounds on the high rocks, and endless sets of cat and mice, others played marbles with needles, or pebbles or coins, throwing these into little holes. Favourite among the games I observed was quoits – throwing rocks at little home-made wooden pins.

At Thunri I saw a group of children engaged in a strange warlike game. Through the middle of the village ran a small brook spanned by a bridge made of two flattened tree trunks placed side by side. Two teams had formed on either side of the stream and, armed with stones, they threw these into the river so as to splash each other's party and prevent anyone from approaching, and ultimately crossing the bridge. Those who were wetted by the spray from the stones were, according to rule, obliged to retreat. Inevitably the rules were not observed for long, and a good scuffle ensued with little fancy hats flying all over the place and small boys screaming after bigger ones, who were running away with their head-gear to use as flying saucers.

5

Bows, Arrows and Beer

Feverish preparations for the archery contest began at midday; beside the stream stones were piled up to form two target banks fifty paces apart. Black leather discs were then placed on the slanted face of the target mounds in the centre of which was set a round, dry clay bull's eye. To one side a crowd erected a large white cotton tent trimmed with blue strips of cloth. Inside the tent rectangular cushions were laid out and then covered with carpets. Carpets were also placed in a large rectangle outside the tent.

At two o'clock down from the monastery came a procession led by a drummer and followed by a cymbal player and two oboists; behind these marched the headman, the richest man of the village and father of the young fellow who had invited me to stay in his house. The headman was a true giant with a booming voice as big as his bulky frame. Standing above everyone else, one felt he was a born leader. Surrounded by a court of monks and assistants he now supervised the scenario for the feast.

Behind a stone wall that protected a clump of poplar trees a goat was slaughtered and cleaned, by a Moslem butcher, as Buddhists are not allowed to kill. Meanwhile men were busy mixing tsampa (roasted barley flour) with a flour made from ground peas. These were then shaped into heavy unleavened, brick-like cakes, banged into shape by mixing the flour with Tibetan tea. While this was going on three huge copper pots of the kind one would use to boil an entire ostrich were brought forward and laid side by side, to be filled from earthen jars with chang, a real flood of the brew – several hundred gallons! I felt certain that such quantities could not be completely drunk in one day. Great copper ladles hung from the edges of the pots, waiting to be used.

Before the festivities began a small willow tree was cut and its stem sheared of all but the top branches, along this pole was attached a strip of dark blue cloth overprinted with prayers in black ink, printed from the appropriate woodblocks kept in the monastery. The prayer flag on the mast was then erected at the entrance to the tent.

When all was ready the women of Thunri came down and squatted against a stone wall along the length of the arrow pitch, their turquoise head-dresses forming a wavering pool of gems. The men in turn congregated around the main tent in their finest great gowns and strange top-hat-like head gear. They sat toying with arrows, while their small bows rested stacked against the tent post.

Nawang Trile, our host, was in the tent, from which there soon issued a religious chant, no doubt a blessing for the occasion. Chang was then ladled out generously to every extended cup that the men and women drew from the breast pockets of their chubas. Some presented simple wooden bowls, others were silver lined, all were filled to the brim. Courtesy required that on being served, one drank a little right away after which the server filled your bowl to the brim. This having been repeated a third time, the server then moved on to someone else.

On the cushions laid out beside the tent were seated the village elders, or rather the oldest men of the village: a group of five tottering ancients with scrawny beards and tattered faces, who drooled over their chang and were very soon drunk and quite gay. I was invited to sit beside them and was joined by some of the young men of the village. Everyone made a point of filling my cup whenever I drank a sip, fortunately the chang was excellent and I do really enjoy a good drink. I soon began to see the landscape in happy terms. The sight before me was indeed a delight, the tent, the flagpole, the two bull's eyes and beyond them the women, while by my side were the weather-beaten faces of the old men, looking like bards recalled from the brink of death. All were drinking with glee and had a naughty twinkle in their eyes. Beyond this joyful scene rose the outlines of great peaks shrouded in mist.

Somewhere a man burst into song as clusters of archers rose and walked to the targets. There they let fly their arrows in a rather inaccurate volley, cheered and whistled at by the crowd. It was somewhat disorganised and the archers, who included the village headman and several monks, showed a poor mastery of the bow, due no doubt to drink or lack of practice. Whatever the reason their skill was greatly inferior to the martial precision of the Bhutanese archers I had seen. There the targets were a hundred and one paces from each other. This simple contest was in a way more fun although I constantly feared that someone would get shot. A great roar of laughter echoed in the valley when a dog ran away with the leather target.

One after the other the immense basins of chang were drunk and the general tone of the conversation slowly rose. Fortunately, to soak up all the drink, some very indigestible cakes were passed around. Reluctantly I had to accept one and began to stoically plug my stomach with it until, to my relief, I was able to pass it on to my neighbour.

Anthropological exactitude would risk being warped were I to describe the subsequent happenings. I found myself growing more and more loquacious and patting everyone on the back while being offered and accepting countless more cups of chang. In the end I thought Thunri the most delightful village in the world and Zanskar the most congenial realm of the Himalayas. I drank to all and sundry, to the mournful world of cities and pollution, to fast cars and radio sets, to St Tropez and other pagan saints of what seemed a distant never-never land to which I no longer belonged, and yet to which in drink I was dragged back by a strange nostalgia. I wished my friends could have seen me now, if only to understand why on occasions in the West I would drift away to this other world, where chang flows free under the mountains and arrows fly through the thin air.

I remembered singing going on all night and I was amazed that there were no fights in the wake of what I suppose was really an orgy. A hang-over is a hangover at whatever altitude and in every language. The following day began rather badly with a great row. The screaming I had heard was that of an angry villager into whose barley field one of Lobsang's horses had apparently strayed. This was a serious offence and one that called for official sanctions; a crime of this sort incurring a heavy fine from the village council.

Lobsang admitted his responsibility and agreed to pay the fine, but the farmer did not seem content and swore in loud tones that he would kill or keep the horse. It took long and patient negotiations to calm the man. In the end I payed the fine and soon we were packing our bags. I then bade farewell to the two young men who had come with me from Kargil and wished them good luck before setting off with three horses for Lobsang's home in the northern part of the central province of Jung.

I had made up my mind that I would go there first to meet the three old aunts with whom he lived; from there I hoped to visit the King of

Zangla, one of the two men in Zanskar who bore the title rGyalpo which in Tibetan means 'the victorious one' and is reserved for independent monarchs.

Lobsang was an enlightening travel companion and as we walked he rolled off the names of local villages and their monasteries, the religious sect to which they belonged and the list of the names of the local *Pembo* or headman, and those of the noble families, *Lumbo*, in the area. Shortly after leaving Thunri and having passed the village of Trakhang the valley broadened, beyond the far bank of the river stretched a vast stony plain, dotted here and there with patches of green grass and various small hamlets. This was the western extremity of the district of Jung which soon spread out to cover a wide area which resembled a dried-out high altitude lake-bed closed in on all sides by lofty mountains. I was now contemplating the very heart of Zanskar, a region remarkably flat and very different from the upper province through which I had passed. The full variety of landscapes in Zanskar was yet unknown to me, but I was beginning to appreciate how different were each of the land's four districts. The upper district I had come through had been a barren valley with broad ledges upon which clung small villages surrounded by terraced fields. Now I was approaching a flat land of grassy fields and long, un-broken vistas. Villages sat dotted out like dice upon a green carpet thrown haphazardly, as it were, upon the plain. This certainly was part of the land revealed by the gods; lush, flat, well-irrigated land is very rare in all mountains and especially out of place and unexpected here in the highest innermost folds of the Himalayas. Some god must have lain open this plain in which I could well understand fairies might want to congregate.

Instead of descending into the plain we skirted it to the north following the river high above its bank. From our vantage point I could look over the central province of Zanskar on to a clump of trees which enclosed and dissimulated the monastery of Sani. This monastery, Lobsang remarked, was the oldest in the land. Here the great Indian Buddhist monk, Panchen Naropa, had resided in the eleventh century and the saintly Bodhisattva (Lama) Guru Rimpoche, the founder of Lamaism often also called Padma Sambhava. I had visited virtually a hundred shrines where he is said to have resided, some in far-away Bhutan, and some in Mustang. I therefore showed no enthusiasm for Lobsang's observation about Sani Gompa.

Seeing I was unimpressed he was reproachful and took me to a spot marked by a little chorten and a cluster of prayer flags. There, under a stone, he proudly showed me the clear imprint in a rock of a human footprint he claimed to be Padma Sambhava's. The saint had rested there while fleeing from the monastery to go to a cave above our heads which Lobsang pointed out to me. This was the first truly unusual footprint I had ever seen and to Lobsang's delight, I expressed my admiration. Once again I appreciated I was not going to get anywhere if I did not believe in all I was told. How indeed could I hope to understand the local people if I did not see miracles where miracles happened and ghosts where ghosts lurked? I must, I repeatedly told myself, truly believe in the marvellous, and in spirits if I was to communicate fully with any Zanskari.

Usually it takes me a week to get rid of the habits of my rational Western self, to stop querying every fact and figure and searching for an explanation to every phenomenon. This period over, I began to believe in witches and ghosts, gods and demons, good and evil spirits and endless other characters that in the West I liked to consider imaginary – in the same manner that Lobsang would consider unreal and laugh at all the dreary statistics in which we believe, such as the height in feet of our tallest buildings, or the exact distance in miles between the earth and the moon, the facts and figures which mould our lives and command respect in our figure-mad world. But what do figures mean, or spirits, if one does not believe in them? The answer is nothing, for it is Faith that counts. Often we would be at a loss to check many of the facts we believe in; we accept them with that same blind faith with which I now accepted the presence of demons and the miracle of the footprint. After all both Guru Rimpoche and Naropa were in fact historical persons who lived in the eighth and eleventh centuries respectively and indeed spread Buddhism to many Himalayan regions. As to how ancient and famous Sani Gompa was, I had still a lot to learn.

Towards midday, turning behind the shoulder of a hill, we found ourselves facing a vast natural amphitheatre on whose green gradients four small villages and several large buildings were laid out.

These hamlets, with their houses linked together, looked like fortresses rising above the plain of Zanskar. I was struck by the sheer elegance of Himalayan houses, houses whose sloping walls emerged from rocky pedestals to rise like mountains; they were decorated with the sober grace of symmetrical windows outlined in black against whitewashed walls. Nowhere in the East can one find an architecture more grandiose or pleasing to the eye. One that depends on form and not on decoration.

This great natural amphitheatre was backed against a grand peak from which tumbled streams that flowed between the villages.

The sun which had been absent over the past three days had reappeared and when the entire skin of my nose came off, I began to wonder whether I did not prefer the bad weather. I had been badly sunburnt in a few hours in spite of a thick layer of cream under which I fried. Later that day, while shaving in a stream, I had a look at my face which I realised must look truly odd and frightening to the local inhabitants for while my nose was unduly large by Himalayan standards, now as well it was that brilliant pinky-red so dear to clowns.

In a grassy field traversed by a clear stream Lobsang decided we should stop to eat and let the horses graze. I agreed and got busy preparing a meal of lentils. I was rather upset that Lobsang showed no inclination to cook for me. Of course he had not the slightest idea as to what food a European might like to eat. However we had become real friends and I hoped he would stay with me throughout my journey. We were now heading for Lobsang's father's house where Lobsang lived when not at his monastery or roaming the world.

The village at the foot of which we were picnicking was called Konchet and, more than the other villages, it resembled a fortress on a spur. This was where Lobsang's brother lived, while his own house lay far up the mountainside several miles from the village. Slowly I began to understand that the house owned by Lobsang's elder brother had once belonged to their father. In this connection Lobsang told me about the odd Zanskari custom concerning what are known as 'little' houses.

When the eldest son marries he then becomes the *dakpo* (owner) of his father's land and house. The father retires from active life and goes to live in a building called the 'little' house. I had heard of a similar custom in Mustang: in Zanskar this custom is so strictly carried out that every family has two distinct homes; the 'large' house, usually a vast structure of up to fifteen rooms, and the 'small' house, sometimes immediately adjacent to it. Thus every village is composed of two types of households; the large active homesteads in which live the eldest son with his wife and small children, and the little houses inhabited by 'retired parents' along with old aunts, grandmothers and unmarried sons, including those who have become monks. A few fields are given to the retired parents who cultivate them for themselves with the aid of the eldest son and other relatives.

Having eaten, and since Lobsang planned to graze the horses for a while longer, I set out with a child to visit Konchet. To reach the village I followed the stream by which I had eaten, reaching two little watermills.

They were powered by horizontal waterwheels, upon which a jet of water was directed through a pipe made from hollowed-out logs. This system is far simpler than the vertical waterwheels of Europe, it is in fact a system allied to that of modern turbines. These mills are used for grinding popped barley (barley grain that has been roasted). When ground it becomes tsampa, the cooked flour that forms the basic diet, if not the only food, of all the Tibetan peoples of the Himalayas.

Leaving the mills I clambered up a steep slope to the fortress-like village. At the foot of the first houses I came upon a wall of stones, on one of which were carved classical prayers such as '*Om mani padma hum*'; others had beautiful carvings of Buddhist divinities and monks, but most unusual were four carved, narrow, vertical stones embedded in the wall. I recognised that at least the largest of these sculptures was very ancient. It represented a rather naïve rendition of a many-headed divinity. I photographed it, not knowing exactly what it was nor of what period. This discovery triggered off in me an interest in old and unusual stone carvings which was soon to lead me to a series of fascinating finds. From now on I never failed to ask if there were old stone carvings in all the places I visited.

My little guide led me on through the narrow streets between the houses perched on the rocky outcrop. I was not let into Lobsang's brother's house as he was away, but walking around it I ran into a fine old man busy weaving on a loom set up in the shade of a house. He was Lobsang's father, he smiled a warm welcome and then showed me how his loom worked. It was an amazing affair because the scarcity of wood resulted in all its parts being made of crooked sticks, which gave the loom a rickety, knobbly, surrealistic appearance. However, this did not seem to impede it from operating efficiently. I am not very learned in matters concerning looms but I understand this was of the Jacquard kind with four pedals to raise and lower the different threads; the shuttle was thrown across by hand. Lobsang's father was using undyed wool to weave long strips of material two hands in breadth. The cloth would eventually either be dyed red with a vegetable root dye or left in its natural colour.

Leaving the village I returned to Lobsang who had saddled and loaded the horses; on my way I was escorted by a horde of naughty village boys who laughed at me because I was the first foreigner they had seen.

When I mentioned my interest in ancient carvings to Lobsang, he told me that near the village, perched high above, were three other large and ancient carved stones. I decided to set out for them on my own while Lobsang went to his house which by now was visible high up on the mountainside.

My climb was to be a rugged one and I suffered the first effects of what was soon to prove a minor attack of high-altitude sickness. As I ascended, the valley floor spread out ever wider at my feet until I could see a tangled mass of rock in the distance. Later I was told it was the site of Padum, the capital. To my left, a steep hill rose straight up from the flat plain, it had as a crest one gigantic chorten. This was the sacred shrine of Pipiting.

I now passed a small village built around an exceptionally vast house which I believed to be a castle, perhaps the home of a lord? Behind the village a row of chortens led to a little monastery; unfortunately it was locked. I asked if there was a *go-nyer* to be found but was told that the doorkeeper had gone to Karsha monastery. Most chapels and small monasteries in the Himalayas are always closed, their main door secured by native spring-operated padlocks. These are made locally, they are composed of a housing into which, through narrow slits, fit small folded springs that once in place open out and stop the lock bar from being separated from the housing. To open such locks one needs a key that, when slid through a gap at the bottom of the housing, can be pulled up so as to close the springs and thus allow them to slip out of the housing again. These locks are beautifully ornamented and so are the keys which are sometimes shaped like chortens: they are also extremely effective, when I am in the Himalayas I always purchase some as they can fool the most brilliant lock-picker in Europe.

Passing the village I reached a lonely chapel, alas it too was closed. But my climb was amply rewarded by the incredible view. I had risen to over one thousand feet above the valley and I could now see a new horizon of great snow-covered peaks: they formed the tormented sea of the Great Himalayan Chain, in the heart of whose folds I was now standing. Looking at the flat valley beneath me, set in a gargantuan upheaval of tormented ranges, I saw Zanskar for the first time for what it truly was: the lost valley of all dreams. From my earlier expeditions I knew that throughout the Himalayas no other such inaccessible refuge as this mountain-locked vale existed. In the setting sun I could see the two rivers glitter where they met, before disappearing to the north down a valley flanked by red, green and black peaks. There was no natural exit to this little corner of paradise which lay in the heart of the world's most inhospitable mountains. Suddenly I began to feel the cosiness of this enclosed universe, whose

Rangdum monastery on its hillock, dwarfed by great peaks

The leading citizens of Thunri competing at their
favourite sport, archery

Gallons of *chang* being ladled out at the festival

A Lama giving the 'Blessing of Long Life' at Thunri

The summer living-room of Lobsang's father's house,
inhabited by the old aunts

Young girls at Thunri, their yellow hats indicate that
they belong to the reformed Gelupa sect

The illustrated cover of a fine old book

splendid peaks would from now on be the constant backdrop to all my activities.

Near the monastery an old man directed me a little further up the mountain where there stood three great stones a little over six feet tall, set side by side like three menhirs. They represented three standing Buddhas; alas, some goodwilled vandal had crudely refreshed their age-worn outline. I was sure however that they were very very ancient sculptures most possibly dating from the sixth century AD, that is from before the Tibetan conquest of Zanskar. Having searched in vain for inscriptions I photographed the stellae and then set off to Lobsang's house.

On the way I passed a group of women busily weeding a field of barley, on the edge of which two long strips of newly dyed woollen cloth were laid out to dry. The young women giggled and laughed at my strange face. I laughed back and surprised them by talking Tibetan. With their permission I took photographs of them against the staggering background of the fierce Matterhorn-like peaks that rose on the other side of the valley. Then, leaving the girls singing away I walked up a parched, grassless slope and followed a little irrigation ditch that led me to Lobsang's isolated home.

If there are places where fairies congregate, and if the Vale of Zanskar is one, then certainly within the realm of fairies Lobsang's house must have a very special place because it is the magic universe of three fairy godmothers.

The setting itself is enchanting: a lone house high upon the barren slopes of a great mountain crowned with snow and ice. Small and rectangular with a flat roof, fuzzy with great mounds of brushwood, the house overlooked all of Zanskar, moreover it stood surprisingly in an oasis of green fields enclosed by a stone wall. Fast-flowing rivulets ran through the fields, bubbling a constant tune, as beside the house they formed a natural fountain.

Facing south the house had three small, shuttered windows, which turned a blind eye to a sea of summits above the green carpet of the valley beneath, patched with grey and dotted with toy-like villages. In the sunset the peaks glistened with gold while a wind descended the mountain and brought the freezing breath of glaciers. Chattering with the cold, Lobsang directed me to enter his house by a ladder of twisted pieces of wood that led up to the roof. On the roof, piles of firewood surrounded a central rectangular hole through which, down another rickety ladder, I descended into the bowels of the house, or rather into its summer living-room, a little patio open to the sky.

Beside a fire I could see three figures huddled in the darkness, only when one of them threw a fresh handful of twigs into the flames did I realise they were Lobsang's three fairy godmothers.

I was introduced first to Ibi, Lobsang's great-aunt, such a small, fragile, dried-up, unreal sort of person that I thought she might be a little bit of a ghost. Then there was Ani-che, the older of two aunts, a tall and wild-looking, strong woman, and Ani-chung (meaning small Auntie), she had a smiling Cinderella-like face and two shiny bead-like eyes. As she hobbled around the fire in a slightly grotesque manner I noticed that she was lame. She appeared to me as some strange, crippled vestal keeping the fire alive, forever blowing and fiddling with it while at the same time, playing with pots and pans, some of copper and others of stone. That night we were all to sleep together side by side in the open room under a canopy of crystal stars.

At home Lobsang lost all his authority and became a pampered child spoiled by the three old ladies. After all he was a monk, a holy celibate student, the pride and joy of his large family.

The very old lady, whom I believed to be on the brink of death, turned out to be the life and soul of the place. Quick, fierce and funny, her wit soon focused on me. Later Lobsang told me the story of his great-uncle. A monk who, at twenty-three had become a trader, leaving Zanskar to travel the Himalayan world on his own. More amazing still was the extent of his journeys.

'Although a monk, he had girlfriends all over the world,' Lobsang explained with a wink. It seemed that he had lived in Calcutta, and Lhasa, also in Sarnath, while every few years he would go as far as Bhutan. He was constantly on the move, trading in dyes, inks and paper for Karsha monastery, buying things here and selling them there, specialising in religious objects, ornaments and textiles for chapel decorations.

In disbelief I heard the old man's fascinating story. He was now eighty-two. I could well imagine him during the days of the British Raj in India, leaving his primitive mountain fastness to journey thousands of miles to far off Sarnath, then to modern Calcutta, or north to Darjeeling mingling there with crowds of turbanned Indians and dark Nepalese. From Darjeeling he had travelled to Gangtok, the capital of Sikkim, climbing from there up the Natula pass into the Chumbi valley and then slowly he proceeded to Shigatse, and on to Lhasa, the holy city. It seemed an impossible trek for a monk, or for anyone coming from such an isolated place as Zanskar.

I laid out my sleeping bag and then opened my various baskets and bags in search of an aspirin for one of the aunts. The old great-aunt looked incredibly energetic for her age. She was in fact quite a character and ruled the household with a stern hand. She was nevertheless kind-hearted and welcomed me like a long lost child.

The tall aunt's story was very different and rather sad. She was a divorcee – a rich one. She had the most magnificent head-dress composed of the largest and finest turquoises one could imagine, this dress was her dowry and a dowry is always kept by women even if they divorce.

'After some years,' Lobsang explained, 'she decided that she did not like being married to the man she had chosen and so now lives alone, or rather with us.'

Divorce is frequent in Zanskar and a relatively simple affair entailing no fuss. If there are children the father keeps the boys and the mother the daughters.

Lobsang's favourite aunt was not his amazing great-aunt nor his divorced aunt, but the lame spinster.

'She cooks the best *thuk-pa* in the world,' he said, 'and she is always so happy. I have promised that when they finish the road to Padum I will take her to Leh to the hospital where she will be cured.'

I gathered that his aunt was suffering from acute paralysing rheumatism of one knee. It was touching to observe how the three women fussed over Lobsang, who was a little embarrassed at my witnessing the way in which he lorded it over the three old ladies. Seated to the left of the fire in the place of honour, Lobsang was begged to recite prayers and bless the food that the old ladies served him with great enthusiasm.

I soon realised that with the money he made trading and hiring out his horses, Lobsang financed the entire household. It was he also who, with his elder brother, ploughed the surrounding fields as his father could do no strenuous exercise. The strong aunt also did her share of the field work, helped by the amazingly agile granny. Yet the really heavy work was Lobsang's burden and during the short summer he had to make certain his father and the three old ladies had enough food and fuel to see them through the long winter, most of which they spent marooned by snow in their lofty, isolated house.

In winter it was very cold so they all moved down to the 'winter living-room'. This was sunk half underground and attainable only after having crossed the several outer rooms by which it was surrounded. In these outer rooms, goats, sheep, yak and horses were kept. They were in fact stables and barns connected by very low doors that kept out the cold. The winter living-room too had only a minute door so placed that it could not let in any draught. There are no windows to this living-room, the only light came from the smoky fire and a tiny skylight a foot square that opened into the summer room above. These living-rooms were heated almost exclusively by animal and human warmth. Only by burrowing underground into the inner heart of their house can the Zanskaris survive a winter which is one of the most rugged in the world.

Before I fell asleep that night, amidst the indistinct forms of the three aunts lying upon carpets around the fire, Lobsang explained that next day we would go on foot to visit his monastery at Karsha. This would also give the horses a day's rest, and allow Lobsang's aunts to prepare food for our journey to Zangla.

When he blew out the butter lamp I considered for some time the ease with which I had adapted myself to their unusual, mediaeval way of life. It was as if somewhere inside me were inscribed all the right reflexes and patterns of behaviour. Although I had been raised in a modern world powered by electricity and petrol engines, somehow there seemed to lie in me another self born to live in the simpler manner of days gone by. Was this only an impression or had hundreds of thousands of years of man's struggling in caves around small fires been built into my genes, an inherited acceptance of such a way of life? Certain scholars believe that much of our behaviour is genetically controlled, for instance our ability to speak and even the nature of this speech and its grammar. If men's languages are different, the nature of these languages are remarkably similar; so are the sounds we make and so is the way we all talk. Granted that every race or tribe has its folklore and culture yet even these remain relatively alike.

I believe that within us lies a pattern not only of our shape, size and colour, but of our social behaviour and expectancy of life. Thus here in Zanskar, living in what my fellow countrymen would have considered extraordinary circumstances, I felt perfectly at ease. Is not, I wondered, a monkey happier in a tree, and perhaps man happiest when in a cave-like dwelling sitting around the glow of a small fire?

There is a magic in dim lights, today, alas, found only in nightclubs where noise excludes the whispering of confidential feelings. It is sad that we have forgotten the close human bonds which are sealed by conversations around a low fire where voices have no faces, so things can be said which it is impossible to say in the bright rays of the sun. Beyond doubt, in past ages the long hours spent around dim fires played a significant role in the formation and the well-being of humanity. Perhaps this is one of the strange but not insignificant reasons for the magical attraction of television screens, whose pale lights draw the family into a world of fantasy; that fantasy which is absent elsewhere in our modern world, yet as necessary to man as food is for his body. We all have a craving for the marvellous, and evenings in Zanskar, especially in the cold winter, are spent around soft fires listening to the extraordinary tales that the inhabitants invent to fill their minds with magical visions.

6

A Bridge of Twigs

If darkness has its mystery, dawn brings its promises, and eagerly I got up to go to the monastery of Karsha, 'the largest in the land', as Lobsang proudly reminded me.

Dawn, like dusk, lent a fairy-tale-like quality to the valley beneath us where the long, dark shadows of night still lingered, although the summits glowed a brilliant pink too strong to look at. A strange feeling of both smugness and desolation prevailed, the contrast between sheltered seclusion and isolation. I could not link this valley with other places I had known: Kargil and Srinagar now seemed as far away as London or Paris.

As we skirted Konchet, Lobsang pointed to a small chorten upon a great boulder just behind the highest house. Closer examination revealed the boulder to be covered with naïve carvings of ibex. This was my first sighting of prehistoric designs in Zanskar. Carvings of ibex are widely distributed in the Himalayas and are believed to have been representations of the ibex god of a neolithic people who lived here long before Buddhism reached the Himalayas.

Who had drawn these lively figures? Several thousand years ago Zanskar had perhaps been a warmer place with, who knows, many trees. Touching the rock I could imagine the primitive carver admiring, while he worked, the same great summits I now saw all around me. Did he really believe god to be an ibex, I wondered?

The carvings certainly testified to an exceedingly ancient occupation of the Zanskar valley proving that since the earliest times the highest regions of the Himalayas were inhabited. This speaks well of man's adventurous spirit and ruggedness, and seems to contradict the theory that man was forced into high and hostile mountains only as a result of population

76

pressure in lower lands.

The chorten above the ibex reminded me that many mediaeval crosses in Europe had also been erected on neolithic monuments.

A few miles from Konchet we saw another boulder covered with carvings of ibex and Lobsang told me that the hills around abounded in similar carvings, some showing men with bows and arrows! Close to this second boulder I caught sight of the ruins of an ancient monastery – Gunmoche. Above it, high in a cliff, stood an isolated hermitage built in a cave. In this retreat, Bja Gompa, there lived a recluse, locked away, as it were, from the world. His food was carried up to him by pious villagers.

After crossing a gulley and a steep slope we came round the shoulder of a mountain; from here, at last, we saw the staggering outline of Karsha monastery.

Tibetans, and especially the Himalayans, have a startling knack of erecting buildings in the most unusual and spectacular places. This is probably because most monasteries are built near or over caves, once the retreat of holy men. There is little doubt that Karsha monastery was originally the site of such a cave as its buildings hang upon the near vertical rock face of a mountain. It is the colour of rusty steel. Few of the monasteries I had seen were quite as large as Karsha; its houses are set one on top of the other, as if painted upon the cliff face to which they cling in contradiction to the law of gravity.

The monastery comprised 100-odd whitewashed buildings of varying sizes dominated by two maroon-coloured assembly halls. It looked more like a town than a European convent.

By climbing a little knoll bristling with ancient whitewashed chortens I came in full view of Karsha. With pride Lobsang pointed out the various buildings. At the foot of the cliff was a vast rectangular two-storeyed structure, 'The monastery's stables and granary,' he explained, adding, 'the building on the left is the village assembly hall and chapel.' The numerous buildings above these as far as the halfway line were individual cells, or rather the small private homes of the monks. Halfway up was a large building, the *lhabrang*, the administrative offices of the monastery from which the vast estates of Karsha were run, the great granary was also on this level. Further up was the library which most unfortunately had burnt to the ground seven years previously along with all the precious manuscripts and woodblock books it had housed. A new building had been built, but alas nothing could ever recall those lost literary treasures. Right above the library stood the two highest buildings, the great assembly halls, one used in summer and the other in winter. All the other buildings were monks' quarters, they included a dormitory for young monks.

Karsha monastery belongs to the Gelugpa sect (reformed Yellow Hat sect of which the fourteenth Dalai Lama, now in India, is the head). The patron of the monastery, Lobsang explained, is Tensing Chörgyal, the Dalai Lama's youngest brother. Karsha is the central monastery for some eight villages of northern and central Zanskar. Every village, apart from having its own chapel, is affiliated to a specific monastery, to which villagers' children are despatched. It is customary that every family which has more than one boy sends its second son or sons to a monastery at the age of eight or nine years to learn how to read and write. Although there is no obligation to do so, most parents are pleased to send their children to the monastery and children are equally delighted to go to 'school', to the nearby monastery where their parents come to see them often and where they spend only a part of the year. There is no question of a specific religious vocation, nor is the young monk required to commit his future. Nevertheless, his head is shaven, setting him apart from other children who all wear long braided hair. The child is also given a sleeveless gown worn over a tight little body-vest, and a woollen shawl with which to cover his arms.

What future monastic life has in store for a young pupil is entirely in his own hands, depending both upon his abilities and to a certain degree upon his own economic situation. Every monk is held responsible for providing for his subsistence and is, in this, similar to most European university students. His family usually provide him with a little money and food, some donating a field for his upkeep, which will later become part of the monastery's estate. The monks can either work the land themselves, or have tenant farmers work for them. The produce goes to the monastery to sustain those monks who work in the monastery as teachers, or who are engaged in any other non food or money-producing activities.

Every monk must therefore have either a job at the monastery or personal means of subsistence. Poor monks may work for a small salary in the kitchens or, if they are bright, at writing or copying books for richer monks. Very rich monasteries, rather like Oxford or Cambridge colleges, are sufficiently endowed to hand out grants of money, or barley to their students and to visiting monks. On certain festive days monasteries distribute grain and sometimes money to all the monks.

Once a year all monks are required to live in their monastery. This period, known as *Yarne*, varies in duration from monastery to monastery.

During this time (usually a month) the monks recite the complete set of the Tantric Buddhist Scriptures, the one hundred and eight volumes of the *Kanjur*.

Like universities in which one studies theology, the monasteries give different diplomas or titles similar to our degrees. The young *trawa* (novice) can become a *geshe* (bachelor) if he passes all the required examinations. These are public cross-questionings; the candidate, sitting on a chair placed in the examination courtyard, has to answer correctly and without hesitation all questions put to him by any of the monks present. These questions are shouted at the candidate in a ritual way. The questioner rushes towards the seated candidate, and shouts '*ka-ye*!' and swinging his arms forward in a mock gesture of throwing something, he claps his hands in front of the pupil's face and asks his question. The candidate is supposed to answer tit for tat, elaborating the meaning of some tenet of the doctrine, or of the name of the divinities. If he answers correctly then the student passes on to superior studies which can lead him to the exalted title of *Rab-jam-pa* (Doctor).

Separate from the academic honours are the various religious orders or titles associated with the observance of certain pious rules; from a simple *trawa* one becomes a *geryen* who respects ten rules of pious conduct, then a *get-sul*, observing thirty-six rules, and ultimately a *ge-long*, abiding by two hundred and fifty-three rules. These rules vary from not to steal, or kill, or lie, or not to have sexual intercourse with women, or not to drink alcohol, to such observances as to saying certain prayers daily. None of these observances are necessarily binding for life and one can, so to speak, 'leave the profession' and get married and this is what many young novices do.

Brilliant monks are in great demand in their native villages and even elsewhere to officiate at the many religious ceremonies associated with daily life, such as the choice and blessing of the construction site of a new house, the giving of a name to an infant, funeral rites, or the chasing of demons. Monks also cure the sick, both as doctors distributing potions and herbs, and by chasing away the demons which bring about disease.

Lobsang had studied medicine in Tibet where he lived for nearly four years. Together we sat at the foot of Karsha monastery, he eating tsampa dipped in water, myself – horrible Indian biscuits and peanut butter, not a very holy or even healthy meal.

'You must meet my great-uncle,' Lobsang said ,'the one who has been to Lhasa. He is a great character.'

Having finished eating I briefly inspected the village of Karsha spread out at the foot of the monastery, on either side of the rushing stream. Several houses were quite large and sported loggia-like balconies. I have always been a little disturbed by these elegant yet rather inconvenient rooms typical of Himalayan architecture, as it is generally too cold to enjoy sitting in them. The absence of glass (unknown in the Himalayas) makes them cold even when the wooden lattices closing the vast windows are sealed with paper.

One of the large houses I admired belonged to the local Lumbo, an aristocrat. Lumbos are of noble blood and it was from among them that the two Kings of Zanskar sought their brides. Their exact role and the number of noble families in Zanskar I did not know, but I hoped to find out from the Kings themselves.

I however learned that the Lumbo of Karsha had once been very powerful, as testified by the ruins of a giant fort set upon a cliff opposite the monastery. Beneath it was a small chapel, the Lumbo's private chapel, presently part of a nunnery. It is certainly one of the most ancient in Zanskar, its eleven-headed main divinity being framed by an amazing sculptured and garland-like aura composed of a pair of whale-like monsters and strange female divinities dangling from a winged garuda (an Indian mythological figure). The style is very similar to those found in the oldest chapels of Lamayuru and Alchi monasteries, which are among the finest in Ladakh. The frescos on the walls of this chapel were also ancient and exquisite. Just above the Lumbo's chapel stood a door chorten, claimed to have been built by the famous Lama, Rinchen Zangpo, the eleventh-century reviver of Buddhism in western Tibet. It is indeed unusually fine, in particular the quality of the paintings upon its vault is remarkable. In it an unusual frieze of ducks in red and blue mingle with the more classical symbols of the Buddha. But most outstanding are the, alas, badly damaged statues that lie in opposite niches in the chorten: one representing a Buddha in the finest Greco-Buddhist tradition, with Greek curly hair and a straight nose; the other too damaged to be easily identified, no doubt represented Maitreya, the 'Buddha to come'. Both these terracotta figures, which are of great finesse, were half covered with funerary offerings – little, chorten-shaped, moulded clay objects in which special prayers written on paper, and to which are mixed the ashes of the dead, are often placed.

At the foot of Karsha monastery, against the rock, stands the village monastery, or rather chapel, built around an amazing fifteen-foot standing figure of Maitreya carved in the rock face. Above this in the same rock are several other carvings of Buddhist figures. These are claimed to date from the time of Kanishka (first century AD). Although I doubted if they were quite so old, I was certain that Karsha was a sacred place before the Tibetan conquest in the eighth century.

Passing a narrow door chorten I entered the main monastery and began a slow ascent up a steep and zigzagging path that passed beneath other chortens winding its way in, out and under numerous buildings. Inside the tunnels beneath the buildings little wooden doors branched off on either side, entrances to the cosy houses of the monks. Lobsang led me through this fairy-like world to a tall house – that of his great-uncle. Lobsang called and a booming voice answered. Then a huge, burly man poked his head out of a window. He opened a low wooden door through which I passed. Coming into a minute entrance hall I turned up some steep steps and clambered into the monk's sitting-room which was on the first floor. Here I was asked to sit down while Lobsang exchanged news with his great-uncle.

'How many times have you been to Lhasa?' I eventually asked.

'Thirty times,' answered the big monk, adding, 'I was in charge of the trade of this monastery. Seven times I went overland via Ladakh, then Rudok and Sakya. Those journeys took fully six months.'

Such a journey seems awesome, if not terrible to us who have come to consider travelling as a short period of waiting between two destinations. Of course this is not how the Himalayans or people of the past saw travelling. For them, as for myself since I left Srinagar, it meant visiting places, and was above all a way of life. Their ultimate goal is often seen simply as an excuse for the journey, at best as a not very urgent goal at the end of a visit to, and through, new and different places. To journey for six months was a pleasurable adventure, a sightseeing tour which few but the sick could consider a burden. To travel meant to make new friends, to learn new songs, to acquire new skills and especially to gain religious merit by visiting as many shrines as possible.

Today in the West we often forget that man is a roaming species, and that even sedentary peoples invent some sort of excuse to travel. In the past there were the crusades, or pilgrimages; today there are jet tour holidays. Alas fast planes and organised tourism tend to defeat the object of travel, which is to move slowly through places meeting different people. For us, human contact is reduced to a word here and there with porters and servants in hotels and they are amazingly similar from

Tamanrasset to Rangoon. The one little human discovery left is meeting the people one travels with.

Lobsang's uncle was very proud of his long journeys across Tibet and India to Lhasa. Located at the far eastern extremity of the Tibetan world, the Zanskaris had far to go to reach the holy city which every devout Lamaist dreams of visiting at least once in his lifetime. Second on the list of journeys from the Himalayas is a visit to the famous shrines of India and Nepal, in particular to the deer park near Benares where Buddha was enlightened, and to Bodhgaya where he is believed to have died.

Lobsang explained how he had been to Lhasa with other monks, accompanied also by his great-uncle. They had taken two weeks to cross the Himalayas, then in India had boarded a train to west Bengal nearly two thousand miles away. From west Bengal they had struck out across Sikkim to Tibet and Lhasa. This southern route was of course much shorter than his uncle's route and revealed all the secrets of modern technology – cars, trains, electricity.

Lobsang was ten years old at the time; he was fourteen when the general uprising in Lhasa against the Chinese obliged him to flee to India, that was in 1959. He was then living in Shigatse, and escaped to India without much trouble as soon as news of the uprising reached him.

Having drunk some tea we got up to resume our visit. Before going I was led to the third floor, a sort of sun roof with a little covered gallery. Such sheltered terraces allowed monks to sit in the winter sun sheltered from the icy breeze.

Nearly all the monks' small houses at Karsha were built on the same plan, comprising three rooms one above the other.

I now realised that the monastery of Karsha stretches up six hundred vertical feet of mountain face. At this moment suddenly my legs would go no further; I suffered a fit of violent heartbeats and feeling faint, had to sit down. I panicked at the thought that maybe I was ill or about to have a heart attack.

On a journey such as the one I was taking there is nothing I fear more than illness, knowing full well that even a slight one could prove fatal, thanks to freezing, draughty rooms and no medical help being available. My only hope would then lie in the prayers of monks, and their not too excellent knowledge of herbs, and with my small medical kit. Even 'flu can be lethal at such high altitudes due to lack of oxygen and there also always lurks the menace of getting a pulmonary oedema, which can be fatal in a matter of days.

My fears were fortunately unfounded; what I was now experiencing was only a severe bout of altitude sickness. Over the past week I had not stopped walking and running around, while my lungs still had trouble absorbing enough oxygen. 'Take it easy,' I heard myself say to a voice inside me that urged me to carry on and visit all the chapels and assembly halls. The latter voice won and I struggled on up to the very top to where two vast buildings were set at either end of a large enclosed courtyard.

The winter assembly hall was in the process of being repaired and its fine porch repainted by an old monk sitting upon some rather shaky scaffolding. Below him lay little pots of brilliant colours with which he painted symbolic designs upon the lintel of the great door. I was let in to the assembly hall, a vast dim structure whose roof was supported by red pillars from which dangled silk banners and religious paintings. Beside the altar stood a small chorten studded with semi-precious stones, while ancient frescos lined the walls of a gallery running just below the roof.

But far more interesting were the several chambers of the other great assembly hall whose entrance was two floors above the courtyard. In the corridor leading to the hall I was startled by the looming figure of a stuffed red bear hung up by its waist, its paws dropping down from the ceiling; glaring hideously, it looked as though it were about to pounce on my head. It is a custom to stuff bears and snow leopards that have been killed in self-defence or to protect cattle and sheep, and to offer them to the monastery. No doubt the offering of the skin compensates for the sin of taking life, although it is accepted practice that one may kill in self-defence.

The summer assembly hall had a large latticed window which admirably framed the central valley of Zanskar, a landscape fit for the gods. One hardly needed practice to meditate on the beauty and grandeur of nature in such a place. The hall was partitioned by an elaborate polychrome latticed screen which separated an altar from the hundreds of pigeon-hole-like shelves in which were kept the one hundred and eight volumes of the Holy Scriptures. These books were two feet long and five inches wide, made up of loose sheets of local paper wrapped up in a silk cloth and compressed between two wooden boards that were elaborately carved and served as a binding. The most striking object in this chapel was the veiled figure of a life-size, eleven-faced divinity with countless arms which I recognised as Avalokitesvara. Against another wall was a fine figure of Dorje Jigchet with hundreds of arms and several horrible faces rising in a tiara-like construction. This divinity is much revered in Zanskar, for he is the tutelary fiend of the Gelugpa sect. I was to see many representations of him in small and large chapels, together with the eleven-headed representation of Avalokitesvara with a thousand arms and an eye in each hand.

What was more unusual was the curious assembly of odd objects upon the altars, not the least strange being a tall, felt hat with a slightly conical top. This, Lobsang said, belonged to the King, and was a sort of ceremonial crown. I had thought it very similar to ancient Portuguese hats seen on countless engravings and paintings of the seventeenth century. It was beige, with a thick red ribbon about its broad rim, and I wondered whether it might not be a treasured heirloom left by an early traveller. Could it have belonged to the Portuguese Diogo, the first European to have visited Ladakh, who might well have crossed Zanskar? What was certain was that the hat was not of a kind generally found in the Himalayas, where hundreds of odd types of head-dresses abound, for there is a different one for nearly every religious rank, ceremony or festival.

It is a custom to place all sorts of odd objects upon the altar of the Lamaist chapels; elephant tusks, cheap European china teapots, or the dried-up human hands of robbers. I had even once seen a tin of Nescafé considered a work of art in a region then totally cut off from the Western world.

With pride Lobsang showed me all the little and great treasures the main chapel contained before leading me to a side chapel where stood an ancient statue of Loepön Dunde, the founder, before which fine silver butter lamps and sacred waterbowls were lined up in their hundreds. I examined some fine wall paintings that fortunately had not yet been restored, or rather repainted, as is the regrettable custom. I also saw a strange pair of bronze animals, a stag and a unicorn ridden by an angel.

Clambering up to the roof of the hall I had a staggering bird's eye view of central Zanskar. I could now see clearly to the east of the monastery where the two rivers united to form the great, fast-flowing and majestic river that descended towards a barren rocky valley and then went out of sight. It was down this valley that I travelled on the following day on my way to visit the King of Zangla.

Having admired the view, I was shown an unusual wooden gong formed by beams suspended with leather straps. This was used to call the *geshe* (bachelors) to assembly. Lobsang then blew a silver-clad conch shell, generally employed to call the monks to the ordinary assemblies.

As I still felt dizzy and unwell I was worried about the march home and decided it was time we set off back to Lobsang's house, a good ten miles away. Unfortunately Lobsang could not refuse an invitation to 'buttered-tea' in the cell of a young monk. This was his little personal house. It had three minute floors, each with a tiny room reached by a toy-like staircase. I could not stand upright in any of the rooms. Lobsang spent a good hour telling his friend how he was now attached to me, a scholar visiting the shrines and places of Zanskar. I realised that all this gossip formed the only and vital basis of people's instruction and information, newspapers of course were unknown along with any other type of news media. For this reason travellers are always welcome and the news they bring amply compensates for the food and drink they consume.

Surely one of the reasons why strangers are unwelcome today in most of the world is that, what with modern communications, they have little or nothing to offer. The current price of wool or meat on distant markets is already known and news of distant relatives comes by post. Radios and televisions now satisfy people's curiosity and the traveller is seen principally as a possible menace, perhaps a thief, or a parasite; alternatively he may be regarded simply as a source of money.

But here in Zanskar everyone wanted me to describe life in my country. They asked what we ate, and whether we had yaks and monasteries as fine as theirs. Many questions I found difficult to answer, while the answers I gave to some questions sounded strange even to my own ears. I was struck by how little there is to say about the West. I had always believed that we had created, through science and a modern economy, an extraordinary way of life, very 'advanced' as we say. Yet when it came to describing our progress it sounded like a rather short list of silly toys. I explained that we had aeroplanes, helicopters, moving staircases and lifts, but now as I described them they did not seem to be such great marvels. Also, I had to face the fact that, apart from automobiles, television, telephones, refrigeration and electricity, most scientific advances fail to affect our daily lives, and when they do it is generally as a substitute for an already existing commodity. Most of our technology is nothing but 'clever associations of chemicals', as my friend Pemba, from Mustang, would have said. As for myself, I had designed a small hovercraft which I called a boat that goes on water and land. Even my own children show little interest in it. In Zanskar I began to accept that our laboratories have not solved in any revolutionary way the problem of existence. Indeed had not the inhabitants of Zanskar perhaps evolved a better way of life?

To live in a land cut off from Western civilisation does not necessarily mean to live in a land devoid of technology. This was brought home to me on leaving Karsha monastery, for right at the foot of the lowest of its buildings I found a very interesting machine. It was a water-driven scraper for making incense from juniper wood.

I had encountered watermills in nearly every village but I had never yet seen hydraulic force harnessed on to anything but a grinding wheel. At Karsha the monks had linked the tiny wheel of a watermill to a rod fixed eccentrically to the wheel so as to rub little logs of juniper up and down over a rough stone. This slow rubbing reduced the wood to a damp pulp which was collected in a sieve made of fine cloth. The conversion of a rotary movement to one of pushing and pulling is in itself a fairly sophisticated technological achievement, and there is no doubt that more sophisticated machines could have been made by the inhabitants of Zanskar had they felt the need for them. Their blacksmiths are so skilled at working copper and silver that they could easily reproduce the most complex mechanism. It is thus neither the skill nor the know-how they lack, but the desire or need for such machines.

The monastery of Karsha was famous for its fragrant juniper incense. 'Where do you get the juniper?' I asked, not having so far seen any juniper tree in the land. I was then told that after four days' walking to the north-east one would arrive at a small valley with several juniper trees. These trees had a particularly fragrant wood, and ground by the method I have described and later dried in the sun, the pulp when burnt gives off a most delicate perfume.

Leaving the little machine throbbing by the riverside I headed home-ward. Our walk in the evening sun was beautiful, but I could not enjoy it much as halfway back my legs seemed to buckle under me. To carry on from resting place to resting place was a terrible ordeal, struggling as I was with a failing heart and weak knees. I prayed that this would prove only a short-lived consequence of having climbed up to 12,000 feet too fast. I was nevertheless worried at being so much affected by the altitude, all the more so because it was my intention to visit not only Zanskar's four districts but also to take a little-travelled and quite dangerously high route over the Shingo-la pass (16,722 feet high) down to India. What would happen if I could not stand the strain? Suddenly I recalled the remark a cardiologist had made to me many years earlier. 'You can't expect to go on expeditions after forty.' I was twenty-six then and forty seemed far away, yet what if the man had been right? I was now thirty-nine.

It was nearly dark when I staggered up to Lobsang's house. There, huddled against the fire, I had a warm drink before sinking into a sleepy

Kârsha, a true monastic city

The central plains of Zanskar seen from Karsha monastery

Monks walking in procession up to Karsha's
main administration building

Monks performing a sacred rite in the main yard
of Karsha monastery

At an early age a child learns to care for
its younger brothers and sisters

Women of Rangdum in all their finery

torpor while Lobsang entertained a young cousin, and the three old ladies fussed around preparing a pea and tsampa soup which I was invited to share.

Eventually I fell asleep excited by the prospect that next day at dawn I would set out to visit the King of Zangla.

My teeth chattered in the freezing air as I got out of a warm sleeping bag and went on to the open veranda at the top of Lobsang's house. Mechanically I rolled up my bedding and slipped it into my kitbag. Then one by one I closed my baskets after collecting a torch here, a notebook there, and the socks I had hung out to dry, thus erasing all the little signs that I had made this house my own for two days. Only for two days, yet I felt I had lived here for much longer. The toothless smile of Lobsang's great-aunt no longer suggested to me the strangeness of an old witch but the charm of a member of the family. Looking at her I could imagine her travelling all over the Himalayan world, a beautiful, strong lady with boyfriends, perhaps even monk friends in distant regions. Then there was the lame aunt still smiling and already shuffling around the fire like an actress in some mediaeval play, and the sleepy face of Lobsang's young friend as he adjusted his flowing robe, and the divorced aunt half awake propped against one of the wooden pillars. We all seemed surprised to find another day. The fire crackled, the water boiled, then my cases were hoisted up through the skylight. I turned around and there was no trace of my presence and I wondered if it all had been true or not . . .

I stepped outside and again I was struck by the magnificent view: a full circle of peaks surrounded the flat sea of the central plain dotted with its villages, refuges in a world unfit for man. If ever there lay a valley cut off from the world, a hidden, secret land, it was Zanskar. I could hardly believe that only recently I had left a world which is polluted and over-populated. Everything in Zanskar I found near to perfection: nothing, so it seemed, was out of place or unnatural. The rusty carcasses of tin cans and automobiles, and the death-like skeletons of electric poles, the hideous rust of corrugated iron, the soiled look of waste paper, the deadly gleam of scraps of plastic were absent; nowhere was there the slightest reminder of mechanical ugliness. I do not know what it is that makes all manufactured objects become so ugly the day they are old, worn or broken. Natural decay is rarely as revolting as say a rusty, broken washing-machine.

There was nothing here to tarnish the harmony of nature in which man has his natural place blending with the earth, dressed and fed by its products, moulded by its demands and formed by its seasons. Every image was an ideal one: the horse with its wooden saddle, the yak-hair mattress covered by a woollen carpet whose design represented clouds and mountains.

Waving goodbye to the three old ladies we stepped down the slope towards a ravine.

It was cold as part of our route still lay in the shade. I had not gone far when Lobsang stopped and showed me a little grassy patch beside a small torrent in which I noticed several rectangular holes cut out of the turf. Lobsang, to my surprise, sat in one, demonstrating that these were baths for taking the medicinal waters which seeped from a little spring nearby. These waters, according to him, were very good for rheumatism, yet were alas unable to cure his aunt. This was the first time I had encountered medicinal springs in the Himalayas, although I had seen several hot springs much esteemed for picnics and bathing. I could not help but smile at such rudimentary baths as these holes in the ground that patients had to dig for themselves. Water was diverted into the baths by digging a little channel from the spring. This was a long shot from the sophisticated installations of Vichy, not far from where I live in France. Who knows, perhaps one day it may be discovered that the waters of Zanskar are the best in the world.

After two hours we reached Karsha monastery. Here we stopped while Lobsang went in to fetch a friend who was to come with us to bring back the horses, as they would not be able to cross the bridge that led to the far side of the Zanskar river. After visiting Zangla, and hopefully meeting its King, I intended to travel up the eastern bank of the Zanskar river until I reached a bridge near Padum, which is the capital, and the residence of the country's other King.

I was keen on unravelling some of the mysteries of Zanskar's history and hoped to find new documents; up until now the only historical document on the country was a copy made from scraps of a rat-eaten book which itself was a copy of a book. It was said to lie in the monastery of Phugtal in the far eastern part of Zanskar.

These so-called 'Chronicles' were in fact a brief list of the names of a few local lords and the taxes they levied; all this bore little relation to what must have been the long and prosperous history of an independent kingdom. I hoped that I might perhaps be able to throw more light on the land's past and its political organisation.

From various chronicles of the history of Tibet and of Ladakh it is

certain that Zanskar became a fully independent Kingdom in the year
AD 930 when upon the death of King Nimagon, western Tibet was
divided among his three sons: Rig-pa-mgon who became King of Ladakh,
bKrasis-mgon, King of Guge, and lDe-gtsug-mgon, King of Zanskar. It is
believed that Zanskar later dominated the ancient Kingdom of Guge,
thus controlling at least for some time all the south-western Himalayas.
Its royal family, the lDes, ruled over a territory four times greater than
that of Zanskar of today.

In 1641 Zanskar lost its autonomy as a result of a dynastic feud and
because of the power of the famous Ladakhi King, Sengye rNamgyal,
who also conquered Guge, Spiti and Rupchu, and placed on the throne of
Zanskar his son, De-chog-rnam-rgyal, whose descendents continued to
rule Zanskar as an independent country. In 1836 after nine hundred years
of independence Zanskar fell under the domination of the Dogras, Hindus
from Jammu, who also conquered Ladakh. The Dogras levied taxes in
Zanskar for a few years but they never held the region very firmly.
Indeed the Zanskaris, after their initial capitulation, rebelled several times
until the old King Richen-den-grub rNamgyal was taken as a prisoner
south of the Himalayas to Jammu, where he died (or was killed). Who
then, I wondered, was the so-called rGyalpo of Padum, the avowed heir
to the throne of Zanskar, the mysterious King of Zangla? There seemed
too many kings for such a small place and I was anxious to find out more
about their families.

Leaving the Karsha monastery behind, we followed the shoulder of a
huge barren mountain, passing a great prayer wall. This was both unusual
in its size and conception, as it was hollow. It had the appearance of a solid
mass of stones, ten feet wide and five feet tall, with a slightly slanted roof
covered with boulders carved with the prayer 'Om mani padme hum'. Small
prayer walls abound all over Zanskar and the Buddhist Himalayas but
this one was remarkable for its height, width, and the fact that it was nearly
a mile long! It would be impossible to count how many inscriptions there
were, for each stone carried one. As well as the many hundreds of
thousands of inscribed stones there were also hundreds of delicately
carved images of lamas and divinities. I was told this wall had been con-
structed by that King of Zanskar who had built a great royal causeway
from Padum to the Karsha monastery. It ran over the flat central plains
and led to a large bridge, now gone, that used to cross the river beneath
the monastery. Looking for traces of the bridge I could not see any, but
could clearly distinguish two rows of white stones still marking the

straight sides of what must have been the great causeway that stretched right across to Padum, which was visible in the distance.

Turning north we headed down a barren valley and entered Cham, the northern district of Zanskar.

In central Zanskar the horizon had been hemmed by snow-covered peaks, but here no snow was visible. To our left rose a great mountain tinted green by copper oxide, while to the east, on the other side of the Zanskar river, we saw a sinister black mountain which seemed to be made of coal. Further south were other summits, some the colour of rusty iron, others of a bright and rather unnatural yellow.

These eroded mineral peaks were part of the mighty Zanskar Range which runs parallel to the Great Himalayan Range for about three hundred and fifty miles. Indeed it extends all the way from Tibet to the head of the Suru valley.

Hidden by the Great Himalayan Range, this range gets little or no rainfall and therefore little or no snow; fields of naked mineral rock strewn upon a bed of sand extended as far as I could see. The general impression was one of desert-like solitude hardly disturbed by the heat waves that rose from the sun-scorched stones.

Having walked and ridden across a vast stony plain, the trail joined the river, following the lip of its steep, eroded bank. Looking down I could see muddy swirls as the Zanskar flowed at the limit of its flood-line, carrying down silt and boulders which rumbled in the riverbed with a thumping noise that, along with the quiet swish of foam, told of a formidable current. The Zanskar river is the largest affluent of the upper Indus, whose waters it joins in Ladakh after having run through a hundred and twenty miles of narrow and unpassable gorges.

The province of Cham is composed of rare, flat ledges above the river, lying between the shoulders of mountains that fall to the water's edge. Penetrating the first of these alluvial plains I could see in the distance a cluster of willow trees surrounding a few houses ringed by green fields. This was the small village of Rinam, made up of five homesteads and two small houses (aged parents' homes). To the south of the village, on the edges of an irrigation ditch, we found a little grass on which our horses could graze and so stopped to eat lunch. Once again the sun was unbearable and my nose peeled, revealing an ever redder and more tender appendage that I now had to seriously protect for fear of third-degree burns. Having eaten a small can of meat and some unleavened wheat cakes given to me by Lobsang, I rested a while before setting out again, down what appeared like death valley. A hot dry wind raced over the burning rocks that singed my feet through the thick soles of my shoes. It was impossible to ride as our horses showed extreme signs of exhaustion and the only incentive I had to carry me on was that Lobsang and his friend had told me how a little further south lay a stream with gold in its waters. Naïvely, I believed I might find a nugget or a little dust; of course I found nothing. For several hours after crossing the stream we progressed in a narrow, suffocating canyon clinging to the river, passing a spot where some fifteen years before a bridge across the river had been swept away.

In places the trail widened when crossing little miniature deserts of sand studded with brittle desert grass, at best fit only for camels. The horses looked miserable plodding along between massive boulders that had fallen from the cliffs above us. It could have been a long and dreary march were it not overshadowed by the exotic excitement of penetrating a truly different world and the anticipation of soon seeing Zangla, the home of the mysterious King of that name.

Towards three o'clock in the afternoon, utterly exhausted, I rode on to a vast plain speckled with little patches of grass where water had spilled out of an irrigation ditch on to otherwise barren sandy soil. In the far distance I could see a row of chortens marking the trade route and announcing a distant village. This lay at the foot of a small monastery, dwarfed by a great eroded cliff whose fantastic turrets and towers rose towards a blood-red gully of tumbled rocks.

I reached Pishu with relief, it is a desolate village rather similar to those isolated American-Indian settlements of the Colorado valley, a halting place for a night rather than a place to live in. Although fairly large and possibly prosperous, the village had a run-down look about it. A dusty main street cut it in two: the houses on one side backed against a sharp cliff that fell to the great river, on the far side of which, to the south, the distant fields of Zangla could be seen looking like an oasis.

I suggested we carry on to Zangla that day, but was told this would be impossible.

'One cannot cross the bridge at dusk,' Lobsang explained.

'Why not?' I asked, not realising what sort of a structure it was.

For the night I was offered a small room in a large house that seemed neat and reasonably clean. Little could I then foresee that this was to result in severe wounds, much frustration and eight full days of furious scratching.

'To bite a flea is hardly food for the stomach but how nourishing for the soul,' goes a Tibetan proverb. I had to agree as, forgetting all taboos about respecting life, and in spite of the difference in size and the Geneva convention, I killed all prisoners!

While Lobsang was getting things ready for our dinner I was invited by some villagers to come and join them in the community chapel. There, sitting cross-legged in a cloister, I found myself surrounded by a merry crowd of beer-drinking men and women busy chanting verse after verse from a small prayer book. Luck had it that I had arrived on the day of a monthly celebration called *Luruma*, consisting of the reading of scriptures by the villagers. Each household, and there were twenty-one at the village of Pishu, in turn provided chang, gallons and gallons of it, for the occasion.

While I indulged in my favourite drink I had ample time to examine the villagers. All were dressed in their everyday tattered woollen robes, the women wearing crudely tanned goatskins on their backs. I had seen goatskins worn in this fashion in Bhutan where they served the purpose of protecting their wearers from the cuts inflicted by heavy and uneven loads. Here, all the women wore jewellery around their necks and several sported fancy dog-eared fur flaps and turquoise-studded head straps. I had, in fact, seen quite a few women wearing their finest jewellery while working in the fields although their gowns might be ragged.

Eventually I was to find out why the older women wore all their riches even on what seemed very unsuitable occasions. This was a result of the history of invasion and pillage that Zanskar had suffered. By wearing all their wealth the women were ready to flee to the hills at an instant's notice.

While we chanted, women continually passed chang around so that slowly the atmosphere became less and less holy as jokes circulated between verses. Children ran all over the place, making a nuisance of themselves by constantly opening the outside door, thus letting in a raging wind that caused a miniature sandstorm whose deposit floated upon my never-empty cup of chang. Most of the adults were busy spinning wool with small, top-like spindles.

While observing all this I was myself the object of close scrutiny, and my shirt, trousers, sunglasses, hat and shoes were poked at, for after all I was one of the very few, perhaps two or three, foreigners to have come to Pishu.

After about an hour, with great trouble I managed to leave the now very drunken assembly; the ceremony had not yet ended. Finally I retired to a nocturnal safari against the terrible fleas. Someone, alas, had forgotten to explain to them the deadly effects of DDT, for they completely ignored the floods of insecticide with which I had covered my body. Leeches in the lower, damp southern Himalayas and fleas in the north are responsible for the real hardships of Himalayan travel. My parasites and I awoke early the next day. I found Lobsang giving instructions to the monk who had accompanied us as to what to do with the horses he was to take back. Several villagers were then hired to carry my bags on their backs. So, accompanied by a small crowd I left Pishu and travelled upstream for about a mile along the cold-looking swirling river, in parts fully 300 feet wide. The recent rain had swollen it so that its surface was very near to the top of its banks.

Walking along I could not see the bridge until I came right up to it, then my stomach began to flutter. It was a suspension bridge, one so long, so low and so narrow that it seemed to defy all the laws of engineering. In Bhutan and Nepal I had crossed many a home-made suspension bridge, some with hand-forged steel chains, others made of thick, twisted bamboo ropes. Some were long, some short, and many ancient with mouldy loose planks; others were lined with bamboo matting that wobbled and bent beneath one's weight as if one were walking on a sponge. None was agreeable to cross yet not one had been as fearful as the Zangla bridge. Approximately two hundred feet long, it was the longest suspension bridge over Himalayan waters. Yet its length was nothing compared to the frightening nature of its construction. The ropes were made of brittle twigs somehow plaited together four strands at a time, and yet the whole rope was barely the thickness of three fingers.

Four such ropes laid side by side formed the only support for one's feet, which presumably had to be placed cross-wise upon them. Two or three similar ropes were slung across on either side to form handrails, they were loosely linked to the lower strands by small lengths of the same brittle rope.

Now I understood why it would have been impossible to try and cross the bridge on the previous evening, given the strong wind. Already in the still dawn air the centre of the bridge swung dangerously like a pendulum.

There are a few facts one should, or rather should not know about primitive suspension bridges. The first is that they have two types of movement, one side to side and the other up and down. The up and down movement is caused by the shifting weight of the person passing over them, it can give a little violent upward thrust that could topple the traveller overboard. The pendular movement is still more to be feared because efforts to stop it generally increase it. But the greatest menace of all lies in the innocent look of the handrails (the two ropes on either side of the bridge). They appear to be convenient aids to keep one's balance; regrettably such an erroneous belief can lead to a quick death, for if one leans on one of the handrails it simply swings out. Someone doing this will find himself clinging on to it and, gripping the lower rope with his toes, irretrievably stuck whilst he lies flat over the river. Handrails are *not* there to lean upon, but at best just to touch, both at the same time, for if not they will move outward in a deadly fashion.

I realised that this bridge, the longest I had ever encountered, was bound to have the greatest rock, swing, and tendency to open out.

What I did not yet know was that, contrary to what one might expect, the swing and the vibrations are less if one crosses several at a time, the extra weight and the break in rhythm, along with the fact that all simultaneously pull inwards at the handrails, reduce the risks considerably.

Wrongly I thought that by crossing the bridge on my own I should not suffer the movements arising from the actions of the others. Boldly and foolishly I struck out alone.

Foot by foot I advanced like a tight-rope walker, feet out in duck fashion, my hands gripping the rough and cutting twigs of the lateral ropes. The first twenty paces presented no problem. Then I began to worry, a worry which turned to fear as, peering at my feet, I saw the water below rushing past making the bridge seem to tilt upstream. Correcting this illusion I leant to one side; it was then that the rope swung out. Clutching both sides and pulling them together I sensed a tremor as the taut ropes vibrated. As the water continued to rush by under my swinging feet I felt weak at the knees. Fleetingly I looked at the other bank, it seemed miles away, I had not yet crossed one third of the span. By now I was really frightened, and thoughts of sudden death filled my mind. I noticed that the handrails, which at the start of the bridge had been at the height of my shoulders, were now somewhere below my hips, getting ever lower. By the time I had reached the centre of the bridge, which was now swinging in all directions, the handrails were at the level of my knees and quite useless to help me to keep my balance. In terror I plodded on, step by step, till at long last I made it to the other side.

Looking back I saw the others come across bunched together four at a time, walking at a pace that must have made mine seem quite ridiculous. At last I could understand why some people in Zanskar had never in their lives visited the other half of the land in summer.

One of our men had a dog and made the crossing with it strapped to his shoulders. Having recovered from my fright I examined the construction more closely and marvelled at the boldness of the design. The ropes were simply run around crossbeams of wood anchored into stone piles on either side of the river. These piles were made of uncut stones placed one on top of each other with brushwood laid in between to act as mortar.

Lobsang explained how every three households in the district had to make a hundred and twenty paces of rope each year. These were produced in the spring from the little branches of a wild bush that grew in the mountains. These twigs, the longest rarely exceeding two feet, were wetted and then twisted into strands, four of which were braided together. On drying, the twigs retained the shape of the braiding, and to all appearances such strands are very strong.

'But,' Lobsang said, 'the ropes rot very quickly and have to be replaced every two years.'

On the other side of the bridge we met a boy with two dog-sized donkeys on to which my bags were loaded. Together we all set off down the Zanskar river towards Zangla. Looking back at the bridge I sighed with relief at the thought that I would not have to cross it again, as I intended to follow the left bank upstream to Padum, where I would cross another bridge which could never, I felt, be as bad as this one. In fact it was worse!

7

The Kings of Zangla

A few hundred yards down from the bridge we came to a grassy field on the edge of the swirling river. Here I noticed hundreds of little rectangular depressions in the turf: this was the second of Zanskar's two spas and the most popular, judging from the number of 'baths' and the ruins of what might have been a bath house.

Our trail followed the river very closely for several miles until at last we reached the rocky bed of a lateral torrent that issued from a deep canyon, formed on one side by six hundred feet of towering rock, upon which rested an incredible fortress. This was the ancient stronghold of the Kings of Zangla.

'The King doesn't live there today; he now resides in a palace in the village at its feet,' Lobsang told me. I was relieved at not having to climb up the cliff yet a little disappointed for I had never seen a more staggering site for a fort. Standing on its sheer cliff the fortress, overlooking a sheer vertical drop, seemed totally inaccessible. Certainly no one could ever have conquered such a place, and indeed no one ever had.

Fording the freezing torrent we emerged on to a desert-like plain cut by the solitary outline of a chorten and prayer wall. After crossing it we came to the first green fields of Zangla, a village of forty large houses and twenty-eight small ones.

The problem of where I should stay now arose. Secretly I wished to stay at the palace, a vast manor-like building, but I could not invite myself. I had imagined that the King lived in this palace, but when I enquired I was told that the palace belonged to the King's son, the young man I had encountered while travelling up the Suru valley. The old King lived in a 'small palace', the royal equivalent to the 'small house' of retired parents, and so I learned that even kings cannot escape the custom of giving their status, title and palace to their eldest son when he gets married.

'I will go and see the King,' said Lobsang. 'Perhaps he will invite you.' He then disappeared leaving our luggage with the small boy who owned the donkeys. I meanwhile set out to examine the village. Above it was a large reservoir that served to irrigate the fields; as a result, Zangla stood out as a green oasis surrounded by the barren stone cliff of a great mountain. It was on one of its spurs that the impressive castle which dominated the village was built. To the south, cut off from Zangla by a stream, rose the half-dozen small buildings of a nunnery, beyond it the Zanskar gorge closed in on the river which here disappeared into a deep canyon.

A few minutes after my return to the village Lobsang came rushing up to say I was invited to meet the rGyalpo. Walking back to the donkeys I hastily extracted a cotton ceremonial scarf from one of my packs. Tradition requires that one should always present a person of rank with such a white scarf. For such occasions I had brought several presents, of which the finest were silver fountain pens. I got one of these ready and followed Lobsang into the 'small palace' of the King of Zangla.

It was a rectangular building no different from most of the large houses of Zangla. I entered by a low ground-floor door leading into the stables. A sharp turn then led to a stone staircase that took another turn before rising up to an enclosed rectangular courtyard, one side of which was sheltered by the overhanging roof, while on the other three sides were little wooden doors. At the far end, three bay windows led into a loggia overlooking the patio. Four tiny golden-coloured Tibetan dogs of the short-haired variety raised a terrible din on my approach. Two girls, about sixteen years old, with Dutch-like turned-up bonnets and dark blue capes over their wine-red gowns were sitting in the yard. One was very attractive and the other rather plain. They shouted to the dogs, while out of a smoky room came a woman whose noble features were marred by a solitary protruding tooth. She pointed to a low door opposite the loggia; beyond it, she told us, sat 'the Victorious One', the rGyalpo of Zangla.

Bending low to pass through the door, and still pursued by the little dogs, I found myself in a minute room almost filled by a raised platform covered with orange and blue carpets. The room had one small window which I noticed because it had a pane of glass, the first I had seen since leaving Kargil. Seated in a corner was a thin old man draped in a vast wine-coloured gown with a straight collar and a beige woollen balaclava

97

hat. This was His Majesty, Sonam Thondup rNamgyal lDe, King of Zangla. I bowed and laid my white scarf before him, somewhat ashamed as it was of the cheapest variety, the only kind I had been able to find. The old man acknowledged it with a smile and asked me to sit by his side upon the carpets. I hastily slipped off my shoes and clambered up on to the raised platform in front of which stood little, low, rectangular bench-like tables.

The King signalled to Lobsang to join us and then shouted for tea. One of the girls I had seen in the courtyard came in, her ruddy face hiding a grin of amused curiosity as she looked at my Western face.

The King, not yet appreciating that I spoke Tibetan, asked Lobsang to tell me to excuse him while he finished the religious rite he was performing. On a low table before the King was laid out a vast, beaten copper pan, half full of water and in which stood a silver tripod. A copper pot rested on this rather like a kettle; it was richly adorned with silver decorations. On the table was a small saucer, a circular shiny silver disc and a silver spoon. To one side stood a little pile of peas. Reciting prayers, the King poured drops of water into the large pan, and then on to the little saucer in which he placed the peas; then, taking water in the spoon and drawing designs upon the mirror with it, he mumbled various prayers. The ritual dragged on for half an hour and I began to feel quite ill at ease though at least I had time to take a good look at the King's face. He wore horn-rimmed glasses and seemed, I thought, an exact replica of the typical American 'granpa' with pale flabby cheeks and gums that betrayed many missing teeth. His expression was warm and friendly and his concentration on his religious rite did not alter this.

At last he put aside the complex vases needed for the ritual benediction and turned towards me.

'Where are you from?' was his first question, to which my answer, 'From France,' illicited no reaction, hinting that he might not know where France was.

'I have come to study the customs of Zanskar and Zangla,' I added. The tea arrived, it was *Chini* or English tea with two lumps of sugar. The King took some rather plain European china cups off a shelf. He did not use the superb Tibetan silver cups on silver stands covered with a cymbal-like lid in which he normally drank Tibetan tea. I appreciated his kind concern and commented on how well-made the English tea was, and accepted some biscuits the King gave me. Finally I decided to go straight to the point: risking being rude, I expressed my curiosity as to who was the King of Zangla.

To my delight the answer to what might have been considered a cheeky question by a less intelligent monarch was explained to me. The King's family, a lesser branch of the royal family of Padum, had ruled the country from AD 1020, for nearly one thousand years. Right up until a hundred years ago, they lived at Zangla, in the town standing upon the rocky crag around the high fortress above the present settlement. From this castle the Kings ruled over the four villages of the north province of Zanskar. Their control over this small territory had never been challenged, not even when the King of Ladakh placed his son on the more powerful throne of Zanskar. Even when, in 1836, the Dogras invaded Zanskar, the King of Zangla had retained his position because of help he gave them fighting against the Ladakhis. It was thus that Zangla, with its fortress and four villages, had retained a separate identity and continued to be ruled by the same family. A buffer state to a buffer state, a mini-kingdom within an already small kingdom.

Then, as if to add weight to his claims, the old King rummaged in a chest and produced the second volume of Francke's *Antiquities of Indian Tibet* in which are recorded in Tibetan and in English the brief 'Chronicles of Zanskar' I have already mentioned, and the detailed genealogy of the Kings of Zangla which had been given to Francke in 1915 by a Ladakhi lama. Francke's study of this genealogy may not be entirely correct as to the dates and names of the earliest Kings of Zangla but there can be little doubt about the authenticity of the claim of the present King of Zangla whose name figures in Francke's book with the mention 'child in 1915'. The rGyalpo was now in fact nearly seventy while his son, Nyima Norbu, was about to become a father.

This genealogy made the rGyalpos of Zangla among the oldest ruling families of Asia. Later I learned that the Indian Government had only recently 'officially discovered' the existence of the King of Zangla. It now pays him a pension of two hundred rupees a month. This is no doubt a compensation for having abolished the rights and privileges of all rajas and maharajas. Certainly this Tibetan-speaking monarch is at the bottom rung of the long list of ex-rulers of India, yet what the Kings of Zangla lack in the size of their kingdom is compensated for by their noble lineage which goes back to AD 1020. As Zangla stands at 11,800 feet above sea-level so their King is also, along with the rGyalpo of Mustang, one of the highest monarchs in the world!

The room in which we were seated was cluttered with odds and ends, mostly hanging from pegs on the walls. In one corner stood a broken-down two-way radio set, while beside it hung a transistor radio. The King later produced a cassette-recorder that had been given to him by some Austrians a few weeks before my arrival.

'Have many foreigners come to Zangla?' I asked, curious to know who might have preceded me.

'Not very many,' the King answered, 'maybe six or eight.' He then took a little steel box and extracted from it an old and worn photograph of a certain Mr Erwin Baktey, whom the King declared to have been the first Englishman he had seen in Zangla. In the photograph a man was standing beside a stone on which was engraved, 'Csoma de Körös lived here, Pioneer of Tibetan Studies.' Baktey had come to Zanskar for the centenary of Körös' stay there and had placed a plaque in Zangla, which Körös and Moorcroft had previously called 'Yangla'.

It seems strange that both men should have made the same mistake in pronunciation, especially Körös who spoke (so one is told) fluent Tibetan and who stayed nearly a year at Zangla. How could he have pronounced the name wrong? Perhaps in both his and Moorcroft's manuscripts 'Z' had been misread as a capital 'Y'. The King at least could prove that Zangla had always been written thus.

From the rare documents left by Csoma de Körös concerning his personal life, we learned that this strange Hungarian student who had wandered across Asia to Ladakh on his own, calling himself Sikandar Beg (Gentleman Alexander), met Moorcroft in Ladakh and that Moorcroft gave him an introduction to the principal minister to the King of Ladakh and also money and encouragement to study the Tibetan language. In Leh Körös met a 51-year-old monk, Palde Sangs-ngye Phuntsok, who, for ten years, had been married to the widow of the King of Zangla. This monk, the physician to the King of Ladakh, was very erudite, having studied for a long time in Lhasa. Körös went with him to Zangla in June 1823. There Körös lived in the castle on the hill. Thanks to the 'Regent' of Zangla, Körös was well launched in his studies of the Tibetan language, and started collecting material for a book. He also met some other monks and decided after the death of his first master, to return and stay with one of them at his home in Teta, this is in south-east Zanskar near the monastery of Phugtal. Thus Körös spent another year in Zanskar, from the 12th of August 1825 to November 1826.

The King mentioned that in the castle on the crag there was still 'the room Körös lived in'. He then explained that since taxes were paid direct to the Tasildar, the Kashmiri representative in Padum (about five rupees a family only), he as rGyalpo had no specific duties. Yet as King he had kept most of his land and retained considerable prestige and he still, as the local lord and richest man, played a leading role in the region's religious and social life.

I was touched by the King's intelligent and kindly personality. He was plainly an aristocrat, a man conscious of the responsibility his family bore towards the villagers over whom they had ruled for so many centuries. In particular he felt a responsibility to protect the inhabitants from encroachments on their rights by an Indian administration, often unaware of local customs. There were, as he reminded me, gold sands in his estates; in fact, the greatest gold-bearing river of the region is in the area of the village of Pimo, part of his dominion. To prove it the King showed me several silver and gold bowls made by the blacksmith of Zangla. The elaborate ceremonial vessels I had admired were also, he said, made in Zangla with silver, gold and copper all mined in Zanskar!

The King of Zangla in his everyday robes, soiled by tea and covered by the hairs of his little dogs, was far from the image one has of a fairy-tale monarch but I had long ago come to know that to be the hereditary ruler of a Himalayan land called for qualities of heart and soul, which have more in common with those of the princes, counts and barons of the Middle Ages than with those of royal pretenders of decadent eighteenth-century monarchies. A king is a ruler, and in a rugged land such as Zangla or Zanskar to be a king calls for rugged characteristics and not dainty manners.

Compared to the King of Mustang, the 'vassal king' of Zangla was a far more refined man. He had on several occasions been to Ladakh and to India, and spoke a few words of Hindi. He had, it seemed, relinquished all but his title and his religious role to his young son, whom I regretted not having been able to talk to.

The King of Zangla was loved by all his people because thirty years before my visit he had 'liberated' his subjects, freeing them of their obligations to pay taxes to him. This revolutionary act resulted in the villagers refusing to pay their taxes to Karsha monastery, which in turn led to a general revolt of the peasants of Zangla against all monastic control of peasants' lands. The instigator and hero of the affair being the King. Elsewhere in Zanskar many villages were still obliged to pay taxes in kind to various monasteries and these taxes could represent up to fifty per cent of all crops.

The King of Zangla was in fact very progressive and what he had lost in riches he had gained in prestige.

Getting up, the King begged that during my visit to Zangla I stay in his house. He showed me across the patio to the 'open gallery' opposite his small room. Here, he suggested, I could sleep and live. I could hardly refuse.

And so it was that I settled in the 'small palace' of the King of Zangla. I was now to live in an open room facing the patio of the King's residence. I would have to share not only in the King's daily life and that of his household but I would, as I was soon to discover, be an exhibit, showing what Europeans are like to his subjects who had access to him at all hours.

With Lobsang's help I arranged the open loggia so that I sat in state on my air-mattress, at the end of the little yard. Before me a wicker basket served as table and the King soon enhanced the 'throne room' (which in fact was where he usually sat) with fine, gaily-coloured carpets.

For three days and three nights this was to be my window on to the intimate life of perhaps the most obscure royal family in the world.

Of course the majority of kings, even those of such a fairy-tale land as Zangla, are above all human beings; in this case the King was a little more human than most because of his wisdom and old age. Life around him, I soon discovered, was very pleasant indeed. Poor by any standards except in dignity, the King shuffled around the house doing most of his own chores, occasionally asking the girls to bring him tea. The household was in fact ruled by the Queen, the old lady I had encountered in the kitchen. It seemed she stood for no nonsense and was as strict as her husband was charming and kind. The King was always fussing over his little dogs or playing with children when any came into his house.

I spent the rest of that day writing up the notes I made of the names of the places I had visited. My writing attracted much attention and there would always be one of the girls looking over my shoulder commenting at how well and quickly I wrote. Although most men know how to write, few girls are taught much beyond how to read the letters of the alphabet and simple words. This however was not the case with the Queen or the two girls working at the small palace. They were no doubt of noble birth and had therefore been taught how to read and write. Today there is a school in Zangla in which all the village children are taught how to read and write in Tibetan. In Kargil the Kashmiri Government has set up

The village of Zangla with its monastery in the background

High on its cliff, the impregnable fortress of Zangla

The new palace of the King of Zangla, a fine example
of local architecture

Tea being served to the King of Zangla during a prayer meeting

The King of Zangla watches as the author's bags are
loaded on to a donkey

The blacksmith of Zangla is also a fine silver and goldsmith

a teachers' college and young men are being trained in modern teaching methods to teach in all the villages. For the time being there was no official teacher in Zangla, only a monk who taught Tibetan to the children.

To write the Tibetan script is child's play compared to writing Chinese, or even Hindi. There are only thirty letters in the Tibetan alphabet and since vowels are expressed by accents the language is a sort of shorthand. In every monastery or chapel of the land one can hear little children shouting the '*ka, ga, kha*', as they call the 'ABC', or sitting in silence, tongues sticking out in concentration while they trace letters on their dustboards. These dustboards are dark wooden boards upon which the children spread chalk dust which they then write over with a wooden pen dipped in water. The water reveals the dark wood and the letters come out black against white; afterwards, in one swipe, the letters can be erased, the board rid of its dust and dusted over again.

As night fell I began to suffer from the cold since my room was entirely open on one side; this was one of the inconveniences of being an honoured guest. All I could do was wear another sweater and cuddle a cup of tea which Lobsang had helped me to prepare on the small Primus stove I had brought with me.

It had been a long and tiring day and I was glad to go to sleep early. Shortly after I retired, all the doors giving on to the courtyard were closed and the four little dogs curled up to sleep at the head of the staircase. That night I dreamt of the swing bridge and the strange intimacy of the home of the King of Zangla. I was really happy.

At dawn I was awoken by the barking of the little dogs and opened an eye to see staring at me the rough friendly face of a farmer, his head capped by a tall hat. He must have thought me some kind of monster and I only hoped I had not been snoring. I got up quickly which was no great problem as I had fallen asleep fully clothed, for it was far too cold to change into anything like pyjamas.

The Queen was already busy in the kitchen, bossing around the young girls who, as they came out carrying water, or to clean a pot or pan, gave me a charming smile that made me feel quite guilty at having overslept. It was nearly six o'clock.

Lobsang appeared explaining he had stayed at the house of a friend next door. While he prepared some tea I set about searching for the royal lavatory. These are one of the nicer aspects of Himalayan homes, sur- prisingly so perhaps, since such things were unknown in many rural areas of Asia or even of Europe until not so long ago. Himalayan lavatories are little rooms with a rectangular hole in the floor, complete with a pile of earth and a shovel. In some highly-sited houses, monasteries or fortresses these rooms are built out from the main building so that everything falls several hundred feet over a cliff, but as a rule everything goes to a ground-floor room that opens on to the outside and into which earth and straw is thrown every day. This is an efficient solution to a problem that many nations have not managed to solve so well. The night soil is used in the fields; it is a much needed fertiliser as most of the animals' dung is used as fuel and is therefore not available to enrich the soil.

In Zangla, more so than in the other districts of Zanskar, fuel is very scarce. There is no wood and there are hardly any bushes, so animal fuel is much in demand. In Europe it would be futile and even revolting to try and burn cow dung, but in the Himalayas, due to the high altitude and lack of moisture, dung dries up very quickly and does not mould or ferment. As dry as tinder and relatively odourless it can be stacked in patties ready for burning. The stack is stored on the flat rooftops, together with any bushes or roots that may have been collected. Alongside the fuel, hay and edible bushes are stacked to feed the cattle, sheep and horses during the long months of winter which they have to spend inside because of the cold and the snow.

I have never made a detailed study of the relative calorific output of horse, yak, cow or sheep dung but the well-known French priest, Father Huc, who travelled from China to Lhasa and back in 1856, claims that the best fuel of all is that of the camel, and grades in terms of heat the various dungs in the following order: camel, sheep, yak, cow and horse. The truth is that none gives off very much heat at high altitudes where, because of the lack of oxygen, to burn such fuel calls for constant coaxing from the little bellows that are found by the hearth of most houses. I have spent many an hour blowing against the pale embers of yak dung which eventually consumes itself, giving off a pleasant incense-like smell; all the same, I have always carried a large jerry can of kerosene around with me because on dung fires water can take over an hour to boil.

When the King emerged from his room I rose to greet him. He then made for the kitchen, returning with a steaming kettle. Beckoning me to follow him, he went down the stairs leading outside muttering something about 'a horse' that I could not grasp. I followed him to a small enclosure where two men were holding down a small foal.

'It's the wolves,' explained the King. 'Had its mother not been so brave and eventually kicked them away, the foal would have been killed.' I saw wounds on the foal's flank where the wolves had bitten it. The King, I now realised, was something of a vet; taking water from the kettle, he mixed it with an ointment which he applied to the wounds.

'There are many wolves in the mountains,' he explained. 'In the winter they often come down to the valleys.'

Kings, castles, wolves, lonely valleys, monasteries and roaming monks along with fleas and rats are, I realise, the stuff of which fairy-tales are made, the very fibre of a world that has only recently disappeared in Europe. At times I had to talk to myself in English to make sure that it was truly I who was identifying with this world which I knew would seem unreal when I returned home. I had a camera with me and as much as I loathed its glaring eye shamelessly probing people's faces, I began to cherish it and its film for this would be the only evidence of what was otherwise like a dream. Yet somehow I felt I had lived all this before, not in other journeys but maybe in other lives because it was all so familiar; my standing there commenting upon the wolf bites, upon the hide of a small foal held down by two men with long braided hair tied back with pink ribbons, and dressed in yellow gowns of thick cloth they had woven themselves from wool spun in Zangla by their wives. I found it natural that I should be holding a copper kettle made of metal found in the hills above me and forged for the King by the local blacksmith, natural that the King of Zangla, the rightful heir to this lonely valley, should know how to cure horses.

The job finished, we walked back into the house and the King asked me to have tea with him in his room. I had by now taken a serious liking to the warmhearted old man who radiated a deep kindness. I understood why I had been told that he was a good King and why he was liked and respected by all. It had nothing to do with his high position, for if the Himalayans are polite they are also very outspoken, and do not hesitate to criticise their superiors if they transgress the behaviour expected of them. Public opinion, often spread and amplified by satirical songs, is very strong among the Himalayans who stand for no nonsense and are critical both of themselves and others.

I do not know whether it is to do with the Buddhist religion or with that particular stage of development in which the Himalayan civilisation finds itself, but I am always surprised to see that individuals are either good or bad and that very few are on the border line. In all their activities the Zanskaris, especially young men like Lobsang and Nordrup, act with great enthusiasm and energy, taking an unambiguous stand as to their opinions and attitudes.

I could not help but feel that we in the West seem to have lost our ability wholeheartedly to endorse either vice or virtue. We have lost our certitudes and seem to amble about in the grey waters of a limbo for the lukewarm. It is characteristic of our modern world that our crooks always try to justify their crimes and our true saints are few and far between. We have I believe as few truly evil men as there are saints. Not so in the Himalayas where crooks are crooks and saints are saints, and little lies between the two. It is this characteristic which makes life with the Himalayans so pleasant, misunderstandings and disappointments rarely arise as one can read a person's character upon his face. What annoys me most in our world is not the evil that certain men do but the hypocrisy which surrounds their deeds. No one can begrudge an honest crook his crime; one usually hates the hypocrite more, and all those who are false. The Himalayans are never sly although some are outright bandits.

In the afternoon I set out with Lobsang to visit the old fortress. On my way I passed in front of the large palace, which was in a very bad state of repair. I was told that the young King was about to restore it and for that purpose earth bricks were being prepared. They are made by mixing the local soil with water and a little straw, then they are placed in a mould and dried in the sun.

The climb to the fort led up the barren scree slope that formed a background to the village. Eventually I reached the first of a long series of maybe two hundred chortens; for the most part they were so eroded by the wind and the rain that they had taken on mysterious shapes, some grotesque, others nearly human, ghosting the abandoned palace and the dead city whose ruins surrounded it.

The fort was an immense, rectangular, whitewashed structure overshadowing Zangla whose new palace and little houses seemed like blocks of sugar set in green fields, hemmed in on all sides by a rocky desert. From where I stood Zanskar appeared like one monumental chaos of dry rocky mountains crowding in the silver causeway of the Zanskar river which, gleaming in the sun, slithered down its valley to disappear in the tortuous gorges that eventually led it to the Indus.

The comparison to a lunar landscape is too often made of any arid region but there could be no better way to describe the northern district of Zanskar which constitutes the realm of the King of Zangla. Not only are its mountains barren with sharp outlines and deep ravines, but these are lit by the same dazzling crude light as is found on the moon.

It never, or at least only very rarely, rains in this part of Zanskar. The reason is that those few clouds that pass over the Great Himalayan Range are blown beyond the Zanskar Range, which is within the rain shadow of the great peaks. From where I now stood I could well understand why no one has ever conquered Zangla, for not only is its citadel impregnable but there is little in the land to excite envy, and poverty helps to guarantee political stability. Yet is Zangla really poor, is all Zanskar poor? Strangely the answer is no, and the contradiction between the land's barren aspect and its true wealth is what makes Zanskar such an amazing place.

Part of the fortress had collapsed, exposing an inner cloister and several rooms. I crawled up through a hole in the wall and found myself climbing a ladder-like staircase, then pacing through the deserted chambers of what had been a magnificent fortified palace. Looking out of a vast latticed window I saw a man coming up the mountain. He proved to be the village headman bringing the key to the chapel, the last room still cared for in the empty building.

A strong wind coming down the valley whistled through the empty rooms raising little wisps of dust that rushed about like ghosts. It seemed a shame that this eagle's nest should have been abandoned for the less grandiose but far more convenient site of the new Zangla.

The village headman opened the chapel and let me contemplate a fine old statue of Tsong Khapa, the founder of the Gelugpa sect. It seemed to be staring intently into the semi-darkness of the chapel. Unexpectedly, by its side were the statues of two Drukpa Kargyupa lamas representing the other sect found in Zanskar. In a corner lay a drum whose echo rumbled through the empty rooms, while scattered about the place were old religious texts – a sad case of neglect.

The headman then led me to a room just off the main top-floor living-room. It was low-ceilinged and cell-like with one small window and the charred remains of what had been a small fireplace. It was here, I was told, that a hundred and fifty years ago Csoma de Körös had lived. Intrigued, I examined the room in the hope of finding an inscription or at least some clue to the scholar's visit, but found none. Books on Körös state that he stayed at the monastery of Zangla, but as there is no large monastery there (only a nunnery) and since his teacher and friend was married to the Queen of Zangla and was the tutor to the royal children, there is little doubt that Körös stayed in this fortress palace. In fact, he has little to say about his visit except how terribly cold it was in winter, so cold that he dared not leave his room.

I tried to imagine Körös' thoughts in this lonely place so far away from his native Hungary. Of course the Europe of 1823, at least in its rural life, was not so very different from Zangla today. Railways were unknown, so were motors, and farmers must have tilled the fertile plains of Hungary with tools similar to those Körös found in Zangla.

I have often been struck by the similarity between the Himalayan rural culture and that of Europe. Such things as milking stools, wooden pails, spades with long handles, wooden jugs and pots, while very similar to those found in Europe, are quite different from objects found in all other Eastern countries. For instance, the Tibetans are the only people of Asia to cultivate their fields with long-handled tools that can be used when standing upright.

If Diogo d'Almeida thought he saw a Christian society in Ladakh because of the apparent similarity of dress, chants and the organisation of the Buddhist monasteries which recalled those he knew in Europe, there are as many reasons to believe that the Tibetans might have learnt of our European agricultural techniques and copied them.

Leaving the fortress and its ghosts I examined the ruins of the houses that clustered around the main building. Of these nothing was left standing except for their lower walls of cut stone; all wood had been removed, no doubt to build the new houses in the valley. None of the ruins seemed to have been the remains of any large monastery, so that settled the question of where Csoma de Körös stayed: it must have been at the fort.

Back down in Zangla, on re-entering the King's small palace, I found the place bustling with activity. Cushions were being laid out against the walls of the courtyard and little tables placed before them. These were of decreasing size, the lowest being only wooden logs. The kitchen was bustling with noise, while in a corner a man was busy shaping little round balls of tsampa which were then coloured red by one of the young girls who poured hot dyed butter over them.

Obviously a ceremony was in preparation and soon several people arrived carrying many sheets out of books. These I gathered were to be read in the course of an assembly somewhat similar to that which I had attended in the chapel of the village of Pishu on the other side of the river.

Taking my place in the loggia where the King would preside over the ceremony, I watched as events got under way. In all about fifteen people attended; these included the King's daughter, her husband and the pregnant wife of the King's son (soon to die in childbirth in a hospital in New

Delhi). This distinguished gathering in which the women were more remarkable than the men because of their magnificent head-dresses, was also attended by some seedy-looking retainers and friends of the family. The old King took the lead by sitting at the top of the patio to my right, for most unwillingly I was sitting at the place of honour. Everyone, including the women who sat in a cluster in the centre of the patio, whipped out, from the folds of their gowns, a wooden drinking bowl. This was filled with excellent chang poured from a vast copper pot by two beautiful girls and a tall young man. Later in the evening his hat came off and revealed a strange hairstyle (common to both Zanskar and Ladakh). The hair had been shaved short on the front and top of the head and left to hang long and plaited on the back of the head. This hairstyle is perhaps designed to accommodate the oddly shaped, tall Ladakhi hat.

'Good chang makes for good religion,' I had to agree. The ceremony progressed and voices were raised as page after page was turned over in between sips of chang. Fortunately the little red cakes were handed round to reduce intoxication. The King was in a good mood, making many much appreciated jokes and telling me to drink up. Later, when the royal family and its servants had completed the religious observance, the rather dull musical chanting of the religious texts was replaced by folk songs. I was told that similar prayers are held once a month in different houses.

The following morning when I awoke it was drizzling and cold. Zanskar was experiencing one of its worst summers in man's memory. This bad weather was to last several more days and cause, as I later learnt, the tragic crumbling of several houses in Zanskar. Looking out I could see that the normally bare summits were frosted in snow. I was concerned, for if this snow persisted I would not be able to cross the Great Himalayan Range over the Shingo-la. More snow not only meant drifts but eventually more water in the rivers which we would have to ford.

I decided that I should spend another day in Zangla. I still had many questions I wanted to put to the King and I had also to visit the nunnery and the 'large palace'.

8

A Donkey in Danger

The large palace proved to be a fine example of Himalayan non-religious architecture. It conformed in its general plan to the characteristic design of all Zanskari houses in that it was divided into two levels, one for summer living and the other for the winter, but here the winter level, instead of being on the ground floor surrounded by the stables, was on the first floor and consisted of a dark windowless room designed to retain warmth. On the second floor were a vast chapel-library and a grand reception-hall, both with wide latticed windows opening on to a rooftop terrace sheltered from the wind by a covered cloister-like gallery.

The chapel contained some splendid books, several with finely decorated wooden bindings and also some statues. The empty reception room had a great hearth of polished baked clay with three rings for kettles and cauldrons, it was decorated with reliefs of Buddhist symbols – a sacred parasol and an endless knot. The whole building was in bad need of repair as it was cracked in many places and I was pleased to see that these were soon to be mended by the young prince, a man I had been told was very dynamic and in whose hands many of the inhabitants, not only of Zangla but of Zanskar, placed their hopes for the future of their small country.

From the royal palace, passing under several door chortens with ceilings painted with mandalas (geometrical designs symbolic of the ordinances of the universe), I went with Lobsang to the women's monastery, or nunnery. This was located on the other side of the little brook that flowed past Zangla. The buildings, about five in all, were clustered around a central assembly hall surrounded by a dark, enclosed passageway built so that in winter the shrine could be circumambulated without having to go out in the cold. To walk around a building is always considered an act of merit, this must be done in a clockwise direction. Also, usually, one should always pass to the left of any religious monument, such as chortens or prayer walls.

Lobsang and I tried to attract someone's attention in what seemed a deserted monastery until suddenly, as if from nowhere, an old nun appeared, leaning on a walking stick, the very incarnation of a witch. She had a hooked nose, was lame and hunchbacked, her hair hung over her face which sported numerous warts and she gave us a toothless leer that would have frozen a bonfire. Fortunately her soft, kind voice warmed our hearts and made us certain she would not turn us into frogs. Evidently she was in need of sympathy and company. She complained bitterly of her bad leg for which Lobsang prescribed a remedy he had tried on his aunt. On hearing the aunt's name the old woman's face lit up and she recalled having been a friend of Lobsang's great-aunt.

I realised then how small Zanskar was, in spite of the two hundred miles that separate its furthermost villages; Zanskar forms a completely isolated and self-contained unit and most of its people are, if not inter-related, at least friends. I was told there are now some forty-eight settlements, although the official figure quotes the number of villages as twenty-eight. The population is in the order of twelve thousand people, a figure which if it sounds insignificant by modern European standards is sizeable for the Himalayas. What is particularly interesting is that such a small number of people should have all the attributes of a nation: their own language (or rather dialect), their own traditions, and of course a very ancient history. There is even a special physical type and indeed Zanskaris, to a stranger, all look rather alike.

There could be few people in the world with a more definitely limited, isolated, and unusual habitat. More so than an island, Zanskar lies cut off from the rest of the world and no ship is ever likely to be wrecked on its shores, for it requires true courage and determination to make the journey over the high and dangerous mountains into its valley. This journey has only been undertaken by a few merchants from Karja, the valley immediately south of the main Himalayan Range. In India Karja is known today as Lahoul: this is a deformation of the Tibetan *la-yul*, which means 'the villages of the gods'. How rugged was the trail that led from Zanskar to Lahoul I would soon find out, for I planned to leave Zanskar by this route.

Returning to the King's house I began making arrangements to hire a donkey to carry my bags on the two-day journey that would lead me up the left bank of the Zanskar river to Padum, the capital.

Later that afternoon much to my surprise Nawang Trile, Nordrup's brother, arrived from Thunri. Sporting a fine red tunic and elegant boots of embroidered material attached to yakskin soles turned up around the foot, and pointed towards the ends, he was unrecognisable. He brought me a bottle of mango juice and a small bag of sugar as a present. Where he had found such unexpected treasures I could not imagine, until he told me that Nordrup, his brother, had returned at last. It seemed Nordrup had been delayed by snow on the Pensi-la and had slipped and hurt his foot. Because of this he had not been able to come back when he had promised. When he finally reached Thunri and discovered my gift of a chuba to his young nephew he immediately despatched Nawang to give me these presents and to help me in any way until he himself could join me in Padum.

I accepted these presents and suggested that Nawang should return as I could manage with Lobsang. Nevertheless Nawang insisted he should come too.

That evening was a sad one as it meant leaving the old King, whom I had come to regard as something like an old uncle. I had been touched by his great kindness and intelligence and his sense of humour. During the evening the rGyalpo recorded Nawang and Lobsang singing religious chants. A tape-recorder had been given him recently by an Austrian party which I understand had included Heinrich Harrer, the mountaineer who with Peter Aufschnaiter, had escaped to Tibet from an Indian prison camp. He had lived there for seven years. Peter Aufschnaiter had recently died in Nepal, I had known him well and regretted missing Harrer by a few days. Harrer, like me, had lost no time in rushing to Zanskar, open at last after having been for so long included in the restricted strategic zones of Kashmir. This restriction, plus its altitude and isolation, had limited the number of Europeans to visit it. How many had ever set foot there is hard to say but it would be safe to suggest a figure of under a hundred, over four hundred years. Of these visitors how many had been to all the four provinces, perhaps not half a dozen? Because of this I worked over-time recording all I could of the local customs. The King of Zangla had given me much information about the traditional administration of the land. He and the King of Padum had used several noble families, called Lumbo, as administrators who had collected all the taxes and looked after the Kings' interests. The highest office had been that of *chanzup* (royal secretary), this person was assisted by a *nierpa* (assistant secretary). Next in order came the *sor-dpon* (royal cooks) and the *chir-dpon* who looked after the royal household, the peasants were called *ulag-pae*, they owed free transport to the King.

Each village had its monastery to which the children were sent for education and to which the population came on special festive days to pray. At village level there was a separate administration led by the *zildar* who was assisted by several *mokdams*, while an older man who held the title of *mKas-dman* served as judge in disputes involving communal land and irrigation. The latter worked co-operatively, every household being obliged to delegate a person to take a turn in guarding the irrigation canals in the summer against possible leaks.

I discovered that Zanskar still, in the main, observed the laws concerning land tenure and marriage elaborated by the famous Tibetan King, Songsten Gampo. These ancient laws are directly responsible for the relative wealth of these Himalayan people who are of Tibetan culture, and are framed to preserve intact, through the generations, a man's house and his fields. The most ancient law (no longer observed in Zanskar) was that every farmer's fields should be of the same size. The second law had it that land could neither be purchased nor sold. This remarkable law is still observed to a certain degree in Zanskar.

Further to protect land holdings, all land has to be transmitted in its entirety to the eldest son, or failing a male heir, to the eldest daughter. The other sons and daughters get nothing. The custom of primogeniture saves farms from being divided and sub-divided till the peasantry is reduced to poverty because of the inadequate size of the land holdings.

This is most important in areas like Zanskar because arable land is too rare to allow the enlargement of land under cultivation to meet population growth.

This law of course left the second sons with no land, and this is where both the celibacy of monks and the custom of polyandry comes in as a natural regulator of population growth. A younger son can become a monk living in a monastery, or at home, or in the village chapel as local parish monk, performing religious duties for his living. As he does not marry his upkeep is no great burden to the community. If however a younger son did not want to be a monk, according to the wise Tibetan laws he can and should marry his brother's wife. He shares her with his brother. This custom called 'fraternal polyandry' allows second sons to benefit from the produce of the father's household, yet does not divide it.

More important there are no reasons why such a family or 'triple' should necessarily have more children than one husband with one wife, so that polyandry in fact helps keep the population stable.

Many Europeans have been startled and shocked by this custom, wondering how two men could get on with one wife. Few appreciate that this custom is no more unnatural than any others that are dictated by the need to survive. After all, Eskimos kill some of their children at birth and leave aged parents out to die. Nothing is unnatural if it is directed to the survival of the species. Polyandry, a method of natural birth control, was practised for thousands of years throughout the world though today only a few Indian tribes and Tibetans practise it.

I have met several polyandric triples, including a co-husband in Thunri, Nordrup's village, where there are three polyandric families. Few problems seem to arise in such unions as brothers have been brought up since childhood with the idea of possibly sharing a wife, and of doing so of their free will. The children in Zanskar call their eldest father, '*apa-che*' (big daddy), and the other 'small daddy'. This of course does not solve the problem as to who is the genetic father but no one seems to mind. The custom is at variance with what is generally practised in other Himalayan lands where the eldest husband is called the father, and the younger, uncle.

The foundation of polyandry in Zanskar and in Tibet in general ensures, as we have seen, the preservation of the household intact with its fields, yet the proportion of polyandric families in Zanskar is approximately one in ten. This is because not all families have two or more sons and in those which do, one of the sons or both often become monks. This was the case of Nordrup and his brother Nawang. Alternatively they may seek out a girl with no brothers and marry her and thus become the head of her household.

Whatever one's personal taste, one has to admire the social system evolved by the early Tibetan King which made the household the pivot of all institutions, including that of marriage. The net result is that after over a thousand years of continuous habitation Zanskar remains a prosperous region without blatant poverty or the need for emigration. It is sufficient to see the children and the adults to appreciate how healthy everyone is, and to see the women's headgear to appreciate the extent of the capital in the hands of the women, not to mention the riches of their husbands.

Zanskar women play a role equal to that of the men; this is generally true of societies in which the individual freedom of all is respected.

Indeed a quick survey of the peoples of the world will show that the treatment of women reflects the general political order. In a society where there are slaves, women are considered chattels; in a true democracy women are considered equals. A servant's servant is his wife and her position reflects society's treatment of her husband. In Zanskar there is very little hierarchy. If, as until recently, the King was acknowledged to be a privileged person, all other householders were by definition equal.

Himalayan feudalism is different from that of Europe and even from that of latter-day Tibet. The peasant is not a serf, subject to a master who owns his land and his person. He is an independent landowner who owns his fields 'until the crow turns white'; but there is a qualification, the man who inherits land holds it in trust. By ensuring that land is not treated as a source of wealth the Tibetans have avoided all the pitfalls that have led other agricultural societies to impoverishment, through the division of land, the sale of land or the tyranny of those who hoarded land.

In this, Songsten Gampo and his successors were the only true agricultural socialists the world has known. In their history books young Himalayans learn that on three occasions the holy Kings of Tibet equalised the fortunes of the rich and the poor.

It is ironical that China, who fulminates about the feudal injustices of Tibetan society and its terrible serf system (a semi-myth), should in fact be reinstating, with its communes, a system very similar to that of the holy Tibetan Kings. In the process of equalising the rich and the poor the Chinese are redistributing the land to communes (enlarged families), and just as in Tibet's ancient past and in Zanskar today, the leaders of these communes can neither buy nor sell the land. The only weakness of the new Chinese system is that the communes are too large to be effective; history proves that individual families tend to work better together than in collective groups of several families. China has also failed to devise a natural way of controlling the birth rate in their communes, which become poorer and poorer or have to exile their excess members to cities and factories.

How rich the Zanskaris are I had yet to discover. But already I was constantly amazed at the land's wealth when considered in relation to the region's barren, inhospitable appearance and terrible climate.

I am convinced that man's noblest conquest is neither the horse nor the elephant but the harnessing of the earth and the weather. If we are the only animals to have no claws or tusks, we have a superior intelligence and it is our brain which allows us to survive by adaptation to unusual conditions.

The amount of brains we need to survive is to some extent dependent on one's environment: the harsher the environment, the more man is obliged to think to be able to live. Ingenuity along with courage have allowed men to populate the Arctic; it has likewise allowed the inhabitants of Zanskar to live and thrive in a region where trees would not think of growing and where all but the sturdiest of animals die. The Zanskaris have to put up with a climate as rugged, if not more so, than that of the Arctic, and they also have to put up with a lack of oxygen and with strong ultra-violet rays which make their world quite different from the rest of our planet.

An arctic desert at a high altitude is how one could best describe Zanskar. To have been able to adapt to such a place and to have created a rich, happy society is indeed a true tour de force, a proof of the intelligence of the inhabitants of the 'Land of White Copper'.

I met with intelligence among all the inhabitants I had dealings with. Nordrup with his quick and fickle wit, Lobsang and his delicate, astute mind, Nawang with his jovial, pertinent comments, the King of Zangla's discreet scholarship and true humanity, and yet my journey had only just begun.

On my way to the capital I planned to visit the monastery of Thonde, from there I would visit the villages and monasteries of central Zanskar before travelling on to the remote and isolated communities of Lunak, the province of the 'black demons'.

Saying farewell to Sonam Thondup rNamgyal lDe was a sad affair. The King came down to watch my bags being piled upon the back of a minute donkey. I felt rather ashamed and conscious that the Society for the Prevention of Cruelty to Animals would have objected as the little thing disappeared under a load it had taken two horses to carry. In the end Nawang and Lobsang carried some of the luggage.

The donkey staggered off and I turned to wave goodbye to the royal household and to the villagers of Zangla, a little kingdom within a little kingdom, lost in the immensity of the Great Himalayan Range.

I was heading for Padum, the capital of the King of Zanskar. Who was he and what would he be like?

It was pleasant to be on the move once again, for one thing it gave me time to recall all I had seen over the past days and somehow I felt that my true vocation was to be on the trail with Lobsang and Nawang. We again passed the mineral springs and the bridge, now I could admire it in a more relaxed fashion knowing I would not have to walk across it.

We were heading towards Tsasar, one of the four villages under the jurisdiction of the King of Zangla; to reach it we crossed a small desert-like plain above the river, which fell down from the great mountains that barred our horizon to the east. The track was small and stony, occasionally marked by a chorten. At one point the river had cut deeply into this plain, taking the track away with it and leaving us to scramble along the crumbling edge of a precipice. Prodded by my two companions the little donkey staggered forwards. I suppose to a casual observer we made an unlikely trio, Nawang in a spotless, red woollen gown, Lobsang in less grandiose red clothes, and then the mini donkey led by myself wearing a battered khaki hat, my face covered with thick layers of white cream.

As we advanced I chatted with Lobsang and I am sorry I cannot recall our conversation. For casual talk is the heart of life, and I have always regretted that history books never contained any casual conversations. As a result we imagine that people in the Middle Ages talked in that silly jargon one hears on films. 'O noble sir, pray tell me where lies the royal route to yonder village.' In fact they spoke in exactly the same way as we do today. I was now struck by how modern my conversations with the people of Zanskar were, though in all other respects they would seem antiquated. The truth is that through the centuries man's mind has changed very little, we still have the same desires, weaknesses and ambitions and they do not need lengthy explanations or formulae for their expression.

'How many hours till we reach Tsasar?' I would ask.

'About an hour,' Lobsang would answer.

'Did Nordrup really hurt his leg? I don't know whether to trust the rascal.'

'He did hurt himself, but he was also delayed because of having to find enough horses to take back all the load left by the truck.'

'I think Nordrup is very nice but he says one thing and does the other.'

'You should not be too harsh on him. He really is a very good fellow.'

'Poor donkey, hope it does not die.'

'We got it quite cheap, twenty rupees, but I will not make you pay because of the deal we have about the horses.'

'I think the King is a really good fellow.'

'Yes, he has a beautiful heart. Everyone likes him.'

'What about the King of Zanskar?' I asked.

'Well, he's okay but not as nice as Sonam rNamgyal.'

'Is he really heir to the title of King of Zanskar?'

'He is, but he's not as well liked as the King of Zangla.'

So we chatted, as an ocean of distant peaks and barren valleys shadowed by mineral cliffs unfolded around us.

Towards midday we reached Tsasar with its green fields spread out on either side of a ravine. On the far side stood a cluster of houses, one built against the other forming what looked like a citadel. In appearance the village recalled some of the fortified hamlets of the upper Kali Gandaki river along the salt route that leads to Mustang. This settlement had certainly been built with a view to defence, it being the southernmost village of the King of Zangla. I entered it through an archway beneath one of the houses and came into a closed yard where I was greeted by several young men who stuck out their tongues, slightly intimidated by the sight of an unusual visitor. Save for the fine door chorten there was nothing to retain me in the village, so I set out for another cluster of houses standing beside a little enclosure in which grew a clump of poplar trees.

Could we eat in the shade, I asked a group of farmers who had come out to look at us.

'*La-les*' (yes), answered a young boy, the son of the owner of the wood. Scaling the stone wall I lay down in the shade listening to the bubble of a small irrigation canal that ran between the trees, which would otherwise have died in this parched land. Lobsang and Nawang untied my baskets while I lay down under the watchful gaze of twenty people peering over the wall spying my every movement; obviously they were trying to establish whether I was properly human or not. I understood what they were saying: they made comments about my clothes, my nose, my bald spot and other remarks so in the end I felt obliged to respond.

'I have been all over the mountains, and visited many lands,' I said. 'Now, in Lo Mantang (Mustang), in Bhutan and in Sher Khumbu (Sherpa country) no one would leave such an honourable visitor as myself without giving him a drink. Who here will get me some chang and some tsampa for my lunch?' The spectators were so surprised at first they did not reply. At last a young man asked, 'Do you really want chang?'

'Yes,' I said. A few minutes later it was my turn to be embarrassed as the young man came up with a wooden jug full of chang and a big wooden bowl with a wooden cover, full of roasted barley flour.

I thanked him and gave him in exchange one of my precious tins of pineapple rings which he ate with caution at first and then in apparent

The gorges of the Zanskar river in Lunak spanned by
one of the many spectacular suspension bridges

The impressive bridge of Zangla

Zanskar bridge, nearly 220 feet long

Twisted twigs make up the ropes for the bridges

Padum, the capital of Zanskar set on a glacial rock deposit,
looks like a mound of ruins

delight. Having rested a few minutes while Lobsang boiled some tea, I set out to visit the local monastery. This I had been told was considered to be the actual site of a chorten erected by Guru Rimpoche, the saintly Padma Sambhava, an Indian, and the principal introducer of Lamaism to Tibet, who set out for Tibet in AD 747 at the invitation of the King, Thi-Srong-Detsen. In the centre of the monastery's vast, ancient hall stood a tall, old chorten so covered in successive coats of whitewash that it had taken the bloated form of a stalagmite.

It is hard to discover what is legend and what is truth regarding holy shrines of 'the Lotus Born' as Guru Rimpoche is called. The assertion that the great saint himself had built this chorten, or been here at all, or left his footprints had to be taken with a pinch of salt.

Having eaten lunch, a small escort of boys saw us out of the village, their curiosity said much for the land's isolation.

About half a mile out of the village we came upon a gorge cut in the flat barren plateau that ran down from a mountain to our left. Along the flank of this valley was an irrigation canal a few feet wide outlined by grass growing at its edge. Looking at this ditch I realised to my surprise that the water was flowing upstream. I had never yet seen a river or even an irrigation canal flow uphill. So I had another look, and then another, and yet from whatever angle I looked at the river it still flowed upstream. I even took a look through my camera to see if this might correct what I believed must be an illusion, but through the reflex lens the river still flowed uphill. I then took a picture which, when developed, showed the same canal imperceptibly slanting upwards in the direction of the water flow.

This made me understand that this optical illusion was caused by several factors: what appeared as a flat desert was in fact slightly inclined; so also were the peaks around me. As a result the entire landscape collaborated to give a false impression of what was horizontal. The relatively horizontal line of the canal thus seemed tilted against the direction of the general slope. There not being a single tree or house to rectify the vertical plane, the illusion was absolute and would not have been noticeable but for the fact that the water seemed to flow against the apparent gradient.

I had heard of the existence of strange optical phenomena in nature but had never witnessed one on such a scale and which resisted analysis, for the illusion remained even after one was aware of its origin. Was the water really flowing uphill? It took a lot of faith in Newton to say no.

An hour after leaving the strange up-flowing canal I was walking along happily preceding Lobsang, Nawang, and the donkey, feeling like a sort of Don Quixote crossing rivers that flowed upstream when suddenly my feet sank ankle-deep in mud. Hastily I pulled them clear. I wondered whether I was not going mad for I had been walking on dry, dusty ground with rocks and little stones sticking out. Surely it was not dry mud I had stepped into, yet everything was dry around me and I had never yet heard of or seen floating stones. Was it the heat, I wondered, that had made me first see water flow upstream and now this!

As these thoughts flashed through my mind I looked back at my two companions and at that very moment saw the donkey sink literally through the top surface of dry earth and sand, on which rested large stones. The situation had become dramatic, Lobsang and Nawang rushed forward in a panic and began to untie the load from the donkey, they themselves sinking dangerously into deep mud as they did so. The donkey, up to his belly in mud and incapable of moving a limb, stood petrified in fear but he was quickly raised out of the oozing black mud and carried by Lobsang and Nawang to safe land.

A close investigation soon explained what had happened; it made us realise that we had been lucky not to have been swallowed up by tons of liquid mud, for a gigantic landslide was oozing out of the mountain to our left. This must have occurred only a few hours before we came on the scene, yet the intense heat of the sun and dryness of the air had made the surface dry up completely so that no one could have guessed that underneath it was liquid, possibly still creeping down the valley. Had we crossed a little further down in a deeper place I might well have met a death said to be worse than drowning.

After all these experiences I was prepared for anything, even a flying yak, yet none appeared and as we plodded on I asked myself, how far is far? A question difficult to answer; but as the day dragged by, finding us at dusk still marching amidst the rock-strewn desert landscape, I began to think I knew the answer. Far is eight hours' walking, very far ten hours' and terribly far fourteen; anything longer is out of reach. It struck me that in the West we never consider any distance as too far, as we have in fact lost all true notion of distance. Distance is something to do with aching muscles and manpower and has, as such, totally disappeared as a unit of length in the West, to become in our world a unit of speed.

I was reaching my limit when we passed near the tiny village of Shilingshit. Lobsang's sister lived here and he suggested I should visit her and meet her husband, one of the very few if not the only, potter of the

Zanskar valley. I readily accepted and cut across the barren plain towards four or five low houses nestling among a few trees.

The village seemed deserted but Lobsang soon caught sight of an old lady and called out to her, to ask if his sister were there. Eventually she came out on the roof of a nearby house and stood there surrounded by several people. Lobsang explained who I was and that I wanted to enter the house to see the potter's workshop. After a long silence the woman came down and told her brother I could not enter the house as her husband was away. Lobsang then exchanged a few words with his sister but to no avail, so I was obliged to leave without satisfying my curiosity.

'You must forgive them,' Lobsang explained, 'the village is small and off the trade route so people here have never seen a foreigner before; my sister's mother-in-law was afraid you were an evil spirit!'

Towards evening it began to drizzle and low clouds capped the valley that we could see opening out to our right, as we once again approached the central province of Zanskar. To our left rose the impressive, steep, barren slopes of a great copper-coloured mountain whose summit was hidden in the clouds. Just beneath the mist I observed the monastery of Thonde, a spectacular sight, its buildings lined upon the edge of a vertical cliff like suicidal pigeons on a wall. At the foot of the cliff a cluster of whitewashed houses spread out, the first of the village of Thonde which was composed of four hamlets scattered on the flat sloping plain that ran down to the Zanskar river at the confluence of its two branches.

It was too late to think of going to the monastery that night. Pushing ahead I reached the first house; it was set beside a large chorten near an immense boulder that had toppled from the cliff. The monastery was almost totally invisible from the foot of the cliff. Around the chorten stood a group of some thirty primitive-looking peasants in ragged home-spun garments, the women with great goat fleeces hanging loosely over their backs in a prehistoric manner. Little boys and girls stared at me with dirty faces and rosy cheeks.

I surprised the little crowd by speaking Tibetan and asking if there was a house in which I could spend the night. I got no immediate reply, for a group of old women nudged each other, crowding around me trying to catch my words, exhibiting their broken teeth and forming a sort of ballet of witches. Whereas many young girls in Zanskar are quite beauti-ful, older women become really hideous, their skin wrinkled beyond belief from overexposure to deadly ultraviolet rays while the lack of dentists give them smiles that would frighten the less arrogant of the fierce divinities of their Tantric pantheon.

With age the Zanskaris develop a dark-brown-coloured skin, the result of continuous sunburn, while the protected parts of their arms, legs and body show them to have a very light colour and under their sunburnt faces many have rosy cheeks. To fight sunburn many women smear earth on their faces over a coating of butter which, if it makes them seem frightening and dirty, protects them efficiently against a sun which by now had all but totally destroyed my nose.

Lobsang and Nawang, with our mini donkey, soon caught up with me and on seeing my escort a monk came forward from the crowd and suggested we spend the night in a nearby house which belonged to the monastery. It was now dark and, having packed my torch in some inaccessible place, on entering the house I had to grope around in a low passageway that twisted and turned before reaching a central patio on the first floor. I realised that the low doorways and twisting corridors served the dual purpose of keeping out the cold in winter and were also a defence in ancient times against brigands.

I awoke the following morning at four-thirty, determined to visit the monastery upon its cliff before setting out for Padum. Leaving Nawang and Lobsang still asleep I crept out of the house, bumping my head and in the process aroused an angry dog. All was dark outside and it was drizzling as I already knew, having found my sleeping bag soaked by a leak in the roof.

Slowly I began the steep ascent to the monastery, easily picking out the small zigzag path lined by chortens and prayer walls. The climb, up some fifteen hundred vertical feet, took me a full forty-five minutes – it was an exhausting task on an empty stomach. I made a point of not stopping to catch my breath and plodded on like a pilgrim, offering my effort to God as sweat poured down between my shoulders and froze cold against my shirt. I was slightly dizzy when at last several fine chortens and a low gate told me I had reached the sanctuary's holy enclosure.

Beyond this limit women are not allowed to stay for the night. Sitting down by the entrance I rested while looking out over the plain below. Although clouds hung low it was now sufficiently light to see the layout of Zanskar's central province like a map beneath me. Just the other side of the river from Thonde an unexpected lone hill rose from the flat plain, upon which stood a gigantic whitewashed chorten whose base seemed to be the hill itself. This was Pipiting, while six miles to the south I could see what appeared to be a mound of boulders, the site of Padum for which we were heading. It was a sad day with rain giving the landscape a dull appearance and for the first time I doubted whether the 'Land of White Copper' was truly a place where fairies might congregate.

My gloom was soon dispelled when I entered the monastery, a fairy-tale village of tiny houses which lined the narrow streets that wound in and out of the great rocks, against which many of the monks' little homes nestled snugly. The minute flagstone streets all led to a small pond over-hung by great rocks and a weeping willow. The site was so charming and so cosy that I well understood why monks were attracted to living in a place with a grandiose view on one side and on the other, the quiet charm of the little pond. Passing beneath the cells I came to a rectangular closed yard, at one end of which rose the orange façade of a large assembly hall, with two open verandas supported by great pillars painted red and decorated in brilliant colours outlined with gold. I stood for a while alone in the yard admiring the building, waiting for a monk or someone to appear. By my watch it was now nearly five-thirty; of course no one here had a watch or any means of knowing the time other than the sun.

I had arrived a little before the official morning call which I was soon to hear echoing through the monastery. This was the romantic wail of a conch shell with its rising and falling tone rather like a foghorn, it echoed against the cliffs to lose itself finally over the valley.

As yet no one had appeared, so I decided to enter the porch of the main assembly hall to examine its paintings, which represented the four guardians of the universe. Fierce-looking seated divinities, they grace the entrance of practically every chapel in the Himalayas. Inside the porch I noticed a staircase that ran up to my right: taking this I found myself on a landing with several doors; one was ajar so I poked my head through it into a room where, seated before a raised hearth, an old monk sat stoking the fire and brewing tea. I coughed and walked in. The monk seemed slightly alarmed but was reassured when I spoke to him in Tibetan and he invited me in for a welcome cup of salty tea. Halfway through my breakfast we were joined by several monks. Two of them were painters engaged in restoring the monastery's frescos and renovating certain halls. The third was a trader, a Tibetan refugee from Dharmsala, the town where the Dalai Lama resided. He had arrived the night before with a load of goods ordered by the monastery. A little later a tall, strong monk with a tough-looking face came in, he was the very energetic Abbot of the monastery. Politely he exchanged a few words with me, asking where I came from and the purpose of my visit, then he suggested that when I had finished drinking my tea he would show me his monastery. In the meantime he talked to the Tibetan trader and the two artist monks. The subject was how much cotton cloth they would still need to cover all the walls of a lateral chapel. He also enquired whether the artists were content with what the trader had brought. The trader showed pieces of cloth he had brought, along with spools of thread, needles and dyes of various colours. The artists looked them over knowingly, commenting on how much more of this or that they would need.

I found the scene most interesting for I was learning about some of the problems that had been attendant on the construction of all the magnificent monasteries I had seen.

In the West we too often take for granted the availability of goods at our local stores and have forgotten how in our own Middle Ages all manufactured goods were hard to come by, because of the lack of mass-produced standardised merchandise and especially the lack of retail outlets. If one wanted a set of knives or swords from Sheffield or Toledo one had to send for them, and to send for them meant, as in the case of these monks, sending a man one trusted on a six-week journey with money for the goods, for his food, and for the return transport of the merchandise. This naturally increased the cost of any item. A further rise in price was due to the fact that, like the swords from Sheffield or Toledo, many items were only made in specific regions, often very remote. Nothing was easy or cheap in those times of slow transport by foot or pack animals. Today many of us in the West complain about the cost of living but what would we say had we to pay exorbitant mediaeval prices!

Having despatched the monastery's business the Abbot took me on a tour of the chapels he was restoring. I have rarely encountered such a dynamic Abbot and it was a pleasure to see how lively the arts and the faith were at Thonde. It is this dynamism that distinguishes the Himalayan world and its culture from so many other civilisations of the East. In the main chapel a complete set of the *Kanjur*, a hundred and eight volumes, was stored behind the fearful statue of Dorje Jigchet, the many-faced fiend. In a lateral chapel the Abbot showed me various ancient swords and spears, and a banner given to Thonde by some abbot from Amdo to thank the monastery for having sent monks to that far region which lay a year's journey away!

I was about to leave when the Abbot called an old monk and asked him to escort me to a very sacred chapel some way off. Accompanied by this lame old man I passed the sacred chortens behind the monastery and reached a rocky plateau on which stood a small chapel. Producing a ring with many Tibetan keys on it the monk opened the lock and led me into a newly painted hall. Here a rather indifferent new statue of the terrible demon Dorje Jigchet made me shudder because of its vivid representation of the fiend, festooned with human eyeballs, intestines and hearts (symbols of the senses and pain), stepping upon human beings.

Parting with my guide I began the descent towards our house, which I could see far below. In front of it Lobsang and Nawang were busy loading the small donkey.

Soon our little caravan set off. As we advanced I passed the village of Kumik to my left and felt a little guilty for not visiting it, for had I not resolved to visit every village and monastery of the land? But there are times when fatigue gets the better of one's determination and so rather too hastily I accepted Lobsang's word that Kumik was not very interesting. Just about level with the village we came upon a stone wall which ran a full three miles from the village to the river, cutting the otherwise barren plain in two. This I learnt was the dividing-line between the pastures of Thonde and Kumik. The wall revealed something of the importance of pasture and grazing rights in Zanskar. Every peasant owned his own field and each village had its own pastures, those in the valley and those in the mountains to which the herds are taken in the summer. With that traditional, obstinate common sense characteristic of farmers these villagers had thought fit to build this immensely long wall to mark out their respective grazing grounds.

The trail soon brought us to the bank of the Zanskar river where, looking over its turbulent water, I could now see the great chorten of Pipiting and the ruins of a vast building which Lobsang described as the 'Jammu Raja's dzong', the fort of the Hindu rajas who conquered Zanskar in 1836.

9

A Modern Lama

No precise documents describe the fate of Zanskar during the conquest of Ladakh by the soldiers of Zorowar Singh, the fearful General of Gulab Singh, then ruler of Jammu.

This Hindu General stormed over the Himalayas and wrought havoc in the peaceful Buddhist regions through which he passed. Unable to occupy a land as vast as Ladakh he concluded shaky alliances with local leaders. As a result his troops were constantly being called back to put down local revolts in Ladakh, which they had conquered but could not control.

After putting down a rebellion in the Suru valley, in 1836, Zorowar Singh hanged thirteen men and offered fifty rupees for each 'traitor' captured. His offer produced two hundred prisoners who were beheaded. Leaving this trail of blood behind him, he marched up to Rangdum monastery, where he learnt of a rising in Leh by the King of Ladakh. Hurriedly the General and his troops crossed the Pensi-la into Zanskar.

At that time the country was only just recovering from three devastating invasions that in less than fifteen years had impoverished the land. The last, in 1823, led by the leaders of Lahoul, had destroyed the great fort of Padum. Since then it had not been rebuilt so the inhabitants could not put up any resistance, they therefore agreed to pay Zorowar Singh an annual tribute of three and a half rupees per household. A small fee, for the people of Ladakh at that time had to pay ten and a half rupees a year per household.

Zorowar Singh asked the people of Zanskar to show him the road to Leh. Submissive but not subdued no one would do this. The road in fact led out of Zanskar past Thonde. Eventually a 'traitor' was found who agreed to lead the troops, he was rewarded with five hundred rupees, two gold bracelets, and a promise that he would become the leader of Zanskar in perpetuity. It is not known if the 'traitor' did ever obtain rights over Zanskar. I doubt it.

The next we hear of Zanskar in the various, sometimes conflicting accounts of the Dogra war, is two years later. It seems that Paldar, Zanskar's south-western neighbour, had rebelled against the Dogras' representatives, killing the entire garrison of twenty men left in the fort of Chatargarh by Vazir Basti Ram. Zorowar Singh, hearing of this disaster and also of widespread rebellion in Ladakh and Zanskar, set out with three thousand men to recapture the fort of Chatargarh. After taking the fort and cutting the ears and noses off his prisoners, he set out for Zanskar by way of the terrible Umasi pass which is at 17,370 feet one of the highest passes of the Himalayas. On the way twenty-five of his men died of frostbite while ten lost their hands and feet. On reaching Zanskar the General found that all the inhabitants had fled in fear; so he decided to camp there for two months until the Zanskaris were prepared to submit to him. Zorowar stayed at the fort of Pipiting from where he sent for the old, deposed King of Ladakh and reinstated him on the throne.

In 1840 the General came to Zanskar a third time while on his way to conquer Baltistan, after which, becoming over ambitious, he invaded Tibet where he died in 1841.

If we are to believe a note by Major Cunningham, there was in 1846 a 'disturbance' (probably a second rebellion) in Zanskar, promptly repressed by Basti Ram.

Doctor Thomas Thomson – the first known European to have visited Zanskar since Csoma de Körös had stayed there – gives us a description of the Dogra fort as it was in 1848: 'A rectangular structure with four round towers at the corners.' Thomson spent only two days camped beside Padum, then he set off for Ladakh via Zangla. He has little to tell us about the situation of the royal families at this time. Francke claims that the King of Zanskar was taken to Jammu as a prisoner and that he and his son died there some time between 1839 and 1846, whether from natural causes or foul play is not certain.

On the other hand, the Kings of Zangla seem to have stayed on in Zanskar 'helping the Dogras'. Their 'genealogy' states: 'It is certain the Zanskaris' spirit of rebellion was broken.'

In 1846 the British, trying to extend their empire, signed the Treaty of Lahore which backed Gulab Singh as Maharajah of Jammu and Kashmir, thus in one stroke giving the British political control over not only tiny Jammu but the vast expanse of the western Himalayas, including the Kingdoms of Baltistan, Ladakh, Zanskar and Spiti, along with the populated and rich Moslem Vale of Kashmir. Thus Zanskar came to be annexed to the British Crown without the British Army ever having gone there, and nine hundred and one years of Zanskar's independence came to an end. Zanskar could certainly not rebel against the mighty British. The Pax Britannica made the Dogra garrisons unnecessary, consequently the fort in Zanskar was abandoned and left to fall to ruin. Unhampered by either the British or the Dogras, Zanskar once again resumed its age-old way of life. Too remote and isolated to justify interference, too poor to excite envy, Zanskar continued as in the past to live very much on its own.

Eventually we reached an enormously wide and nearly mile-long prayer wall, the most impressive I was to see in Zanskar: a great rectangular mass of hundreds of river boulders carved with the prayer '*Om mani padme hum*'. This invocation, which is ceaselessly recited by all, is also written on strips of paper to be placed within prayer wheels, printed on prayer flags, carved on chortens and on any prominent rock or boulder. However it has strangely enough no direct significance in Tibetan. It is in fact a magic formula whose meaning is vaguely claimed to signify 'Hail thou jewel of the lotus'. Anyone passing such a wall is believed to gain the merit from all the prayers carved on it. Several of these walls in Zanskar contain inscriptions telling who built them. I was told that this one had been erected by one of the Kings of Zanskar but I was unable to find an inscription that might have recorded his name.

Rain, along with snow that was melting at higher altitudes, had swollen the branch of the Zanskar river we were now following. In great swirls of foam, accompanied by a steady roar, it rushed down full of rocks and silt. We began to clamber down the steep embankment nearly opposite Padum which still looked like a gigantic ruin. Suddenly I saw below me the bridge we had to cross, or rather the two bridges that spanned the roaring river. My heart sank; for the first was a suspension bridge: shorter yet much higher than the Zangla bridge. It dangled over the river like a piece of wet string hanging from two great rocks set in midstream. The second bridge was a topsy-turvy affair of huge flagstones laid upon two half-rotting tree trunks precariously resting on boulders.

Our hardy donkey had to be abandoned on the left bank, while we set out to cross the bridge. Fear is a weak word to describe what I felt. To begin with I nearly slipped off the smooth wet rock up which I had to climb to get level with the end of the swing bridge. Next I realised that the handrails were so low as to be below my knees and therefore below my centre of gravity. If I were to lose my balance even slightly it would be fatal. To top everything a blinding drizzle rendered the twig ropes, consolidated by a lone steel cable, slippery. The second section of the bridge wobbled and vibrated as its flagstones rattled on their dubious supports. Once on the other side, I admired Lobsang and Nawang as they crossed several times to bring over my bags.

Leaving the donkey to its fate we struck up the steep incline that led to Padum. From nearby, as from afar, the town still looked like a mass of ruins. In fact it is built upon a glacial deposit of huge boulders stacked in a haphazard and perilous manner, the immense blocks lying loosely one on top of the other rising to form a hill. Its summit is crowned by the massive stony rubble of the ruins of what had once been the proud fortress of the Kings of Zanskar. Behind this chaos the houses of Padum were hidden, many were built under the overhang of the great rocks, most were badly whitewashed and looked very miserable. The town, owing to the boulders, was not built on any definite plan, its narrow alleys meandered around stone blocks to meet at a huge chorten that marked the centre of town. Painted white, trimmed with red, the chorten had fine reliefs on all four sides. They represented a pair of lions, a peacock, a horse and an elephant. Now that its crowning castle has been destroyed, apart from its one hundred and twenty houses, Padum has little to commend it to the casual traveller. It does not even have a monastery or an assembly hall of any size. However, I later discovered that the inhabitants were busy building a monastery on the ruins of the ancient fort.

Padum, as the capital of Zanskar, is the main trading centre which explains why perhaps forty percent of its inhabitants are Moslems, mostly Baltis from Kargil who have been settled there for several generations, as can be judged from a visit to the old Moslem cemetery that stands to the north of the town.

When we reached it, the rain had turned all the alleys into mud and made a sad place of Padum. I could not help but feel some regret that the capital of what I by now liked to think was a little bit 'my' country was in such a mess.

I urged Lobsang to find me a good house to stay in as, although it was only two o'clock, I was soaked to the skin and exhausted. Since half past four in the morning I had been walking without a pause and without anything to eat except for the tea and tsampa I had taken at dawn and the few biscuits I had munched on the way.

Eventually I was led to the first floor of a fine tall house with frills decorating the outside of its large latticed windows. This house, the finest in Padum, stood next to a larger yet less luxurious house which I was told was the home of the King of Zanskar.

I was led into a low room, its walls were hung with Indian printed cloth and the floor was covered with Himalayan carpets. The owner, a chubby Zanskari merchant, allowed me to sleep in his living-room.

A few minutes later he produced some tea and we chatted about the town, while Lobsang and Nawang disappeared to the home of the latter's brother who was the father of the boy for whom I had bought the chuba.

Aided by a little *arak* (distilled barley beer), a sort of whisky, my spirits were soon restored. There is nothing like a good drink to chase away a freezing drizzle and I was rapidly involved in heated discussion with my host about Padum. He was a fairly well educated man. After I had asked him about some old statues, I soon found myself leaving the warm comfort of the house to see some ancient stone carvings that lay to the north of the town.

Following my chubby guide I walked along the crest of the steep bank of the Zanskar river past large, crumbling chortens. Two hundred yards out of town I was shown a menhir-like monolith ten feet tall; on it was carved the figure of a standing divinity. Its awkward stance and unusual features convinced me that it was very ancient. By its side stood two smaller images, equally old. My guide then took me down the riverbank to a colossal rectangular boulder some thirty feet high, half embedded in the earth. On its southern side five magnificent buddhas seated upon five thrones stood out in relief, each was supported by animals: a lion, a horse, a peacock, an elephant and a winged garuda. These five celestial buddhas seemed less ancient than the carvings I had just seen. Beside them was a fifteen-foot standing figure that rose on the same rock face to the right of the five seated figures. Several chortens were carved on the eastern face of the same great rock.

Although there was no doubt as to what the figures represented, it was less obvious why they had been carved there and when.

I knew that before the invasion and settlement of the Zanskar valley by Tibetans in the eighth century, the Ladakh region together with the Kashmir valley had been Buddhist; so no doubt Zanskar too had been populated by Buddhist peoples. Could the oldest of these carvings, along with some of the others I had seen, be pre-Tibetan – that is, prior to the eighth century AD? And if so, what could they teach us of the days before the Tibetan conquest of this lonely valley? Was Zanskar then inhabited by Dards, or by Baltis, like the valley of the Suru river, or did it have a Mongolian population before the arrival of the Tibetans? If so, who were these people?

My enthusiasm for these sculptures seemed to spread to my guide who, with an agility I had not suspected of him, drew me down the steep embankment through wet grass on to a steep and rocky slope to another large rock a hundred yards upstream from the first. Looking up I could see the slightly faded outlines of five standing buddhas, they had delicate auras around their heads and seemed older than the other five.

'This place is holy ground where we place the ashes of the dead,' commented my guide. Then he showed me the grim reality of his words by pointing to some human bones lying in the mouth of a low cave beneath the sculptures.

By Lamaist tradition the inhabitants of Zanskar have several ways of disposing of their dead. Either they burn them (an expensive and trouble-some method in Zanskar because of the lack of fuel), or they throw them in the rivers – a solution more favoured in this than in most regions of the Himalayan world; or they cut up the corpse and expose it to predators, wolves and giant carrion-eating eagles. In certain cases they also bury their dead. These various forms of disposing of the dead represent the return of the body to fire, water, earth and wind; the four elements con-sidered to be the component parts of man.

If the body is burnt, then the ashes are mixed with clay and moulded into holy statuettes, often in the shape of little chortens, which are placed in certain caves or chortens, or other holy places, including the altars of chapels. The death of any person in Zanskar is followed by two to three days of religious ceremonies, during which monks come to help the soul on its journey to its next reincarnation.

This journey is a frightening ordeal as the soul roams for forty-three days through the land of spirits, *bardo* as it is called, a sort of purgatory. It is the story of what happens to human souls between two reincarnations which forms the content of the *cham*, religious dances held annually in the larger monasteries. These dances tell of encounters with animal-headed fiends and many other fearful demons.

During the funeral rites the monks look for tell-tale signs on the body which can help forecast into which of the six spheres of existence the soul is to be reincarnated. There is also the possibility of a man being reborn once again as a human; this is not a very good rebirth for 'life is suffering'. Worse, one can be reborn as an animal, or as a ghost tantalised by yearnings to quench unsatiable desires, or one may go to the hell of hells which has a burning hot and a freezing action, in both of which the worse tortures are practised. There is also the possibility, depending on one's virtue in life, of being reincarnated as a Titan, a warring spirit which takes part in endless battles. The sixth and relatively happy possibility is that of being reincarnated as a god, yet even this is not all bliss, for one is hounded by the terrible knowledge that one day one will die and be again reborn in another sphere of existence. Eventually, through the accumulation of merit, one can reach perfection – the fusion of one's soul with the Absolute, with truth; this is what is meant by attaining enlightenment, Nirvana. Only then can man leave the clutches of the wheel of life to become one with perfection.

If nobody likes the thought of dying, the Zanskaris take a less tragic view of death than we seem to in the West. After all it simply gives access to a new life which, if one has been virtuous, should be better than the last. Lobsang for one seemed quite fearless of death, so strong were his convictions. Death in an agricultural community like that of Zanskar is defused of the horror with which we surround it in the West; here death becomes as it should, a visible and natural event of everyday life.

Fascinated by the ancient rock carvings, I made my way back to Padum with my guide and host to another heart-warming drink. There we found Lobsang and Nawang speculating as to the day on which the great festival of Sani would be held. Sani is the large monastery set on the central plain just the other side of the river from Thunri, Nordrup's and Nawang's home village. No one could agree as to whether it was to be held in one, two, or three days' time.

'Anyhow we will know on seeing the fire,' said my host. He was referring to two big bonfires which are traditionally lit at Sani the night before the festival, as a way of advising all that the great occasion was about to take place.

Since my arrival I had heard a lot about the festival at Sani. Lobsang had told me that it attracted crowds from all the four districts of Zanskar, both members of the Yellow Hat sect and those of the Red Hat Drukpa sect.

So far I had only seen monasteries affiliated to the Yellow Hat sect but I was now told that the monastery of Padum, which rose a mile away from the town, belonged to the Drukpa sect, a monastic order affiliated to the national Bhutanese church. Although there is no great rivalry between the sects (as there is between Catholics and Protestants) it was unusual to find the Yellow Hats and the Red Hats sharing a festival.

I was about to dine when someone burst into my room shouting 'Wolf!' Wolves had indeed been spotted on the other side of the river, and everyone feared the donkey we had left there would be killed, since the owner of the beast had failed to come and collect it as had been arranged. After having nearly died in liquid mud and having travelled overloaded for two days the poor little beast was about to meet the worst of possible fates. I felt quite as sorry for the donkey as for its owner. Lobsang left immediately to cross the terrible bridge in the dark and sleep under a rock with the donkey so as to guard it from the wolves! Amazingly he did not seem to mind the discomfort and was as jovial as ever as he bade me goodnight and set out to donkey-sit in the cold.

In the arduous weeks that lay ahead I was to have many other occasions to admire Lobsang's courage and resilience.

10

A Thousand Pilgrims

That night I dreamt of wolves and shivered for Lobsang until I was awoken at the crack of dawn by someone shouting.

'It is today; we have seen the fire!'

Slowly I understood what this meant.

'The Sani festival is to be held today.'

I got up, cursing the festival, yet determined not to miss it.

I had originally planned that Lobsang's horses, which we had left at the Zangla bridge, should be sent to join us at Padum. They had not turned up and by now there seemed little chance that they would appear in time so I started for Sani on foot. I thought I would spend the night there while Lobsang got the horses and provisions ready for us to set out for Lunak, the rugged province that stretches for nearly a hundred miles along the upper Zanskar river.

I had now decided that rather than leave Zanskar by the route I had come, I would cross the entire Himalayan Range and eventually reach India by cutting through the great mountain chain to the Kulu valley. This was an important decision since it meant crossing either the Baralacha pass, some 16,500 feet high, or the less travelled and more fearsome Shingo pass at 16,722 feet. I chose the last pass, partly because I like a challenge and partly because the Baralacha pass now had a strategic military road leading to it. This road was washed away in many parts but originally it had been built to connect Leh, the capital of Ladakh, with India; it ran across the district of Rupshu which, along with Zanskar, forms the highest land mass in the world.

Most people thought that these passes would now be closed by snow because of all the rain that had fallen over the past week. What decision I would take depended on Lobsang, for I could not hope to travel without him on this long and arduous expedition. He was not very enthusiastic about the journey so I did not press the matter with him.

In the meantime we all set out for Sani monastery. It was a fine morning with the sun shining upon the surrounding peaks which glittered whiter than ever after the recent snowfalls. Half a mile out from Padum we could see the silhouettes of pilgrims for miles across the flat plain, converging towards the shrine.

Soon we ran into a small group, joined them and chatted happily as we went. They were dressed in their finest robes; the women resplendent with jewels, while some of the men wore magnificent black velvet robes. Several parties on horseback overtook us. In one such group a father, mother and their child rode the same pony in a flutter of brocade capes and flowing gowns. I could easily believe that in the Middle Ages the pilgrimages to Canterbury had been very similar, with crowds slowly gathering along the trail bound for the same goal, and animated by the same faith.

We passed groups of pilgrims who had stopped to rest, and who cheered us on. We were like a marching army in a great column, as far as one could see the trail was packed with pilgrims, all out to receive the solemn blessing which would be given at Sani by holy monks. It was an occasion not to be missed and a tradition as old, if not older in fact, than the Tibetan presence in Zanskar.

It was past midday when, four hours after leaving Padum, we came in sight of Sani, visible from afar because around the monastery were planted half a dozen plane trees, the tallest and possibly the oldest in all of Zanskar. Later, in the distance, the houses of the village of Sani appeared. They were set in two separate clusters; one beside and the other beyond the monastery.

Since evidently we could not return to Padum for the night, I asked Lobsang to find me a place to stay while I set out for the monastery.

The main attraction, I soon appreciated, rested in the crowd of pilgrims, for there was not to be any grandiose display of religious pomp; neither dances nor spectacular rites. Yet maybe two thousand people had gathered at Sani, and more were still arriving, mostly on foot but some on horses. The festival, I was told, served also as a horse fair, people buying and selling stallions and mares as a sideline.

All the pilgrims wore their finest clothes and showed them off as they circumambulated the monastery, walking around the rectangular wall that enclosed a garden planted with tall, old poplar trees. Here stood the large monastery, with two little chapels, set around a courtyard surrounding a strange egg-shaped monument, the famous Kanika chorten. Six other chortens dotted the exterior wall around which the pilgrims marched, as they recited the prayer 'Om mani padme hum'. Others just chatted and joked, thereby giving a truly festive air to the gathering. In a little chapel situated above the entrance doorway a monk gave a special blessing: the *wang*, for the accumulation of merit and the multiplication of virtues. The crowd of pilgrims presented white scarves to the monks, receiving in return a little strip of cotton to tie around their necks, and the ritual blessing on their heads by the imposition of a vase of holy water.

For an hour I stared in fascination at the scene. Never had I seen such a splendid crowd; jewels framed the faces of the women, faces that seemed to come from the palette of great masters attached to a feudal court. Equally fascinating were the children: little girls in red or yellow bonnets (according to their religious sect) studded with wild flowers, among which I occasionally saw a blue poppy obviously picked on the high summer grazing grounds where many of the pilgrims had been attending their flocks. Boys sported pompous top-hats made of maroon or black velvet embroidered with silver thread. It is nearly impossible to describe such hats, their rims cut out in the front and their sides fluted and padded. In Ladakh I had noticed that these hats were worn by both men and women; but in Zanskar only men and little boys wore them, for here the women had their strange, dog-eared headgear, while the little girls wore the bonnets I have already mentioned. No film director in the West could have staged a more flamboyant pageant. Looking at this assembly I tried to imagine what the great festive occasions in Lhasa before the departure of the Dalai Lama might have been like, and I reflected that this was possibly the last truly unspoilt assembly of Himalayan pilgrims. Had not the Sherpas of Nepal discarded their traditional gowns? And had I not already witnessed how elsewhere customs were rapidly being changed, under the combined influence of the Indian authorities and the invasion of sightseers?

Looking at the healthy and prosperous crowd I prayed that Zanskar would preserve its customs forever, as I recalled the squalor of the masses in India, the lost dignity of all those peoples and tribes who, in contact with the Western world, have lost not only their identity, but their pride.

'A man without traditions is like an animal,' a young Mayan woman had told me a year before. She had seen the change from complete cultural isolation to the steam-rolling effect of modernisation; the world of blue jeans, sunglasses and ragged imitations of Western clothes.

Indeed what is man without culture and tradition? What is man without all those, maybe artificial, but beneficient elements that make him rise above the basic animal quest for food and sexual gratification? It is culture in all its forms that truly differentiates us from animals. Our ability to invent rites and customs is our most human trait, and their loss is quite definitely a loss to humanity at the expense of animality.

I was much intrigued by Sani, its simplicity recalled its great antiquity. The entire monastery and the small yard behind is surrounded by a covered passage that allows one to walk around the building even in winter. Little cylinders on creaking, vertical axles and containing printed prayers were set in the walls of the monastery so that the devout could spin them as they walked round the shrine. The main hall harboured many books placed behind an altar with rows of Buddhist images, while the walls were covered with frescos that had badly deteriorated. On the first floor was a fine small chapel to which I was invited by several monks and local dignitaries. We sat and drank several glasses of chang. On leaving I clambered down and visited the enclosed yard behind the assembly hall. Here rose the strange Kanika chorten, which made Francke, who had heard of it, think it was a pre-Tibetan monument linked with the Buddhist Afghan King, Kanishka, of the first century AD. The chorten is the centre of special devotion, nothing apart from its weird shape would suggest to me that it might be nearly two thousand years old, but of course it could be that the site simply retained the name of its founder. It was said that under the chorten lay a hidden lake of milk.

More remarkable than this chorten was a strange chapel to one side of it, one of whose walls was decorated with clay sculptures of religious scenes; these surrounded niches in which small statues were placed.

The shrine, called the Gyanchut chapel, is linked by legend with a semicircular group of ten standing stones carved with unusual figures that lie near the monastery. They represent a large female goddess ten feet tall, with smaller figures on either side of her. These were the finest and most ancient-looking sculptured stones I had seen, and proved that long before the monastery was built the site had been held sacred. These stones were collectively known as *Durchot-de-Chen-rdal*.

Beyond doubt Sani was one of the oldest shrines in the land. How old is a matter for further investigation. Quite probably Sani was the site of a temple in pre-Tibetan times when Zanskar was the site of a flourishing ancient Buddhist community now long forgotten.

After having received a special blessing in Naropa's chapel behind the monastery, I went to the house where Lobsang had left my bags. On the way I ran into the young French and Belgian boys who had accompanied me to Thunri. They had stayed in that village and were considering leaving by the same route we had come.

I had so far met no other foreigners except for six Japanese students who had come to Zanskar at the same time as I. They had split up in little groups and travelled to different places. They spoke no Tibetan or English and I no Japanese so we had little to say to each other.

I now heard that the group of Swiss tourists we had met on the way in had been so delayed on their march to Padum that they never reached the capital, and had to return after a brief stay in Zanskar. In a way I was relieved. Mass tourism, I knew, would only bring with it unwanted changes and could, I believed, in no way benefit the local population.

Lobsang had found me a small room in the house of the headman of Sani, a young fellow of about twenty-nine. I was surprised at first by his youth, and was even more surprised when he told me he had been head-man for eight years. Of course I had forgotten the custom of a father transferring all his land to his son when he gets married, for not only do children inherit their father's land, but also his prestige and position. The remarkable corollary of such a system is that Zanskar is run by young people who occupy all the most important offices which we in the West generally reserve for older men. Indeed in most of Europe men over forty-five usually have the monopoly of practically every important political, social, administrative and economic function. But forty-five is the usual retirement age in Zanskar. This custom had scandalised the Chinese who, in one of their criticisms of Tibet, claimed wrongly that the Tibetans 'had no respect for the old'. Certainly management by the young is one of the greatest innovations of the Tibetan social system. This custom stems from Songsten Gampo, the first King of Tibet whose armies settled Zanskar in the seventh century. As a soldier he appreciated the capabilities of young men and understood that if they were not given the reins of power, society would be bound to stagnate. It is a fact observed in many agricultural societies (in which power is vested in the patriarch and landowner) that children are prevented from taking any active role until their father dies. We are all familiar in the West with the sight of old men clinging defiantly to authority, refusing to give up their place and persistently fostering outmoded and antiquated ways. This system may make for stability, but it is not conducive to dynamism or progress. In the Himalayan system dynamism is present everywhere because the young wield effective power.

Since people tend to rise towards their responsibilities, it was no surprise to me to note the remarkable maturity of the young headman of Sani. As could be expected, he was very busy on the occasion of the festival, playing host in his home to the most revered monks. He was also lodging the police officer from Padum, a thin, bearded and turbaned Sikh who seemed out of place in Zanskar. The policeman was the only obvious reminder that for India and Kashmir, Zanskar was conquered territory. The man spoke no Zanskari and practically no English, so he conversed with the Zanskaris in Hindi through an interpreter.

I had, as it happened, a letter for the policeman from the Chief of Police in Kargil, and so dropped over to have a chat with him the following morning. The poor man seemed a little lost among the people of Zanskar. Not only did he find the climate terrible, but he also found the customs very strange. The fact that the Zanskaris drank intoxicating liquor shocked him about as much as the fact that there were no crimes in Zanskar. An annoying state of affairs for an eager policeman. Serious crimes in the Buddhist Himalayas are quite unknown. This so surprises the Indians that they never fail to mention it when speaking of Ladakh.

Through his interpreter the policeman explained to me how the local village council and the local Zanskari magistrates took care of most offences and complaints so that he had little or nothing to do.

'At best we get a few fist fights when the people have drunk too much at festivals such as this,' was his only comment.

From him I learned that if I were to cross the Himalayan Range to leave Zanskar, I would have to seek authorisation from the Tasildar, who was residing in the King's mansion at Padum. In fact, permission would not be vital for me but it would be necessary for anyone who might accompany me, for Zanskaris are not allowed to leave the state of Kashmir without a special pass. By crossing the Himalayas I would enter another Indian province, that of Himachal Pradesh. The matter was further complicated because what one state permitted, the other condemned. While the Kashmiri Government might allow me to cross over the high passes into Himachal Pradesh, that state considered these same passes as within restricted areas! It all sounded a little disheartening, but eighteen years of experience in dealing with Oriental bureaucracy had taught me that with a little patience and if one is in no hurry, everything ends up all right in the end.

The following morning I was woken by Nordrup's booming voice. He stood in the doorway showing his shiny teeth and grinning with delight at seeing me again. I was pleased to see the rascal and, when I was up, I enquired slyly about his leg, which I gathered had been a rather 'lame' excuse for not turning up as promised.

'All those matters are settled,' he answered, 'and now I am ready to go with you where you please.'

We discussed our plans. I intended to visit the province of Lunak and then to carry on up the Shingo pass down into Lahoul, from where I gathered a truck or jeep could take me over the 15,300-foot Rotang pass into the Kulu valley. What I needed was a good horse and both his and Lobsang's company, not only as guides but as companions and friends. Nordrup seemed reluctant, he said the route over the Shingo pass was very dangerous. Only a few weeks previously a horse had fallen into the Zanskar river from one of the many difficult passages along the route and peq drowned. Also there was much snow, and rumour had it that a snow bridge the other side of the pass that crossed a turbulent stream had collapsed, virtually closing the route.

As always when travelling in little-known areas, I found myself at the mercy of rumours and other people's opinions. Could I trust Nordrup? I felt I could, for now his best friend, Lobsang, was my friend too, and his brother Nawang Trile, I knew to be perfectly honest. Although Nordrup might be more turbulent and rather quicker than the two others, he was nevertheless certainly not dishonest. Or at least so I believed – and I proved to be right.

What should I do? Give up my plan and return by the way I had come, or try and go over the Shingo-la, regardless of the rumours and the collapsed snow bridge.

Finally I decided to stick to my original plan. Glaring at the one poor map I possessed, I realised that this decision was about to lead me over about one hundred and twenty-five miles of some of the world's highest territory.

That morning, as I chatted with the headman of Sani, inevitably our conversation touched on the monastery.

'Sani monastery is the oldest in Zanskar,' he explained. 'In it Guru Rimpoche once stayed; when obliged to flee, he leapt to the distant cliffs that you see over there,' and he pointed to the cliffs on the other side of the river.

'I know,' I added, 'I have seen the footprints.'

'It is a fact that the holy saint came to Sani, it is all written down in a book I have here,' the headman went on.

This sentence had me asking to see the book, and soon the woodblock-printed sheets of the biography of *Guru Nyima Osher* (Guru Rimpoche) was produced. The young man then tried to find the passages that mentioned Sani. The book contained some three hundred loose leaves and, as always when you are searching for a specific passage, it just disappeared. For half an hour my handsome host wearing his elegant chuba, squatting cross-legged on the floor, flipped through the pages, unable to find the reference he was looking for. Soon he was helped by a friend who sat down beside him and took part of the book. Later he was also joined by an old man, and lastly by Nordrup, who was given some pages and in turn leafed through them in search of the reference to Sani. For an hour everyone read out aloud while I sat slightly embarrassed at having started all this commotion.

Eventually there was a cry of victory, the young headman had found the reference to Sani and showed me the page. Unfortunately I could not read literary Tibetan, so I arranged to photograph the sheets.

It was a fine morning, the first sunny day for some time, as I strolled out to the monastery with the headman. A crowd of pilgrims were already busy doing the rounds, yet the big rush of the preceding day was over. Under a tent beside one of the chortens a merchant had set out his wares; a Balti from Suru, he sold such goods as matches, sweets and glass bangles. He attracted considerable attention and this reminded me that except in Padum I had not seen a single shop in all the villages I had so far visited. The truth is that the people of Zanskar do not yet live in a monetary economy; indeed they buy little or nothing beyond jewels, and these, no doubt, are paid for in cattle and grain.

There can be few more closed economies than that of Zanskar, whose 12,000-odd inhabitants not only make their own clothes and shoes and grow all their food, but mine their own gold, silver and copper. They also gather upon their apparently barren mountains the herbs that produce their medicines. The result is a strong, sturdy and independent race of men and women who would make the average Asian peasant look sickly by comparison.

Their society is a strong contrast to our own in achieving what are, in fact, similar ideals. The high standard of living of the inhabitants of Zanskar is acquired entirely by relying on their own products. We, on the contrary, owe nearly all we have to an intricate structure of exchange that relies not only on machines but on complex international market structures. If, for example, we want light we have to purchase a bulb, wires, and then join a large network. If we want to wash our linen many of us depend on electricity and machines for which we pay in money. The Zanskari alternative is a do-it-yourself method, such as was practised all over Europe and America not so long ago, but which today seems alien to us. The proud self-sufficiency of the American settlers at the beginning of this century is now, we must admit, replaced by the servile dependency of a consumer society, made up of men enslaved to jobs because of an ever-increasing need for money with which to buy things he once had, either for free, or that he could easily obtain through his own ability.

The appeal of the modern system is that people believe that in purchasing things they economise on labour and time. To wash one's own clothes in a river is thought of as a terrible chore, to walk several miles is described as hardship and a waste of time. Time is built up to be so precious and to do anything for oneself is a waste of it, which can be saved by buying this or that service. What our advertisers and industrialists forget to say is how much time is wasted in acquiring money. Approximately eight hours a day with very few holidays. The five-day week is the price of money, time spent and not saved to be able to save time!

The people of Zanskar have to work much less than ourselves; to them eight hours of solid and uninterrupted work would be unthinkable, except in emergencies. I always remember the reaction of a Tibetan friend of mine, Tashi, for whom I had found work in a European school. His job was to look after pupils, both in classrooms and on the playgrounds. Coming from Tibet he had never heard of work as we understand it, after his first day at the school he came to see me looking desperate.

'What is the matter?' I asked.

'It's terrible,' he said. 'They want me to spend eight full hours at the school working all the time.'

This was too much for him, because it meant a total alienation of his liberty. Yet none of us would have thought of complaining.

I had had ample time to observe the activities of the people of Zanskar and I concluded that few of them ever thought of work as a chore, for all their activities were directly concerned with their own well-being. They drank the milk of the cows they tended, they ate the barley they reaped, and wore the clothes they wove. Their daily activities are not seen as a burden, but are in fact considered amusing. For people truly do enjoy productive activities, even if these are tiring. There is, after all, nothing unpleasant in being tired or in perspiring; do not people in the West enjoy a good sweat playing squash, an exhausting and apparently repetitious chase after a very undisciplined rubber ball? One's approach to work or even the very notion of work is, above all, a psychological attitude to activity. To carry heavy stones for someone else is a chore. To build one's own house can be most rewarding and pleasant. In fact man is happy mainly when active in a physical sense, and possibly much of the drudgery of work as conceived in the West stems from the lack of physical exertion involved in bureaucratic activities. Another factor that makes work unpleasant is doing something alone. Work shared is always more pleasant and can turn out to be amusing. But only if the activity is for oneself or one's family, and as long as there is a direct relation between the energy expended and the reward. To stretch out an arm and pick an apple has never been considered tiring; to sit in an office to earn enough to buy an apple is inevitably seen as tedious.

Beyond doubt the most common physically exhausting activity in Zanskar is to move about up and down the mountains, yet to travel is also the most rewarding of activities for every step brings a new view, and the effort to climb up- or downhill is proportionately rewarded by a faster change in scenery and more dazzling vistas than if one were walking along a plain.

It was with apparent glee that Nordrup shouldered my bag when, after having said goodbye to my friends in Sani, we set off towards Padum.

11

Pipiting

I now had time to become better acquainted with Nordrup. It was evident that he and his brother Nawang came from a less opulent family than Lobsang, and that, unlike Lobsang (the cherished darling of his three aunts), Nordrup had not had a very happy childhood, his mother having died when he and his two brothers were young. He had had to rely on his wits to make his way in life, and his quick intelligence had served him in good stead at the monastery where he had rapidly mastered reading and writing and quickly learned all that is needed of a young monk.

Having few family ties in Zanskar and being of a restless nature Nordrup had decided to travel. This was not too difficult, for a monk is welcome in nearly all the Buddhist monasteries of the Himalayas and if Zanskar is physically isolated, its inhabitants have a very strong feeling that they are part of the vast Himalayan world which is theirs to share and in which they feel at home. Stretching from Afghanistan to Burma, we must appreciate that this world is far greater than the accessible world open to the nationals of European countries. For the Frenchman or the Italian, his culture extends to the not very distant boundaries of his nation; anything beyond is foreign with all the strangeness of the exotic – places with other languages, other religions, countries that at best are visited hastily out of curiosity but hardly as places in which to live. For the Tibetan-speaking Himalayan, journeys to lands thousands of miles away can be undertaken with the assurance of finding there people with the same language, customs and religion.

In order to travel, a monk needs little or no money for monks are always welcome in every household they pass on their way as, in fact, are most travellers. Hospitality to travellers and food are generally free of charge, a custom which was once worldwide. The Himalayan's diet of tsampa further makes travelling simple as this cooked flour is eaten cold and keeps for a long time. A small bag of tsampa can see a traveller on his way for weeks. Nordrup had proudly showed me the tsampa bag he had brought over from Thunri for the long journey to India. On high, windswept and snow-covered passes he need not light a fire to cook his dinner, and is thus freed from the burden of carrying fuel or making lengthy stops as is required by rice-eating travellers such as the Chinese or the Indians.

Nordrup had travelled extensively. As a child he had visited Tibet, later he had roamed around Ladakh, staying in various monasteries and returning later to do business for his monastery of Karsha. On several occasions he had been to Manali, the town at the head of the Kulu valley and our ultimate destination. There he had bought cotton cloth also needles and horseshoes for his monastery, and even horses, including those that were due to arrive with Lobsang. Thus it was that Nordrup knew the route we would be taking very well. It had been on one such journey to Manali that he had decided to travel on to Dharmsala where the Dalai Lama now lives. Travelling by buses, Nordrup had been fascinated by Dharmsala with its Lhasean nobles and great monks living in what seemed to him modern luxury, as he associated cars and electricity with the Dalai Lama's exiled court rather than with modern India. It was while at Dharmsala that Nordrup had heard of the great Tibetan refugee settlements in Mysore several thousand miles away. With a letter for the abbot of the monastery near to the largest refugee community in Mysore state, he had taken more buses and then a train (in fact the first train he had ever seen) to travel two thousand miles across tropical India to the refugee camp. He had then spent several winters in the sun of southern India teaching the little refugee children how to read and write. When summer approached and the heat became unbearable Nordrup set out north for Zanskar to find the passes just open. He returned to his monastery a little wiser, richer and more contented. There he told Lobsang of his adventure; as he had been to Lhasa, and was an intrepid traveller, the following year they went together to Mysore. Spending winters in Mysore had become a routine, while in the summer they worked for their monastery in Zanskar, using the monastery's horses and some of their own on business trips, while saving up for the coming winter. Both could speak Hindi tolerably well, which helped them to do business with the Hindu administrators of Ladakh.

It had been on one such trade mission to Kargil that I had met Nordrup. He had come down with ten horses which he had left at Rangdum, but as he was delayed in Kargil some of his horses had been rented to other merchants. That was why when we returned they had gone, leaving Nordrup's cargo stranded where our first truck had broken down. Having to find his horses again and rescue the cargo explained why he disappeared, placing me in the care of Lobsang.

Nordrup hoped that what I would pay him and Lobsang would be enough for them to buy goods in Manali, and that after selling these goods in Zanskar their profit would be sufficient to allow them to set out in October for Mysore once again.

I always find the lighthearted way in which the Himalayans go on immense journeys a little startling, since we in the West make such a fuss about much shorter travels. It also reminds me that, contrary to what one might imagine, the inhabitants of feudal Europe (even simple folk) travelled much more than we do today. To go to Rome from France or England overland was a journey undertaken by hundreds of thousands, as was the journey to Compostella when this shrine became popular after the closing of the Holy Land. Today the furthest a French or English farmer or employee usually goes is on a charter flight to Mallorca, because travel today has become purely a matter of economics.

A spotless blue sky now capped the flat central plain of Zanskar across which we plodded, passing through little hamlets where we were greeted by old men and women. One very pretty girl in a long grey-black robe falling to the ground had a delightful minute Tibetan terrier. With typical Himalayan humour Nordrup called out.

'What a beautiful mistress you have, little doggie. Where did you get her?'

Not having understood Nordrup's joke the girl came up and showed us the dog, explaining that she had had it since it was a puppy and she a child. Her charming manner and straightforward approach to foreigners was normal for Zanskar, but anywhere else it would have caused frowns.

Relations between men and women in Zanskar are quite uncluttered by the complexes and taboos that plague the Hindu and Moslem people. Indeed the Lamaist concept of the sexes is so egalitarian that I myself felt slightly embarrassed at the straightforward attitude of women towards men. We in the West still have a long way to go before we come to conceive of each other simply as human beings rather than as sexually differentiated persons.

Leaving the young girl with her delightful dog we soon came upon a small river running down from one of the nearby summits. Here we stopped to have something to eat. It was very hot and the river was shallow enough to be relatively warm so I decided to wash my hair. This was the first time, for until now the water had been so cold that it called for great courage even to wash one's hands. Ice-cold water explains why the Zanskaris are not very keen on washing, a characteristic they share with most Himalayans. Because of the earth that the people smear on their faces as protection against sunburn, early Victorian travellers to the Himalayas regarded its inhabitants as dirty, which they often equated with sinful. Major Alexander Cunningham for instance went so far as to describe the Ladakhis as '. . . in general they are all, both men and women, not only ugly but hideous'. While Dr Gerard, an earlier traveller, said, 'Some have the shaggy appearance of wild beasts.'

Having eaten and washed, I let Nordrup carry on towards Padum while I struck out for Pipiting across the barren plains. This is the village surrounding the large chorten set on a hillock that dominates the central plain of Zanskar.

For an hour I walked in a straight line suffering from the heat, while the day before I had suffered from cold. The fields surrounding the village of Pipiting were sown with peas and barley, the two main crops of the lower regions of Zanskar, that is those areas between 11,500 and 12,500 feet where a little wheat is also grown.

In summer it was difficult to fully appreciate how terribly cold the climate of Zanskar was during most of the year. In winter freezing winds howl over the central plain and for months the temperature stays below minus thirty degrees Centigrade. All streams freeze and water is only to be found by breaking the ice over the largest rivers. Lobsang told me that snow lies in such depth that it is often impossible to go from one house to another in the same village. To reach neighbouring hamlets, deep channels have to be cut through the snow. Occasionally wolves prowl in these narrow passageways, and when this happens villagers organise beats, cornering the wolves who then jump out of the channels into snowdrifts where they are stoned to death as they flounder about.

The fields are frozen hard and it is quite impossible to graze animals so they are enclosed during winter, except for the yaks which are allowed to stand by day in the little yards surrounding the houses, for it is a fact that the yak is the only animal that can survive the Himalayan winter in the open. How wild yaks survive in such deserted lands, what with the snow and the cold, is a mystery particularly in view of the apparent absence of any forage. Moorcroft, who first explored Ladakh in 1820, was a veterinary surgeon of the early school and as such took a most enlightened interest in animal fodder during his famous journey.

Not only did he discover flowers and plants that to this day bear his name, but he observed in eastern Ladakh a fodder so rich that small quantities sufficed to fatten cattle. The yaks in particular ate this bushy weed whose nutritional content far exceeds that of all known grasses.

Moorcroft recommended the eventual export to Europe of this Himalayan plant, but so far as I know nothing has been done about it for I have been unable to find in Europe anyone aware of the *Prangos* Moorcroft described. Yet this fodder is so much prized by the Zanskaris that when we were there they were already making stores of its dry, brittle stems alongside stacks of hay, weeds and alpine flowers to be eaten by the flocks in the cold weather.

If it was a near miracle that sheep or cattle could be raised in Zanskar during the long winter months, it was even more amazing that human beings could survive there. One of the reasons why the Zanskaris can live in such an inhospitable, cold and high land is that they have developed an artificial means of melting snow in spring so that they can sow their barley in time for it to ripen before the rapid return of winter. For this purpose in autumn farmers pile up earth in their fields and even in their houses, where this earth does not freeze. When May arrives, and there are still a few feet of snow on the ground, the peasants take this earth and spread it over the snow covering their fields. The dark earth then concentrates the sun's heat and melts through the snow so that these fields are free of snow long before the surrounding countryside. In consequence ploughing and sowing can begin while there is still snow about. This technique assures that the barley will ripen before the first September snowfalls.

Such an ingenious system is characteristic of the Zanskaris' determination to survive in a world fit at best only for gods and fairies.

However, many of the villages, in particular those of Lunak, have such a brief summer that even using the melting-snow technique the barley does not have time to ripen during the short summer. Therefore it is cut before the grain is ripe, and although this brings in a slightly smaller crop the unripened grain is quite digestible, and dries out rapidly in the high air.

It is remarkable that grain can be harvested in Zanskar, but of course strong ultraviolet rays compensate to some extent for the short season and

in fact, in spite of the high altitude, barley gives good yields. This is all
the more surprising since in the higher villages, where only barley is grown,
there is no crop rotation. In the lower villages crop rotation (peas, barley,
wheat) is practised (or peas, barley, barley, peas). In intermediate villages,
barley, wheat and alfalfa are rotated. Perhaps one of the reasons why the
soil does not become sterile is because constant irrigation (every five days)
brings with it additional top soil, and because the fields are well manured.
Weeds are pulled up as soon as they appear; and many are eaten, a variety
which looks like march is particularly popular.

Just as I was surprised to find apricots in Kargil, I was astonished to
meet with the common garden pea in Zanskar. Peas grow there in
abundance and, although not cultivated in the highest villages, delicious
wild peas with small, furry pods are to be found at an altitude of up to
15,000 feet, which must make it the highest growing common vegetable.

I noticed that every house had a minute vegetable garden in which
onions, large radishes, cucumbers and some potatoes were grown.
Potatoes do well in the Himalayas, to which they were imported by the
British in the middle of the eighteenth century. The Sherpas who live
around Mount Everest exist almost exclusively on potatoes. Yet in Zanskar
their cultivation is extremely limited. When I asked why, Nordrup told
me that potatoes were notorious for cooling one's body and favouring
rheumatisms. I would be interested to know whether there is any truth in
this theory.

When I reached Pipiting I found the village apparently deserted, and
strolled amongst its unusually large houses hoping to attract someone's
attention. It seemed that everyone had gone to the Sani festival and had
not yet returned. Eventually I spotted a man peeping out of a small
window and called to him, saying I was looking for the doorkeeper of the
shrine.

'You are in luck,' the man answered, 'he is in here.'

Minutes later a young monk came out and asked me if I would like to
enter the house as the doorkeeper could not come right away. I accepted
and found myself clambering up narrow steps and being ushered into a
low room where two old monks and four men were sitting, all were
busily reading prayers out of a book. They did this in a sing-song chant
that recalled that of our own Christian monks. I sat discreetly in a corner
wondering what the ceremony was about. In Zanskar, more than in any
other place I had visited in the Himalayas, religion and chang seemed to
go hand in hand, and now I was given a cup while the old monks con-

tinued their chanting, their orange bonnets shining in the late afternoon sun that seeped through a little wooden-framed window. The sight of these monks caught in a sunbeam would have inspired any great master. The two old men's heads cocked together, their necks strained as they tried to read their prayers. The four other members of the party had beautiful though savage features, and sunburnt faces that breathed warmth and humanity. I was now so completely absorbed by the present that the world I had left seemed very far away.

How simple it is to lose one's past, how easy to forget one's identity. I felt much closer to the feudal past of Europe than to a world keen on fast cars and electronic equipment, and what I wondered could be more blissful than chanting in the afternoon.

The last prayer over and my cup empty for the third time, one of the old monks bade me follow him as he hobbled downstairs into the street.

Marching behind him, I was escorted towards the famous chorten by ten ragged and mischievous children who made fun of the doorkeeper and did all they knew how to make a nuisance of themselves. For certain they were brats with no complexes. If in most of Asia children look solemn and brow-beaten, Himalayan brats, and especially those of Zanskar, are odious, noisy, active little monkeys always playing fearful games such as pushing each other over cliffs. It is a miracle that any survive.

The famous shrine of Pipiting is to the east of the village, the gigantic chorten being built on the crest of what must have been a glacial deposit. I climbed to the foot of the chorten, and stood admiring the view: to the south, set upon the rock face, rose the white blocks of Karsha monastery, to the east the white cliff-top chapels of Thonde, while to the north-east I could just see the entrance to the gorges that lead to distant Zangla. Far, far to the west I imagined rather than saw, Sani under the shade of its great trees, and beyond it the valley leading to the Pensi-la. To the south-west was Padum, and above it a monastery I planned to visit, while beyond, a narrow, dark valley led to the mysterious Lunak province to which I would soon travel.

Looking at this view was to be my farewell to the more accessible central regions of Zanskar and it was not without sadness that I viewed the incredible panorama and said goodbye to this small, forgotten chapter of the history of humanity.

Coming down from the chorten, still pestered by the children, the old monk showed me into a little chapel containing fierce masks showing the famous third eye, they hung above an image of the eleven-headed

Sani monastery with Kanika chorten, one of the oldest
and most sacred monuments of the Himalayas

At the Sani festival, a woman re-adjusts the massive
turquoise head-dress

The author examines the, so far undated, pre-lamaist sculpture
of Buddha which stands beside the Sani monastery

Jumping down from a glacier, one of the many incidents of travel

Slow, but sure-footed, yaks are the best transport animals
over high passes

Help for a donkey floundering in the mud

Phugtal monastery, the jewel of Zanskar

Avalokitesvara. I was struck once again by the over-rich and intricate Himalayan art which is such a contrast to the straightforward clarity of the Himalayan soul. In Tantric Buddhist iconography there is so much foreign influence – both Indian and Chinese – for it to portray accurately the mentality of the Tibetans. I think the only art that reflects the attitude and mind of the Himalayans is their architecture. This is majestic and sober and blends so well, as do the people, with the magnificent natural surroundings that are the ever present 'decor' of their lives. Nowhere in the East has architecture achieved such a grandiose simplicity; perhaps nowhere in the world has man understood better the role of form, volume and space and their relation to nature than the anonymous architects who have raised so many a magnificent building to honour their gods and their kings.

It should be remembered that the vast Potala complex at Lhasa with its nineteen storeys was built in the late seventeenth century and, for a little under three hundred years, was the world's highest skyscraper, while the grand palace of Leh, the huge fortresses of Bhutan and the magnificent buildings of Mustang and of Zanskar must certainly rate among the most sober and impressive buildings of Asia.

Leaving as is the custom a few rupees with the old monk for the upkeep of the chapel, I set off on my way back to Padum. Still followed by a flock of children, I asked them if there were any old carved stones in the area.

'No,' said one, 'Yes,' said another, and 'No,' said a third. Grabbing the one who had said yes I made him lead me to what was indeed an ancient carved stone representing a Buddha wearing a tri-pointed hat. Later the children showed me another strange divinity. These stone images which were still held in good respect (as testified by the prayer flags about them) recalled that ancient valley's past about which we know little or nothing.

Was Zanskar part of the Kushana Empire before the Tibetan conquest? And if so, how could one explain the presence of so many rather primitive sculptures? For surely the Kushanas, under whom the admirable Buddhist statuary of Gandhara and Mathura had flourished, might have produced something a little grander than the primitive figures I now saw here and had seen at Sani and Padum? Alternatively, were these figures more ancient in origin, like the ibex carvings? Had Zanskar, the 'Land of White Copper', been the mythical land of the gold-searching ants? Certainly there was more gold here than in the Suri river and until recently the gold washings from Pimo were famous. Who had ruled Zanskar before the arrival of the warring Tibetan hordes? Maybe one will never know. What I found strange was that none of these pre-Tibetan Buddhist sculptures were to be seen incorporated in a 'modern' Buddhist temple. The only exceptions were the rock carvings around which the village chapel of Karsha is built.

Leaving Pipiting I set off for Padum along the banks of the Zanskar river. The sun was low and being tired I dragged my feet, pausing to look at the ruins of the dismantled Dogra fortress, then pushing on to fields that stretched south of Padum. Gazing at the swirling river I was lost in thought when I saw coming towards me the unmistakable silhouettes of two Europeans. For a moment I looked at them as one might spy a foe. I had never been keen on meeting fellow Europeans in lonely places, because their presence inevitably forces me out of the other self I become on long journeys. Who could they be? When we reached eye-level, the shorter of the two men came forward, his hand extended in a gesture that I might have thought a little out of place in Zanskar had he not startled me by saying in a matter-of-fact voice, 'Peissel, I presume.'

I could hardly have answered 'Livingstone,' and so made the naïve statement, 'How did you guess?'

'Everyone in Padum knows who you are, because the Tasildar (local magistrate) is reading your book on Mustang. We are staying with him. You should pay him, and us, a visit.'

The two young men were German physicists from Cologne University, and we agreed to meet that night at the house of the King of Padum where they were staying as guests of the Jammu magistrate.

When I returned to my quarters I found that Nordrup had prepared some hot water, so I indulged in the luxury of a cup of cocoa. Then I went over to see the Tasildar who was staying in the house next door. It was a large, rundown building in which the King of Zanskar had rented him a couple of rooms. I knocked on a low door and, hearing no answer, poked my head into the room. A servant gestured to me to come in and sit on cushions beside a man who looked about thirty years old. With his head on his chest he was busy praying, his lips mumbling as, rushing through his devotions, he turned to a small altar, lit an incense stick, muttered a formula and then rang a little bell.

Having finished his offerings to various Hindu divinities (for he was a Hindu from Jammu), the Tasildar turned to me and spoke in English. At first I had trouble in understanding him, for his accent was made worse by a cleft palate. Fumbling under a low table he pulled out a copy of my book about my journey to Mustang and flipping through its pages sought a photograph of myself to compare it with the original. When satisfied, he showed keen pleasure at meeting me and asked his assistant to prepare us some tea.

Then he explained that he was the first resident magistrate in Zanskar, a post he thought no one would envy as the winters were but one long misery of freezing weather, during which he never left the house or even the room in which we were in. For months on end the thermometer stayed below minus thirty degrees Centigrade and it was totally impossible to travel. He was serving a two-years' compulsory tour of duty and I could see that the strain of living in this foreign land had reached the point at which the Tasildar was counting the days till his departure. I could not blame him, for compulsory residence at 12,000 feet above sea-level in a land which had none of the amenities to which he was accustomed and whose people spoke a language he could not understand, was certainly not bliss.

I learned from him that 'officially' there were twenty-eight villages in Zanskar, with 'officially' eight thousand inhabitants, and that it was hoped that the motor road would soon cross the Pensi-la and open Zanskar to the 'benefits' of civilisation in the near future. When I asked him what benefits he had in mind, to my surprise the Tasildar admitted that he was dubious as to what might be gained from the existence of the road. I realised that this magistrate was a sensitive, clever man, possibly the first government official who questioned the value of the Indian programme for 'civilising' the Tibetan-speaking districts of Kashmir. In the past, the Indian Government's admitted policy was 'to wean away from Tibet' the people of these regions, whom the rather superior Hindu administrators of New Delhi regard as primitive barbarians. In India few indeed were the people who understood the sophistication of the Himalayan social organisation, or valued Tibetan culture.

Fortunately today matters are changing, for instance one of the ministers of the Jammu and Kashmir state is a Ladakhi, Sonam Norbu, a man of good education and great influence both in Srinagar and New Delhi! The Queen of Ladakh has also recently been elected a member of the Indian Parliament.

As regards the road, I feared that any sudden influx of goods would upset the sturdy economic stability of the Zanskari way of life. For instance, the road could lead to a scarcity of grain because the people would sell their surplus to get money to buy the knick-knacks and gadgets which would arrive by truck-loads from India.

The magistrate admitted that, at present, there was little the Zanskaris needed or wanted from the outside world, and that even his services as chief magistrate and administrator were rarely solicited as each village had its own traditional system of administering justice and settling disputes. As a result his main activities were concerned with Balti traders inside Zanskar and the problems of tourists. He reckoned that some eighteen foreigners had reached Padum in the past two years.

As well as the Tasildar and the Chief of Police, a forestry officer and a school supervisor lived in Padum, while recently two doctors had arrived there for the summer to set up a first-aid dispensary. These six men, and two Ladakhi road engineers, constituted the Indian presence in Zanskar, and its intention to change the lot of the inhabitants of the 'Land of White Copper'. But I wondered if they could improve on a system that had supported a healthy population on a land so arid, so high and so cold, particularly as those sent out to effect the change, except for the Tasildar and one schoolteacher, all left at the end of the short summer, unable to survive the winter conditions.

Except for the need for some modern medicines, I could find little enthusiasm among my friends for any of the plans for development. The road, although welcomed by Lobsang and Nordrup who, because of their wanderlust, appreciated rapid communication, was generally regarded by most of the inhabitants as the forerunner of an invasion of the country by Moslem squatters and traders. People who were profoundly disliked by the normally tolerant Buddhist Zanskaris because of the Moslems' fanatical religious attitudes.

I left the Tasildar having made an appointment for early the following morning, when he would give me permits for Lobsang and Nordrup that would allow them to accompany me across the Himalayas to the Kulu valley.

It was a slightly sleepy Tasildar whom I met again the next day over a breakfast of fried fish. I ate the fish with delight mingled with a feeling of guilt.

'There are plenty of fish in the rivers,' explained the magistrate, perhaps unaware that for Buddhists to kill a fish is a terrible sin, in fact, the worst form of taking life as fish cannot cry out in self-defence. The conversation then turned to shooting, and the Tasildar showed me with pride the horns of an ibex shot by a friend of his who had come to visit him.

Ibex, I knew, are very numerous in Zanskar and constitute the main food supply of the many wolves. They live in large herds on the highest slopes, rarely coming down to the valleys. In winter however, they can be seen quite close to the villages.

No one to my knowledge has ever made a detailed study of the wildlife of Zanskar, though it would certainly merit investigation; the great Himalayan hunters of the British Raj seem to have by-passed this country on their numerous hunting expeditions because of its remoteness. Nevertheless, they did observe that the high, nearly snowless Zanskar Range marked the westernmost penetration of ibex (*Capra ibex siberica*), the best specimens of which have horns up to 50 inches long. The rugged ridges of these horns are believed to indicate the age of the animal. One sees many ibex horns stacked up on village shrines to the pre-Buddhist land gods.

The ibex are the most famous as well as the most common of the wild animals of Zanskar. Above an altitude of 14,000 feet *Ovis ammon hodgsoni*, locally called *nyan*, are also found. They are 12 hands high and have long legs adapted for fast flight on the high Tibetan plateau (from where they enter Zanskar). Large specimens of *nyan* have been known to weigh 250 lbs. Their coats are generally light brown, but with white withers and pale heads and horns. Because of their keen eye-sight and exceptionally sensitive sense of smell, they are considered to be among the world's most difficult game to stalk.

Another member of the large goat family in Zanskar is the little known *burrhel*, or blue sheep, *Pseudois nayaur*. Like *Ovis ammon hodgsoni*, they are to be found only above the tree-line, living in rocky wilds where they are often prey to wolves, and they have been sighted as high as 19,000 feet – the limit at which man can survive without oxygen cylinders. These sheep are often about 9 hands high. They have black marks on their faces and chests, and black stripes which run along their backs and the middle of their flanks and down the front of each leg. *Burrhel* are said to change colour in winter, but few have been seen except through field-glasses. Their horns follow the line of their bodies, the ends curving gently backwards. These sheep are a prize trophy for hunters, and alas today in Ladakh are menaced by trigger-happy military personnel who wreak havoc not only among ibex and wild sheep, but also among snow leopards, bears, and even the beautiful Tibetan wild asses, the famed *kyang*, which are found in the Chang Thang (north-east) region of Ladakh and in Rupshu, east of Zangla.

One of the most formidable inhabitants of Zanskar is the Himalayan red bear, also called the snow bear and, by zoologists, *Ursus arctos isabellinus*. They are rarely seen below 10,000 feet and hibernate during the long winter months. Their position is often given away to huntsmen by the presence of crows; these birds hope to benefit from insects that the bears turn up in their search for berries.

Other mysterious inhabitants of the Zanskar Range are the snow leopard and the black Himalayan wolf. About them, as about the Tibetan wild ass, everything remains to be discovered, for they have so far eluded all study by Europeans, who know of them only through accidental encounter or hearsay.

When the discussion got around to the question of permits for my companions, the magistrate seemed reticent and suggested that it would be much simpler and safer if I returned the way I had come, that is by the Pensi-la. The journey I wanted to make was, he said, dangerous; a horse had been lost there only a few days ago. I pointed out that I was quite used to Himalayan travel. The magistrate then produced a second objection, that it might take a considerable time to reach Kulu, and since my permit to stay in India was running out it would surely be better for us to return via Srinagar. His insistence merely strengthened my determination; it was true that my permit was nearing its end but I had been told this could be renewed, so I wrote a letter to the Kashmir authorities asking that this be done. I wanted the letter to be posted but I learnt that there was not, as yet, any postal or even runner service between Zanskar and the outside world. Eventually I gave my letter to a Zanskari merchant I met at the bazaar, who was about to set out for Kargil.

Meanwhile the magistrate suddenly said, 'Come and see me this afternoon with your two companions.' This sounded hopeful so I began to pack my bags. Nordrup had warned me that it would take from eight to ten days to reach the southern face of the Himalayas and the first Indian road. Since I planned to visit the Lunak district on the way, I estimated we would be about two weeks on the trail. Wishing to travel as light as possible I decided to give away or sell some of the excess stores I had brought with me, and so went down to one of the little stalls in the town where a trader promptly agreed to buy some of my wares at a fair price. As I was selling him some rice an old man with a pointed, scraggly beard and a weather-beaten face listened, then asked if there was anything else I would sell him.

'I have some packets of tea,' I said, showing him the packets I had brought with me to sell.

'How much?' the man asked.

'Whatever price you think is right,' I replied, showing the tea.

'Six rupees,' answered the old man, taking my tea and paying me on the spot. As he walked away the shopkeeper whispered:

'That is the rGyalpo.'

Such was my first encounter with the King of Zanskar.

Having finished my packing I set out to visit the monastery which overlooked Padum, its whitewashed buildings emerging from a cluster of poplar and willow trees. This was one of Zanskar's four Red Hat Bhutanese Drukpa Kargyupa monasteries. On my steep climb I had a bird's eye view of Padum with its one hundred and twenty houses nestled amongst the boulders of the hill on which it was built. Eventually I reached the first outhouse of the monastery shaded by what looked like a forest of trees. Shade was real luxury, both to the eye and the heart in this barren land with its burning midday sun. Little bubbling irrigation canals added to the charm of the place. Was it due to the weeks I had spent contemplating a desert landscape, or to the rustle of the leaves – a sound I had forgotten – or to a craving for the colour green? I could not tell; but the willow garden clinging to the mountainside which surrounded the small chapels of the monastery, appeared to me to be paradise.

I was excited by the prospect of striking out across the Great Himalayan Range, linking in one march the high central Asian tundra with the damp Indian plains. I was also intrigued by the accounts I had heard of Lunak province, with its rock-top monastery of Bardhan and its cliff-side monastery of Phugtal.

Even the Zanskaris seldom went there. Lunak was a province apart. 'The valley is very narrow, there are places with little sun,' said Nordrup.

'The track is dangerous. We could lose an animal, and if it is too bad we will have to turn back or abandon our horses there,' Lobsang had echoed. Others protested, 'You are a fool to try the route. Why not go back to Rangdum,' and 'There will be too much snow. All the rain we have had, will have fallen as snow on the pass.'

For the last time that afternoon the magistrate had tried to discourage me, but I did not change my mind and he issued two permits for Lobsang and Nordrup which would allow them to enter the province of Himachal Pradesh with me. All I wanted before I left Zanskar was to see the King of Padum, but he was away.

The following morning was filled with excitement; ahead lay a ten-day journey over some hundred and fifty miles of the most rugged mountains in the world. Lobsang had arrived late the night before with six horses and it was agreed that I would choose those that I preferred. I did this and made certain that we all had ample provisions. I had alterations made to some of the harnessing of the ponies and provided myself with better stirrups than the pieces of dangling string which had been prepared for me.

When all was ready I went to pay a last call on the Tasildar, and there to my delight I ran into the King of Padum. I had seen him as a sort of rival king to my friend the rGyalpo of Zangla and had imagined that he would be charmless. But we began to talk and I changed my mind. The old man, who had his grandson with him, explained how it was that he was in the first place King of Zanskar. His great-grandfather, Tsetang Namgyal, a relation of the King of Ladakh and of the royal lineage of Henesku, had been sent to Zanskar to take possession of the title and the property of the King of Zanskar who had died (some say poisoned) a prisoner of Gulab Singh in Jammu. As a relative of the Ladakhi branch of the family that had ruled Zanskar from 1644 to the time of the Dogra invasion, the King of Padum was in a way the legitimate holder of the throne of Zanskar. As in Ladakh and in Zangla the rGyalpos of Zanskar had retained much prestige, and a portion of their past wealth, although not officially recognised as rulers by the British and later, the Indian Government, as was the King of Zangla.

Although less erudite than the King of Zangla, and for some reason (possibly because of his Ladakhi origin) less liked, the King of Padum was nevertheless a most charming, unassuming and sophisticated man. It was amusing that the Indian administrator should be a paying lodger in his palace, and it was evident that of the two men the more sophisticated was not the conqueror from Jammu.

12

The Vale of the Demons

It was late in the morning, ten o'clock, when at last I bade farewell to the King of Padum and the Tasildar. Hurriedly we detoured the town, setting off up a narrow path dominating the river. Our route for most of the day followed the sheer mountainside that fell to the Zanskar river. Riding was quite dangerous, for the ponies had great difficulty in keeping balance.

For three hours we walked without pause. On the far bank we saw a magnificent village, the houses of which formed a fairy-tale palace standing above a few green barley fields fringed with willow trees. This was Chila, a village that could only be reached by crossing the bridge at Padum. I was tired and hungry when at a bend in the trail the improbable silhouette of Bardhan was suddenly revealed. Nature had thrust a cylindrical cliff, three hundred feet high with sheer, unscalable sides, into the Zanskar river. The feet of the tall pillar bathed in the river's foam, while its western flank touched the side of a mountain that rose to a snow-covered peak. On the top of this amazing rock rose a large monastery, surrounded by a circular wall that looked as if it were a continuation of the sides of the cliff. The scene was one of impregnable gloom.

Lobsang and Nordrup decided to halt a hundred yards short of the monastery by a little spring that gave birth to a small pasture where we thought the horses might get something to eat. While Lobsang and Nordrup started to boil water for their tea I set out to visit the monastery. It took me a little time to find the entrance; a goat track, that linked the shoulder of the mountain to a footpath hewn into the rock, clambered up in a spiral to a gate that led into the monastery. This gate was so placed as to be right above the sheer drop into the river so that any unwanted guest could be conveniently pushed over to a watery death.

When a huge mastiff rushed towards me at the gateway, I nearly made a fateful step backwards. Fortunately a handsome young monk, perhaps twelve years old, appeared in time to grab the brute. I was then led under buildings into a closed courtyard lined with high structures. The yard was sunny and protected from the bitter wind that blew along the river, and appeared very cosy by contrast to the austere exterior appearance of the fort.

A senior monk greeted me, and we became great friends when I discovered he had been to Bhutan. We exchanged reminiscences about the fortresses and monasteries we knew in the land of the dragon, to whose church this monastery was affiliated.

Before being shown into the main assembly hall I was taken to see a magnificent copper-cased prayer wheel at least ten feet tall, its gigantic cylinder decorated with exquisite reliefs in dark and light copper. I had never seen such a large copper-cased prayer wheel before as most are made of wood. To turn the cylinder, which must have contained at least half a ton of paper inscribed with prayers, there were little handles which an old monk grabbed energetically, causing the wheel to revolve slowly and strike a small bell at each turn.

To us, prayer wheels and prayer flags may seem a rather naïve form of devotion. In fact those who use them do not believe that the prayers are actually recited by this method but that the physical action of spinning a prayer wheel, or walking around a prayer wall, or planting a prayer flag, are in themselves meritorious activities. The merit gained by such actions being used to offset wicked deeds, for bad deeds and likewise evil thoughts are believed to be compensated for only by good deeds and thoughts. All this is to cancel out evil thoughts and actions one may have performed not only in this life but also in past lives.

That even the wind may be harnessed to glorify Buddha is after all natural, for do we not raise flags and standards to the glory of our nation and of our kings, and of our God? In the Himalayas nearly every action performed by monks and of the lay folk is linked to religion. They are constant reminders that we are to be reincarnated only according to our merits. This piety has been effective in making the Himalayans one of the most 'civilised' races in the world. Rare are those who do not practise compassion, kindness and self-control.

The interior of the main assembly hall at Bardhan was strangely similar to a Bhutanese chapel. Two elephant tusks flanked an altar whose central image was that of the holy Abbot Thubchen, founding father of the sect. He sat cross-legged with a flowing beard and a fan-like crested hat. On the wall to the right of the altar were four fine mandalas painted in rich hues of dark red, deep blue and green, ornamented with gilded figures. The Abbot told how in 1947 Pakistani troops had stolen all the treasured jewel-studded and gilt divinities that had once adorned the altar. Because of its strategic location, the monastery had on several earlier occasions been besieged and sacked by impious soldiers.

Next to the main chapel I was shown to the *gungkhang*, the chapel of evil spirits. This is the antechamber of black magic and sorcery which is much practised by the Red Hat sects. Here were preserved demon-faced masks, many with the famous third eye; here too bows, arrows, ancient muskets and swords were stored. These *gungkhangs* are always sinister places with hideous masks grinning at frescos depicting death and pain. There were few arms at Bardhan, no doubt as a result of the pillage, but in Bhutan such chapels contain real arsenals for it must be remembered that in the not so distant past Lamaist monks were often called to battle, and it was evident that Bardhan, set on its impossible rock which commanded the river approach, had always had a military value.

Having visited the monks' cells which opened on to two galleries that closed one side of the interior yard, I made a small donation and left the monastery to join the others for lunch. On my way I observed the ruins of a fort that further defended the monastery from the mountain above it. I opened one of the few remaining tins of meat with almost religious fervour. These sixteen tins of meat which I had purchased in Frankfurt on my way out to India contained the only meat I had eaten since leaving Srinagar. Lobsang and Nordrup, who were horrified by my diet, asked me to share their lunch which was, they said, 'a very special dish', tsampa kneaded in tea and then shaped somewhat like a bowl in which they poured hot butter. It was good and filling and certainly very nourishing.

By two-thirty we had rounded up the ponies and loaded them. I had counted on riding a good deal of the way but soon realised that the track was too narrow and rock-strewn for safety. So far we had not seen any villages on our side of the river, passing a lone rope bridge and on the far bank the hamlet of Pipcha – we then walked far above the small village of Tiyne with its spotlessly whitewashed houses. For hours we continued to follow the river, occasionally descending into lateral gullies, down one of which ran a roaring stream that battered a rickety bridge which soon it would sweep away. The amount of water in these torrents, the product of melting snows, worried Nordrup considerably.

'*Yapo mindu*,' (No good), he explained. 'There is so much water further up we may not be able to ford some of the rivers.'

I tried to cheer myself with the knowledge that these streams hold less water in the morning. In fact some of them flow only in the afternoon since it takes so much time for the snow which feeds them to melt.

The track was forever rising and falling, up and down the steep shoulders of great mountains whose peaks we occasionally perceived directly above our heads. I was told that in winter Lunak is completely isolated from the rest of Zanskar by constant avalanches, indeed the trail is sometimes closed right up to the end of June. Frequently we crossed the tracks of avalanches that had loaded the trail with rubble. Occasionally we ourselves caused minor avalanches down scree slopes, over which the horses had to be led one at a time.

Towards late afternoon, to my surprise, the track led on to a steep slab of frozen snow, it was obviously the remains of some avalanche that had not yet melted. On the ice one of the packhorses lost its balance and began skidding dangerously down the slope, but just stopped short of a four-foot drop down to some rocks. Grabbing the pony's tail Nordrup held on for all his worth until the beast stood up, a little shaken. Lobsang then jumped down from the slope to see whether the pony could jump off the ice without risking breaking a leg in a pothole between the rocks. The first pony jumped off the snowdrift successfully, but the second fell, and although he did not hurt himself, broke the straps which held his load. The third and fourth ponies jumped down without incident. The track now went down to the water's edge and there followed a sandy shore lapped by eddies of swirling water.

The summits of the mountain were a gleaming gold as we began again to rise above the river that soon became only a silver line running down a deep and narrow canyon. A steep, zigzagging track led us to an unexpected pass marked by three beautiful, whitewashed chortens. On the other side of these monuments, backed against a hill, stood the dozen white buildings of a monastery called Mune. The view from the chortens, looking south, revealed tormented, barren, eroded mountains dominated by great peaks staggered one behind the next as if extending to infinity. They gave a frightening dimension to our expedition for we would, I knew, have to cross all these ranges.

At sunset a strong wind began howling up the canyon and rushing through the pass. To spare the horses Lobsang and Nordrup decided to camp on the pass itself in the sparse shelter that the chortens offered against the blasting wind. Secretly I wished to spend the night in the monastery but Lobsang pointed out that it was getting dark, so as there was little time to argue I erected my tent in the lee of one of the chortens; it chatted in the stiff wind. Outside I could hear laughing and joking as Lobsang and Nordrup ordered a small crowd of monks around, asking some to fetch water, others to bring us a little wood and dried yak dung. I sent a monk to the monastery to get some arak in return for the pills I was obliged to hand out for various ailments: one monk had terrible toothache, another stomach pains and headaches. My distribution of pills soon drew a large crowd. From the monastery came the muffled thud of drums and the tinkle of bells.

It had been a long day and Padum already seemed a distant memory. In the dark I played around with a saucepan of sticky rice, but was too tired to be hungry and a little sad that the arak was foul. How much I regretted the culinary talent of Calay, the Nepalese cook who had made so many of my Himalayan travels into gastronomical tours. This journey was a little on the austere side when it came to food.

At the crack of dawn the first rays of sun struck the white chortens whilst the dark valleys remained in gloomy shade. It was cold, yet so dry that I had forgotten what mist, haze, or dew were like. While Lobsang searched for the horses which had strayed on a nearby mountain, I watched the sun move slowly, like a gigantic spotlight across the incredible scenery.

When a beam struck the first white buildings of the monastery the valley echoed to the wail of a conch shell calling the monks to assembly. For a long time, rising and falling like a foghorn, the sound trailed into infinity, filling everything with a slight shudder of strangeness. Once again I felt the exhilaration of solitude among a land of demons and gods.

Before raising camp I set out to examine the monastery which, in the design of its twin assembly halls set within a greater building, presented signs of great antiquity. Two monks were busy painting some of the windows and I feared that they might be obliterating the badly worn, but old, frescos of the halls. Mune monastery belongs to the Gelugpa order, an old monk explained to me, as he led me to the dark kitchens from which I only just escaped before having to drink salty tea.

From Mune, the trail led us up a rocky slope which dominated a small village sprawled upon a ledge above the river at the foot of the monastery. The barley fields of this village were irrigated from several reservoirs in which, at night, water was accumulated. When the reservoirs were full they could be drained to irrigate the fields. This technique is used when the available water is insufficient to allow it to run continuously through the fields.

Having travelled a few miles we came to a low pass and saw stretching before us an unexpectedly large plain. A stream reached it from the great peaks to our right, and crossing it joined the Zanskar river. At one end of this plain stood the village of Raru, its houses backing against a rocky outcrop. We did not go to the village but passed the ruins of what had been a fort at the far end of the fields. Lobsang pointed to a small trail which set off to the south-west, eventually leading to a pass 18,752 feet high. This was the amazingly lofty Poat-la, which leads over into the valley of Paldar.

The ruins of yet another fort reminded us that the province of Lunak, due to its isolation, had always been relatively autonomous. Several Lumbo were still living in Lunak. Once they ran local affairs nearly independently of the King of Padum. One such noble family was that of the Lords of Teta, who had been the owners of the famous 'Chronicles of Zanskar', the only historic document specifically relating to Zanskar (except for the brief genealogy of the Kings of Zangla) that the scholar Francke had been able to collect.

It was this document which stated that Zanskar was a land 'where the fairies congregate'. This 'Chronicle', itself incomplete, was said to be a copy of an original manuscript which belonged to the monastery of Phugtal. It was to search for this that I intended to visit the Phugtal monastery, even though it lay off our track. I could not hope to see the copy (if it still existed) at Teta, for the Lord of Teta was away, supervising the building of the road over the Pensi-la.

On leaving the plain of Raru we had a treacherous climb up the steep face of a cliff that overhung a narrow canyon, through which the Zanskar river flowed. Our trail was now of the kind dear to illustrators, one on which at every sharp bend the ponies were obliged to stick their necks far out into the void. We had to hold on to their tails to stop them from losing their balance, a very tedious operation which did not seem as funny to us as it must have looked.

All morning the track was both tortuous and dangerous, and I began to doubt the wisdom of my decision to leave by this route. Riding was now out of the question and Nordrup repeatedly suggested that we had better abandon the horses and most of our equipment and proceed alone. To cheer him up I pretended that compared to other trails I had travelled, notably in Bhutan, this track was just a joke. My declarations did not seem to convince him as we now began crossing a series of nearly vertical screes, down which our every step triggered a small avalanche. The horses were led across one at a time, Lobsang holding the bridle and Nordrup the tail, as they rushed across the slope in a cloud of dust and a scurry of falling rock. To stop or to stumble would have resulted in sliding down the near-vertical slope into the pounding river below, where an instant death would have awaited the victim.

I was told it was at this place that a few weeks ago a horse had been lost, and I well believed it. For miles the track hung precariously to the slope. We were now able to admire on the other side of the river the village of Ichar, with its houses clustered on a cliff looking like a great fortress. This formidable bastion was in fact a human hive backed against a great peak hanging above the roaring river. I had been told that there was an ancient chorten built in the eleventh century by Rinchen Zangpo, who built the chorten of Karsha. Eventually we reached a swing bridge that crossed the turbulent river, but due to weariness and lack of time I did not cross it and contented myself with looking at the village from afar.

At midday we halted on a steep slope, sitting on the track to eat, while the poor horses clung like flies to the slope where they could eat some flowers and grass that grew around a little spring. I identified some mulberry bushes. Who had planted them I wondered, for although they are known to grow wild in certain areas of the Central Asian highlands, these I felt sure had been deliberately planted. Alongside the mulberry bushes were several shrubs with little edible orange-red berries the size of red currants which had a bitter-sweet taste. I have not been able to discover the Western name of this berry, which also abounds in Bhutan. Their fruit is delightful to eat but must not be confused with a similar bush with nearly identical berries, for these are foul tasting and possibly poisonous. I can vouch for this as in my greed I often munched the wrong ones. The bushes with the sour berries are those whose branches are used for making the ropes of the suspension bridges. At first I had doubted if it were possible to make rope of such short and brittle twigs but Nordrup explained that before being plaited they had to be soaked in water.

As we sat eating on the trail we were disturbed by a small caravan of donkeys pushed along by a young boy and a handsome old man. He stopped to have a chat while looking at me with unmasked curiosity. Immediately we enquired if he had come over the Shingo-la pass but learnt that he lived in a village just beneath the pass. No one, he explained, had come over the pass recently, and then suggested that the best route for us was to take the Philtse pass into the Rupshu district and from there cross over the Baralacha pass to the district of Lahoul. Nordrup seemed to agree with him but I objected, explaining that we were not allowed to take the Baralacha pass as this was considered within the strategic army zone.

'We will see,' I had to conclude, for I felt both Lobsang and Nordrup were quite nervous about crossing the Shingo-la, and I feared that they might simply decide to turn back, leaving me stranded.

Later I realised that this was entirely to misjudge the characters of my friends, for in the event no one could have been more energetic, rugged, or daring than they; from dawn to dusk they joked and laughed while running after the horses, shouting to them, grabbing their bridles, heaving them up high steps or holding them back as we descended steep stretches.

Talking and living with Lobsang and Nordrup I began to appreciate that an extremely active life, which called for considerable exertion, is not only stimulating physically but also mentally. The more Lobsang and Nordrup perspired and toiled up the mountains, the wittier they became. Never once did I hear them complain of a steep incline or about having to chase after a pony that had taken a wrong turn and strayed off the track. Moreover, they were always keen to rush around and made me feel ashamed at being so feeble and dim-witted as I panted and groaned step after step, hour after hour, wishing the climb would soon end. Although I was in pretty good physical shape and quite acclimatised, I still felt the effects of the altitude, and to walk a mile at 12,000 feet seemed to me like walking two. Since we had left Padum our route had risen continuously, occasionally reaching 14,000 feet when we clambered up the steep sides of the canyon in which the river was now locked.

Since leaving Raru at dawn, we had not passed through a single village although we had seen three nestling on ledges on the opposite bank. Towards evening we entered a region of white rocks and eroded cliffs shaped like towers and dungeons, our little caravan advancing between them like ants in a gigantic sandpit. After several steep climbs we reached a little tableland, on it were two houses and a few barley fields, which cut a neat green pattern out of the barren land. On the other side of the river, which was accessible by a bridge which we could not as yet see, there rose a large solitary manor house surrounded by rich, terraced barley fields that glittered in the setting sun.

Far up the valley we could see the fields of the village of Surle looking like a green carpet on the white rocks. Just short of the village Nordrup and Lobsang found a small patch of grass on which the horses could graze and so decided we should camp here for the night. One of the drawbacks about travelling with horses in the Himalayas is that stopping in villages is nearly impossible in summer because the barley fields have no protective walls, and therefore horses can not be set free.

While Nordrup started pulling up scraggy bushes in an unsuccessful attempt to make a fire, I pitched my tent in a small hollow that offered some protection from the wind. In the end it was my kerosene stove that cooked the supper. No sooner had I downed the last gulp than I withdrew; by my watch it was eight-thirty, a good time to go to bed.

That night in my dreams I lumbered up mountain trails repeating the exertions of the day, my mind fully absorbed by the world in which I was living, conjuring visions of that other world in which I had once speeded along in the comfort of cars. My dreams would inevitably end up focusing on what was for me an obsessive preoccupation; food. I would see, in my dreams, the most exquisite of dishes loaded upon a buffet tantalisingly near me. I can still picture them today: the entire hams with parsley, roasts with glistening crackling, huge silver dishes of everything that would inevitably vanish, leaving me hungry to sip at dawn watered-down chocolate, as I was reaching the bottom of my last tin. This chocolate was followed by a breakfast of tsampa or maybe lentils or rice, with curry powder and water as sauce, to which I added a little rancid ghee. According to the strict plan I would allow myself one of the remaining four tins of meat every other day at one of my meals. I also ate a little peanut butter on home-made bread (I baked two loaves on the journey); this bread would keep for days, especially as neither Lobsang nor Nordrup could muster the courage to eat any of it. I was so proud of my bread as it looked like real circular country loaves, even if it did taste a little mouldy since something had gone wrong with the flour. I would bake the bread without an oven (a trick I had learnt from Calay) wherever there was an abundance of fuel, which was rare indeed. In lieu of an oven I would drop four small pebbles into a large saucepan, put a smaller pan (with the dough) inside it, and place the lot on a fire, covering the lid with burning embers.

An hour before dawn I was awoken by Nordrup. I planned to make for the monastery of Phugtal, which lay some seven to ten miles off our route. It stood above the main branch of the Zanskar river which split into two a few miles from where we had camped, the right branch leading to the villages of upper Lunak and eventually to the Shingo-la.

Lobsang would continue up the right-hand branch with the horses and wait for Nordrup and me at a hamlet called Ial where the grazing was known to be good.

A sense of mystery prevailed over our departure; in silence we advanced to the rhythm of our heavy breathing and the occasional roll of a stone. Pale pre-dawn light was casting its dim hue around us when we reached the village of Surle, whose inhabitants were just getting up. Nordrup and I went towards the river, heading for what I knew would inevitably be some fearsome swing bridge. I was cold and miserable and the thought of crossing a perilous suspension bridge was like having to pass an exam or go to the dentist; it weighed down on my stomach and stopped me from being able to enjoy the thought of being underway to visit what sounded like one of the most staggering of Zanskar's monasteries. I could not forget the genuine terror that had accompanied my crossing of the Padum bridge, not to mention the one at Zangla. Although not by nature a person to be easily frightened, I was truly in anguish.

The sun was only beginning to touch the summits of the peaks above us when we reached the edge of the river and clambered up to a rickety-looking bridge.

I was now really scared and asked Nordrup whether he too was frightened.

'No, one quickly gets used to them,' he said with a smile, adding, 'Two men drowned when the old bridge to Zangla collapsed some fifteen years ago but there are very few accidents.

'Follow close behind me,' he suggested. 'Like that the bridge will swing less.'

As I looked down in the cold light of dawn, I saw the swirling water rushing by, creating the illusion that the bridge was moving. Cautiously I looked at Nordrup's shoes, then at my own, trying not to notice the river that seemed to beckon me. A slight vibration along the ropes made me shudder. I found myself counting each step, and then it was all over and I had reached the other side. At least, I thought, this was the last swing bridge I would be crossing, for after visiting the monastery we planned to carry on up the far bank of the river until we reached the first 'horse bridge', a solid wooden structure. In fact I had not yet seen the last of Zanskar's little engineering horrors but as innocence is bliss I sat joking with Nordrup unaware of what lay ahead.

On getting up we resolutely attacked a steep climb that led to the village of Char, a cluster of ten run-down houses set amongst barley fields overlooking the river. Panting and shivering, for we were still in the cold morning shade, we reached the first houses and gladly accepted the invitation of a young boy to enter his home and have tea.

Bending low, we followed him through a door and climbed up some dark steps to an upper room where carpets were spread out on the floor, and in which various terracotta divinities were stacked. His father, the boy told us, was about to build a chapel in the village in which these would be placed. The images were very ancient and I wondered from where they had come.

While waiting for the tea I strolled out of the room and poked my head round a door, surprising an old woman who sat busy using a long stick to churn something brewing in a huge copper cauldron set upon a roaring fire. In fact she was making chang for some celebration but seemed to be the perfect image of a witch preparing a magic potion as she glared at me, her toothless grin making her look most alarming in the light of the red fire. The boy soon came back with some excellent salted tea and handfuls of fresh peas. We sat in silence podding them as fast as we could and eating them between sips of tea, a welcome if unusual breakfast.

Having far to go and much to do if we wished to join up again with Lobsang that night, we left the house, thanking the boy for his kind hospitality. In my hurry I must have been careless, for the next thing I remember was lying on my back clutching my head. Already I had cracked my skull about ten times on low beams, but this time the beam had been of stone and had knocked me out. Staggering up in pain I stumbled out of the house.

Nordrup's sympathy alas, could do little to alleviate my pain, and I felt very sorry for myself as I staggered on up a steep climb clutching my head while panting from the lack of oxygen. How on earth had I come to be here, to eat raw peas for breakfast and then charge off with a gash in my head to a monastery called Phugtal, located in the black demon district of the 'Land of White Copper'? All this in search of a document that I would probably never find and which, if miraculously I did locate it, would not interest anyone – not even Himalayan scholars, all too preoccupied with their own pet projects to care about what had once happened in a land most people do not even know exists.

Fortunately the pain slowly disappeared and the sun at last began to warm our bodies, announcing a day of such magnificence that nothing really seemed to matter. As we rose, the river Zanskar unfolded beneath us – milky-blue, running into the grey waters of its main affluent, both seemed like little coloured ribbons set out in a lunar landscape that rose to great peaks which, high in the sky, proclaimed the splendour of nature. Like eagles on a ledge, we looked upon such beauty in silence. Nordrup was as affected as I by the majesty of nature and could only repeat '*pe kyipo re*', meaning really happy, or rather really delightful, as happiness, delight and beauty are often considered synonymous in a world that understands that aesthetics are the most important factor in the shaping of man's happiness.

Far beneath us we had a bird's eye view of two little homesteads surrounded by barley fields. We would pass through these on our return along the far embankment of the Zanskar river.

Carrying on, we found ourselves high up the vertical sides of a steep canyon falling to the river which we could no longer see. The track clung to this cliff face, cut into a rock whose bright and rusty-red colours betrayed the presence of iron. For two more hours we plodded on, edging our way across several avalanche paths and disturbing rocks that plunged a thousand feet down the canyon. I prayed that I would not slip, recalling how twice I had tripped and nearly plunged over a cliff. My first such fall was in Bhutan where I fell flat on the edge of a ledge, with one arm and one leg above the void. Then again in Nepal I once found myself flat on my face in a similar position, inches from a fatal fall. I prayed this should not occur again. I always marvelled that one did not trip more often in the course of the thousands of hours spent walking, millions of precarious footsteps each placed within inches of disaster. Man must surely have a sixth sense and Providence may not be a vain word, for very few people in fact fall over cliffs.

The sun was now hot – it was nearing nine o'clock – so it was with great relief that we at last found a stream, the first we had seen since leaving Char. I had a good drink and as Nordrup had brought along some soap, we washed, plunging our heads into the freezing water. I washed my hair which in the high-altitude sun dried in a few minutes. I then decided to give my socks a quick wash as they had reached a state I would rather not describe. This proved a difficult and smelly job and, as the socks would not dry, I had to carry on with wet socks in my hand and bare feet in my shoes.

It was in this guise that I reached Phugtal. The monastery was announced by two dozen chortens that led to the side of a barren, eroded cliff, the colour of light sand, rising some nine hundred feet above the Zanskar river. There, in mid-cliff hung the most incredible monastery I had ever seen, a cataract of little white buildings glued, as it were, to the surface of the cliff, emerging from an immense, dark cave in which were several large, red buildings. It was this gigantic cavern which gave the monastery its name, Phugtal – *phug* meaning cave; it was situated several hundred feet up the cliff overhanging the river, and to reach it one had to scramble up ladders and steep steps that linked the tiny white cells of the monastery.

As we approached this hornet's nest I heard the metallic din of sacred music. It was our good luck that we arrived at Phugtal in the middle of the *Yarne*, that is the time in which all the monks dependent on the monastery are requested to congregate there to read the whole hundred and eight volumes of the *Kanjur*.

Seated on the roofs of the assembly halls, overlooking the precipice, the community had seen us approach. We were greeted at the entrance by a young monk who showed us which ladders to use to make our way up to a terrace set in front of two assembly halls and chapels that were built inside the cave. Here we found some thirty monks, all holding pages of the scriptures which they had been reading when we interrupted them. They stared at me in amazement and I felt embarrassed with my bare legs and rather dirty clothes.

Nordrup explained that I was a scholar who had travelled all over the Himalayas, and sheepishly I acknowledged this compliment and said how beautiful Phugtal monastery was, while trying to hide my wet socks which refused to fit into any of my pockets.

According to those present I was the fifth European to visit the monastery in 'monks' memory', but as I was to discover monks' memories do not go back very far.

13

The Cave of Phugtal

Escorted by a dozen red-robed clerics we were taken into the heart of the cave, passing under its dark dome to a little staircase that descended into a spring. This was a magic spring and I certainly found the holy water a blessing as my mouth was parched; for although it was only ten-thirty we had been on the road for five hours.

Raising my head, I could barely see the roof of the cave sixty feet above us. It formed a dome over this vast room, on one side of which a great arch opened on to the precipice, at the foot of which flowed the blue-white waters of the Zanskar river. The proportions of this immense, natural cave were so perfect that it seemed to be man-made. High in its semi-obscurity, I could hear the screech of bats mingling oddly with the cooing of doves. In front of the opening hovered a pair of birds with jet-black feathers, whose antics gave an extra dimension to the void. In the far end of the cave stood several small shed-like buildings that had perhaps been monks' cells but were now transformed into store-rooms. The central spring was surrounded by piles of brushwood, while the front of the cave was occupied by a large assembly hall, and a two-storeyed chapel. The assembly hall opened on to a terrace overlooking the void. This terrace, without a railing, was the central point of the monastery. Between the two buildings was an ancient chorten so over-painted by successive coats of whitewash that it had become bloated and deformed like a stalagmite and indeed perhaps this is what it had once been. Such 'god-made' chortens are frequent, but this one must have at one time been built up for it now stood fifteen feet high.

The monastery looked straight out of the cave and cliff to the other bank of the Zanskar river, where there was a small village dominated by distant peaks.

A strange atmosphere pervaded the place, perhaps it arose from the smell of damp, the cooing of the pigeons and the shriek of bats. The monks, who seemed like actors in a feudal play, started chanting once more, as they sat cross-legged on the edge of the precipice.

I did not know for certain how to begin my quest for the ancient documents I had come to seek. I asked to meet the Abbot but learned that he was absent. I was then introduced to his substitute, a rather gruff old man. Nordrup advised me not to mention right away the matter of the manuscripts but suggested first things first, and that we try and get something to eat. I knew his appetite to be both fantastic and impervious, and so I escorted him to the kitchens.

These kitchens were level with the main terrace, cut out in a niche in the cliff. Bending very low (my head still hurt) I entered what seemed to be the smoky den of a magician, a circular vaulted cave with a large opening in its roof through which great billows of smoke escaped, their plumes glittering in the sunbeams that streamed into the room. On one side stood a stone furnace three feet high and some twenty feet in length. On it stood all manner of pots and cauldrons, the largest would have been big enough to boil two men in it, while the smallest were brass teapots.

A tall, red figure emerged from the smoke and bade us sit down in a corner, then he placed a low, bench-like table before us. We now had a smoke-free, ground-level view of the kitchens and I was able to see the outline of the half-dozen monks all busy at various tasks. In one corner a young man sat bending over a large brass plate with mounds of butter in it. He was, I understood, taking out the yak hairs! By the fire another monk was busy throwing great handfuls of brushwood into the furnace, where they exploded into flame and gave off a brilliant red light. The monk who had asked us to sit down was the head of the kitchen, the holder of one of the key jobs in the monastery. Seated by our side, he asked me where I came from and made light-hearted jokes about my person and strange attire. He reminded me a little of the head of the kitchens at the great monastery of Hemis, in Ladakh, with whom I had spent two rainy days cooped up before another gigantic stove around which two dozen scullions danced, helped along by blows from a copper ladle upon their shaven heads. Being the guts of the monastery, the kitchen is always a place of no nonsense and some bad language.

On a lesser scale at Phugtal great activity accompanied the brewing of tea. First a cauldron of tea-leaves and water was boiled, and the result was ladled out into pots. Butter was then thrown into a long cylinder with a piston inside it to churn the butter with the tea, to which salt was added. A monk rammed the wooden piston rod up and down, thereby mixing all the ingredients, after which the long cylinder was raised and the tea poured into another huge cauldron on the fire – and kept there until one by one the monks came in with their teapots to be replenished. Tibetans and Zanskaris alike can drink up to fifty cups of buttered tea a day, and as there were forty-five monks in attendance at Phugtal one can imagine how much they drank. Of course this tea serves not just as a drink, but also to moisten tsampa flour.

We were offered tsampa to add to our tea, to make what is considered an ordinary meal. In fact, butter, salt and whole-grain barley with warm water and a little tannin from the tea constitutes a complete diet. Maybe not the best tasting of menus but certainly one that gives energy. All those present had been brought up on this diet, and they were a tough bunch as one could see by their muscular arms, visible because of the monks' sleeveless gowns. These monks all came from various villages in Lunak.

Having eaten, we left the smoky inferno and walked to the edge of the terrace where my lunch nearly fell into the river below, for I felt very sick indeed as I looked at the terrible drop and wondered how many monks had fallen to their death from this spot.

I tried now to broach the reason for my visit with some of the more intellectual-looking monks, questioning them as to what they knew about the existence in the monastery of old manuscripts, and or tax records (*bo yig* in Tibetan). My queries were met by blank expressions that seemed to me inspired more by suspicion than ignorance.

Evidently my straightforward approach raised the worst fears. I had forgotten that to many of the monks I was the first foreigner they had seen or talked to – and I was asking to see their old books, the most sacred and secret treasures of the monastery! Here, books in themselves, apart from their contents, are always considered sacred, and because of this they must be placed higher than statues in the chapels, and before being read they have to be placed respectfully on the reader's forehead; this alone carries a blessing. Matters concerning history are more often than not considered 'top secret' – or at least not to be revealed to just anybody.

Now here I was, a funny pagan with hairy legs and no socks, who had nothing with which to impress these virtuous scholars. Moreover, I looked like a clown, with 'yellow' eyes (as light eyes are called in the Himalayas) and a red nose, something unknown in Zanskar. Certainly one hundred and ninety miles of dusty trails had done little to make me the image of the kind of person to whom a monk at Phugtal would eagerly hand over the treasures of his library. Besides this, the Abbot was away and his second-in-command was not very literate, so of course he was suspicious of Hindu Indians and Kashmiri Moslems, to say nothing of me.

'We have no books of that sort,' came his reply.

Looking round at the monks' faces I realised that they would have liked me to drop the matter. Nordrup, who was as stubborn as I and perhaps a little cleverer, suggested that rather than argue we be allowed to pay our respects to the statues in the various chapels.

The monks were delighted for they were very proud of their sacred images and frescos which they adorned with what they considered most precious, and to each of which they attributed miraculous powers. We were ushered into the main assembly hall where, between reading verses of the *Kanjur*, two rows of monks were busy munching tsampa. Our entry caused a stir and some jokes while, rather embarrassed, I examined the frescos and the statues on the altar. Some of the paintings seemed relatively ancient, but what struck me most were the elaborate and definitely very old, carved figures: animals and flowers that formed a garland around a statue of a seated Buddha, which was set against the right wall of the assembly hall. This recalled the old Lumbo chapel at Karsha and the ancient chapels of Alchi. There I took a photograph and passed on to the two-storeyed chapel under the overhang of the cave. The first storey led to a dimly-lit room filled with a jumble of objects: statues, masks and books along with a model of a mythical palace described in the Lamaist Scriptures. There were also ancient drums with their curved batons. The veiled images represented fierce divinities riding horses, lions and donkeys, depicted in an aura of terracotta flames painted in bright blues, yellows and greens.

In the kitchen I had been told the story of the monastery's origin. Three Indian sages had discovered the cave and settled in it when along came the saintly Lama, Chansen Cherap Zampo who, on meeting the three holy men, suggested that a great monastery be built there. The three men answered that the cave was too small, so the Lama, performing a miracle, made it grow to its present gigantic size. According to this account the monastery was originally of the Sakyapa (Red Hat) sect. But contradicting this account is the statement that Rinchen Zangpo founded Phugtal.

This Lama was responsible for the revival of the Buddhist religion in Guge and its propagation in western Tibet in the eleventh century. That he might have founded Phugtal is probable for he is known to have founded a monastery in Rupshu, just the other side of the head waters of the Zanskar river. I formed the impression that already in antiquity the great cave was a sacred place but I was unable to find any ancient stone carvings to support my view. If there were no ancient stone carvings of pre-Lamaist days, there were remarkable and very old frescos in a lateral chapel situated outside the cave. These reminded me of the twelfth-century paintings of Alchi monastery in Ladakh, and might well prove to be amongst the oldest frescos of the Himalayan world. I examined them in detail and took photographs, but I was aware that to make any significant study of Phugtal, or indeed of any other major monastery, would require a visit of many weeks or months; much more time than I could dispose of in this preliminary survey of Zanskar.

In the chapel with the old frescos a monk took me aside and asked if I could translate what was written on a stone which he now showed me. It was a simple slab of dark local stone on which was carved:

Csoma de Körös lived here 1825–6
Pioneer of Tibetan Studies.

This stone was identical with the one on the photograph that the King of Zangla had shown me of Mr Erwin Baktey. Körös had in fact spent a winter partly at Phugtal and partly in the village of Teta. It was a winter he considered wasted, as the monk he had counted on for continuing his studies proved a disappointment. Thus I learned that I had had an august predecessor at Phugtal and that it could claim to be the first monastery to have welcomed the father of Tibetan studies.

My speaking Tibetan and my genuine interest in the divinities and shrines of the monastery had inspired some confidence in the local monks; so after some further encouragement from Nordrup, they suggested that maybe they did have some 'old' papers tucked away in a dark room located beneath the two-storeyed chapel. My heart beat as under the eerie dome of the cave I saw great sheets of manuscript-covered paper circulating amongst an eager crowd of monks. Most of these documents were slightly rat-eaten but were certainly of interest in tracing the monastery's history. The monks snatched them from each other, as eager to read them as I was. My request to see them had, it seemed, suddenly given these neglected documents a new importance. I asked Nordrup to examine them quickly. Several were titles to land and lists of donations, but the document I was looking for was not there, nor were there any lists or even mentions of royal names. For nearly an hour we examined the manuscripts, persuaded that there must be more hidden around, yet almost certain that our quest was doomed because of our lack of time. 'To find the document you want you must stay a week or more,' Nordrup said. Unfortunately I could not stay on because of what it meant in expenses (I was paying for the horses on a daily basis), but especially because my Indian visa was about to expire.

Convinced that the Phugtal monastery still contained many answers to the unsolved mysteries of Zanskari history, I contributed generously to its upkeep before taking leave of the monks. Climbing down ladders and steep steps we finally left through its small gate. Looking back, I gazed at the amazing cluster of its cells, they looked like swallows' nests set around the dark mouth of the cave in which now, as for centuries past, the deep voice of monks at prayer would be echoing. If there was ever a holy place set aside by nature for the elevation of men's souls it was surely here.

I rejoiced in this visit, yet my joy was quickly marred for we were soon obliged to cross the river by one more of those fearful swing bridges. Fortunately this one was not very long and, once over, I began to agree that Nordrup was right when he said it was all a matter of habit.

By nature a late riser, I always marvel at what one can do in a day if one gets up at five o'clock in the morning. In spite of the hours spent reaching the monastery and the four hours examining chapels and manuscripts, it was now only two o'clock. This gave us ample time to reach, or so I hoped, the grazing grounds where we were to meet Lobsang.

We were travelling close to the edge of the Zanskar river which ran at the bottom of what seemed a furnace of burning, barren rocks. Every mile or so we saw prayer walls with little inscriptions telling who had built them.

Towards four o'clock Nordrup and I felt hungry and at that moment we reached the first of two isolated homesteads. Nordrup was quick to note that one of the fields was sown with peas ready for eating. Sitting down he grabbed half a dozen plants, which we ate. Such an act, Nordrup explained, is customary and generally accepted. I had my doubts and felt guilty when a woman came towards us, evidently to see what was going on in her pea field. Quite unabashed, Nordrup walked over to greet her, and, giving her no time to complain, complimented her on her fine farm land. Amazed at his cheek I tried to change the subject by asking the woman if she would sell me some chang or arak. The woman replied that she would willingly sell us some arak, and asked us to come to her house. Following her we found two little, half-naked children and a tame goat playing in a small neat room with mattresses covered in carpets facing low tables.

Nordrup and I sampled the arak and then without blushing accepted some fresh peas. We now had a problem in that we had no bottle or container to carry the arak we planned to buy, and the woman could not spare one. My solution to this dilemma was for us to drink all the arak we had planned to buy. As a result it was in high spirits that we left the lone farm. A few miles away we passed the other building, an immense mansion that had no doubt been some sort of fortified outpost. It stood above the confluence of the Zanskar river and the lesser tributary we were to follow, which is known as the Kargya river. This we crossed by our first 'horse bridge', an elegant wooden affair with flagstones and a balustrade.

On the other side began a long and painful ascent up a track overlooking a sheer drop. This was livened by a meeting with a handsome man in his early thirties who came stumbling down towards us, completely drunk. At every step he reeled and leaned dangerously over the precipice, then as if by a miracle, stumbled back on to the trail. He stopped to have a chat with us, forgot what he wanted to say and then wishing us a good journey, reeled off to what I felt would be certain death.

'We should have stopped him; surely he will fall into the river and die,' I said to Nordrup.

'Yes, but what could we do? We could not carry him,' was his reply.

It was practically dark when, as we reached three large houses, mastiffs began to bark. Here we found Lobsang, in a little hamlet of herders, which stood upon a great slope covered with boulders. Clumps of mountain flowers and low brush grew over these boulders, giving the whole scene the semblance of a pasture.

The owner of 'our' house was a tall, handsome young man with a long, elegant face, whose beautiful wife had three small children. They ran around in fluffy, miniature sheepskin gowns, postponing bedtime for as long as they could till eventually they were all piled together on a rug set upon the earth floor before the little yak-dung fire in the living-room. In the same room Lobsang had laid out my sleeping bag in one corner. I ate a little rice in the semi-darkness and then fell asleep utterly exhausted.

I was up at dawn, had a wash (of sorts) in an irrigation canal beside a chorten, and then helped load the horses. I no longer cared when we would arrive, for each day brought its problems and its long hours of toil so that in the end our destination became a secondary matter. What was more real was the fear of the pass, the conscious, constant knowledge of danger ahead.

We had penetrated into the Kargya valley, a subdivision of the Lunak district, a region whose rulers had been the Lords of Teta, the owners of the Zanskar 'Chronicles'. This valley is about forty miles long and leads up to the heights of the Shingo-la.

In two hours we reached the first barley fields of Teta, a village of some forty houses set out in three clusters, while a large house standing apart surrounded by a few stunted willow trees was the residence of the Lumbo, the local chieftain.

Compared with the rest of Zanskari houses, these were small and low with walls mostly of stone. They seemed very primitive. After a brief stop to chat with some villagers we carried on, descending to the river and crossing to the left bank. The valley now broadened out. It was barren and dark as we had reached the altitude of 14,000 feet, the limit at which humans can live.

The village of Teta and the village of Trangze, where we stopped to have lunch, were among the highest villages I had so far visited. While Lobsang and Nordrup let the horses graze and attempted to make a fire with damp horse dung, I inspected the houses of Trangze which lay strewn about the valley floor at the foot of a whitewashed monastery.

The houses were very low because their rooms were partly underground. By burying themselves in the earth, the local people managed to stay warm at 14,000 feet during the terrible winters, in a land with no fuel!

After braving the noisy attacks of several large mastiffs, I found the monastery's doorkeeper, a little man wearing rags who hobbled up to the chapel which, standing at nearly 15,000 feet, must rate amongst the world's highest buildings. Before the altar was the biggest butter lamp I had ever seen; the size of a large wash-basin, a full four feet high. Made of beaten copper, this monstrous lamp had in fact caused the monastery to become famous throughout the region.

Clouds obscured the sky as we set off up the ominous valley and entered a bleak no man's land, the higher limits accessible to life, just beneath the silent glaciers. We had once again reached the altitude at which trees cannot grow, even if irrigated. In fact nothing can be grown at 14,000 feet except barley, for not even peas or wheat would mature. Amazingly, soaking in the ultraviolet rays, the barley here seemed to thrive, although it had often to be cut before ripening because of the early September snowstorms. It was now mid-August and it seemed as if already the brief, frigid summer had gone. Anyway here it froze every night of the year. For Nordrup and Lobsang the inhabitants of this part of Lunak were roughneck hillbillies, and there were jokes about their naïve simplicity compared to the 'city slickers' of Padum, or the enlightened inhabitants of the rich and warm central province. I could not help but smile when I thought of how all Zanskaris would rate in the West. How could we appreciate that here all the elements of a society as complex as our own were to be found? A world with its elite, its aristocracy, its centres of learning, its smart villages, and its outback, the Kargya valley – most possibly the site of the highest agricultural community in Asia.

The Guinness Book of Records states that the highest human settlement is a mining camp at 17,000 feet in the Andes, and says that there is a little Andean town at over 14,000 feet. If the Andes holds the world record, its position in regard to the Equator makes the climate on the high plateau much more hospitable than that of similar altitudes in the Himalayas.

As we advanced towards the next village called Ralta, Lobsang told me that copper had been found here, in the bed of the stream we forded at the entrance to the village.

The religious belief that to plunder soil is evil, along with the lack of a monetary economy, has always made the attitude of Tibetans towards mining, even for gold, quite incomprehensible to Europeans. There are many gold mines in western Tibet, and many gold-bearing rivers in Zanskar, yet the local population have never tried systematically to exploit this wealth. To work metal is considered sinful, and this task is undertaken by the *gara* (local blacksmith), a class apart and one treated as second-rate citizens. If there is no caste system among Zanskaris or other Buddhist Himalayans, they do consider Moslem butchers and blacksmiths as strangers or outcasts, along with the *beta*, or musicians; these for them are people with limited rights whose daughters and sons are only allowed to intermarry with members of their own groups.

Most of the mining in Tibet used to be performed by Indians, Hindus or Moslems, who paid a relatively small fee to the local district officials, for which they were allowed to mine as much gold as they could over a certain period of time.

Just beyond the copper-bearing river at the entrance to the village of Ralta we came upon a strange circular construction which looked like the hollow base of a tower.

'This is a wolf trap,' Lobsang explained and he showed me how the interior walls curved inwards, and where a ramp of earth led to the outside edge of the circular wall.

'In winter,' he continued, 'a goat is placed inside the trap to attract the wolves, which come up the ramp and jump into the walled enclosure from which they cannot escape. As wolves travel in packs, several are caught at once. Their howling soon attracts attention and they are stoned to death by the villagers.'

The wolves found here are mainly of the white or grey Himalayan variety, for the rare black Himalayan wolf of Zanskar lives in the ranges to the north. Lobsang said that most villages in the area had similar traps. Wolves are a plague in Zanskar and the farmer's worst enemy, preying on his livestock, killing his horses, calves and sheep. In Europe, not so long ago, wolves played a similar role, and through folklore we have inherited a certain atavistic fear of wolves. Wolves in Zanskar reminded man that he shared nature with animals, his rivalry with beasts being the primeval struggle for survival. Today, in the West, it has become a struggle we only conceive of as a fight against, not nature, but other men.

Passing by the few apparently deserted houses of the small hamlet of Rale, we came upon a grassy pasture on which a stone throne was built. This I first took to be a monument erected to greet a great and pious lama when he was on a tour, but it was covered with little piles of white stones. Nordrup explained that it was in fact an altar, and that the white stones were offerings to the divinity who lived in the cliff, at the foot of which the altar throne was erected. Subsequently I saw several such cliff-side shrines or altars, surrounded by low cairns, stones stacked one on top of the other, piles of pebbles built in honour of the mysterious *Lu*, the little-known pre-Buddhist Bon divinities of the Himalayas, secret spirits which inhabit water, rocks and the earth. In Bhutan I had encountered a Bonpo sorcerer who had told me all the names of the demons of the soil, of water and the cliffs and then of their attendants. For two days I had taped this complex list of names which had survived from the ancient magic religion of Central Asia. Most of the names were those of divinities believed to inhabit certain local mountain peaks, others of spirits living inside unusual rock or cliff formations. Today, many Buddhist shrines and monasteries are places that have been converted from the worship of the elusive *Lu* of old.

The Lunak province was literally the land of the black spirits, a primitive and isolated region still haunted by archaic beliefs.

Chasing away the gloom, a ray of late afternoon sun illuminated the green grass that covered the valley's floor. The roaring torrent we had been following had become no more than a small brook flowing through spring fields. The high valley divided and we carried on up its left branch, leaving to our right two villages. Finally, as we entered a broad valley, we saw in the distance the white houses of Kargya, the last village of Zanskar and also the highest. Having with me no precise means of measuring the altitude I could not ascertain its exact altitude, but calculated it could be no lower than 14,500 or 14,600 feet, thus making it one of the very highest villages in the world. Straight up the valley, beyond the village, we could see an incredible granite mountain looking like the bow of some ship ready to plough down on us. This amazing rock rose higher at each step, as we walked past a series of great prayer walls which proclaimed, here at the extreme limit of Zanskar, the faith of the land's inhabitants. Stone after stone, by the thousands, was carved with the invocation '*Om mani padme hum*'.

In the far distance, to the right of the granite spire, rose great snow peaks; somewhere between them lay our objective, the Shingo pass.

I was panting heavily when we reached the first of the thirty houses that compose Kargya. A tall, ruddy-faced farmer came forward and suggested we sleep in his home. I followed him through a low doorway into a dark passage that twisted and turned down a narrow stone corridor which linked the stables and the rooms for goats. At last I reached the living-room – like the stables, it was underground. It was too cold in Kargya to have a summer living-room as elsewhere in Zanskar, and so during the entire year the inhabitants slept in their dim cave-like quarters, the heart of a rabbit warren surrounded for warmth by cattle. A small skylight lit with a pale hue the pit where a family had to burrow itself in for ten months of the year to survive.

Since the living-room was really too gloomy and the corridors too

On the roof of the main assembly hall set in a cave,
the monks of Phugtal read the Kanjur

Wolf trap: a goat is tethered inside, the wolves run up the ramp
and jump in. Unable to get out they are later stoned to death.

Crossing the dangerous river at the foot of the Shingo-la

Coming down the Shingo-la on a trail rarely travelled

Nordrup, the author, and Lobsang on their arrival at Keylang

difficult to negotiate with our baggage, I declined the kind offer of hospitality and after lengthy discussions with other villagers it was decided that we should sleep in the village assembly hall, a neat little building with two rooms, one of which we turned into a kitchen.

That evening, like so many others, though I would have liked to lie down and rest my feet, I felt obliged to set out and climb above the village to investigate the local monastery. So, my heart beating fast from the high altitude, I set out with two villagers to admire their chapel, perhaps also one of the highest buildings in the world. I mention this because I like to think there was some special value in huffing and puffing uphill when, dead tired, I could have stayed at home. The chapel proved uninteresting, its frescos painted anew and with only one image, a sad-looking recent work of art. Yet here, on top of the world, Himalayan man has proclaimed his faith, his sacred traditions, the very thing that makes him human – his belief in man, in the world, in life, in good and evil and in the virtue of wisdom. However poor, however primitive was Kargya, its inhabitants had struggled to build a place of worship. They too believed in a meaning to life beyond the bitter and seemingly fruitless struggle for survival.

Returning to the village I found that most of the population had come over to look at my camp. Girls sat in a row in front of my sleeping bag while the men stood behind waiting respectfully for my return, keen to see a man from another world. Few people must know better the meaning of isolation than these, the most isolated of the Zanskaris, and therefore few could appreciate more the joy of meeting a stranger. I was offered flowers and chang, and then the girls began to sing. Good humour prevailed that evening as I lit the last of my candles for this unplanned farewell party. In turn I was asked to sing and gave a rather pathetic version of '*Auprès de ma blonde*', a song not quite appropriate for the dark-eyed maidens before me. Later there was a dance, and I listened to the shuffle of the big boots and the fluted voices of the young ladies, and I thought of the long chain of hardship and struggle that had in the end made it possible for man to live here. I thought of the trials and tribulations of nomadic wanderers migrating from deserts to the foothills, then from the foothills up to the valleys and finally of man's slow adaptation ending here at Kargya, at the doorstep of heaven in the highest reaches of our globe. Kargya is the end of a long, evolutionary road, of a long struggle against the secret intelligence of nature's laws. Finally man had conquered all the obstacles: the cold, the scarcity of fuel, the absence of wood, of fire and warmth, the insect bites, the teeth of the wolves and the claws of the leopards. He had overcome the worst of hardships to raise his house so that when the day's work was done he could congregate, conscious of his brotherhood with fellow man. When night falls there is nothing better to do but to sing and to love and raise the voice of prayer, melodies that reassure us that we are all the same bewildered animals embarked for eternity.

14

Ecology Zero

Next day as I left Kargya I looked over my shoulder for a long time; I was leaving my own land, for here I had lived a dream I once thought impossible. I had found again a forgotten land where time stands frozen, where people believed their souls to be as real as the feet they walk with, a land where happiness reigns in spite of the worst hardships.

Now before me lay a struggle against nature. As we prepared to tackle the Shingo-la, and the dangers of its arduous trail across the mighty Himalayas, I realised this was to be the test of friendship between Lobsang, Nordrup and myself.

The great summits that we had seen from afar were now almost within reach as before us lay that strange world of rock, eternal snow and ice, a forbidden land into which neither plant nor animal dared venture.

Towards midday we reached the foot of the towering rock peak and the extreme limit of vegetation. Here only wild peas grew, we ate them with pleasure before striding off among great boulders as we listened to the forgotten sound of marmots. Behind a rock I found a parting gift from Zanskar, a blue poppy. With it in my hand and howling with pain from the cold, I forded the glacial waters of the torrent we had followed now for so long. On the right bank I could see the glacier from which it emerged. We stopped to make some tea and eat, then carried on slowly, till we reached a high, lonely chorten. It was the last I was to see. Further up, on the edge of grey frozen rocks, we saw a little stone hut set against a great boulder. Here we spent the night.

Excitement prevailed as we huddled together around a smoky fire of damp dung which burnt only because I had sprayed it generously with kerosene.

'We should leave very early,' said Nordrup, 'for we should have crossed the pass before the sun comes out and melts the snow. What worries me is the crossing of the river, at the foot of the pass. In Kargya they told us that the snow bridge had collapsed. If it has, we will have to ford a big torrent.'

In spite of the cold (we were at 15,000 feet) Lobsang and Nordrup insisted on sleeping outside 'because of the wolves'. They explained that they could then hear if our horses were attacked. I spent all night worrying about my friends out in the cold, and was haunted by visions of glaciers and invaded with the creeping sadness of leaving the 'Land of White Copper'.

At dawn I looked at the sky. Over the pass hung a dark cloud. Lobsang immediately set out to catch the horses. Half an hour later he returned upset; the horses were nowhere to be seen. With Nordrup he set out again, only to return having found no trace of the beasts. I recalled the wolves, but my friends laughed. With an energy I admired, they now set off in opposite directions, appearing later upon the crest of far-away slopes yodelling to each other. Our plans for early departure had fallen through. It was nine o'clock when, after a three-hour search, the horses were found, hidden inside a cave high up the mountain. Had they been chased there by wolves? Nordrup told me that horses often sleep together facing a cliff, thus presenting a row of hooves to possible attackers.

All four ponies were loaded; the packs, now considerably lighter, had been split up between them. Then slowly we set foot on the damp, icy stones of the glacier, edging our way up amid the loose rubble of recent avalanches. There was no trail as the constantly changing face of the mountain, together with the snow, had rubbed out previous traces of a track. I wondered how many people might cross the pass each year, perhaps a dozen, or even fewer now that there was the alternative of leaving Zanskar by the Philtse pass which joined the strategic road over the easier Baralacha pass.

As we reached 16,000 feet, breathing became increasingly difficult. From here, looking up I could see the pass half veiled in clouds that soon rolled down to envelop us in a grey shroud. It began to snow. To the thump of our hearts and the deep sighs of our breath, we slowly placed one foot before the other, finding it an effort even to shout to the ponies. On the first steep slope of snow they had to be guided over one by one; if they had lost their footing it would have meant a slide to death. Beyond the first snow slope we climbed on to a patch of loose stones which covered a glacier whose ice was visible in gaping crevices. Lobsang took the lead, picking his way between the crevices. It was a long, slow climb until we reached snow again, upon a seemingly endless slope that melted into the mist. The horses began to show signs of severe strain, often they stopped, panting heavily like dogs, their heads leaning down to the ground. The poor beasts had already suffered a good deal over the past six days, days in which they had had rarely more than stunted grass to eat. Occasionally one horse would lose its footing and begin to slide backwards; on these occasions nature had taught it to stay motionless until it stopped slipping by itself. On our way up we came to a sudden dip where the ice had collapsed into what was a stream of water that ran under the glacier. To cross this we were obliged to jump a crevice, where to slip would mean sliding under the glacier to a freezing death. For a moment the mist lifted and through the clouds we caught glimpses of the surrounding summits. They were now at eye-level, mysterious and awesome in their cloaks of spotless white pierced with jet-black, ice-covered rock. It was a frigid hell rather than the abode of the gods; the only beauty was the eerie silence in which one could hear, as it were, the creeping of nature and feel the slow formation of the mountains, the primeval thrust of creation. Solitude hung about us as once again I felt the strong bond of friendship that united us in our common effort.

Slowly but noticeably as we struggled up, stopping ever more frequently to catch our breath, the terrain levelled off. For several hundred yards we walked on snow over flat land and then still in mist, as if from nowhere, I heard Nordrup shouting, '*Lha gyalo!*', 'The gods are victorious!' His cry of joy echoed strangely in the mist and was followed by the distant rumble of an avalanche. We had reached the 16,722-foot summit of the pass. There, enveloped in mist and surrounded by snow, stood a low pile of stones supporting what seemed like a little bush of branches to which clung rags of cloth. These were worn-out prayer flags, the mementos of pious travellers who, like us, had toiled up the Shingo-la. We had reached the southern portal of Zanskar over one of the few great Himalayan passes, those strange gates across the world's highest land mass.

To celebrate reaching the summit we decided to eat by the cairn, we unpacked one of our wicker baskets and feasted on tsampa and biscuits.

'From now on it will all be downhill,' I heard myself saying, unaware that the most difficult and dangerous obstacle was to come.

'The name of the pass,' Nordrup explained, 'is derived from *shing-kurr* (meaning carry wood), because to cross it you must carry wood as there is none here, nor dried yak dung or goat dung or any other fuel.'

As we rested after our lunch, a slight wind swept away the mist and revealed that we were actually on the edge of a precipitous cliff that fell to a glacial lake, surrounded by summits from which avalanches crashed down into its cold, blue waters. With the going of the clouds, brilliant sunshine brought life to the jagged summits, illuminating one by one a succession of peaks – the barrier over which we had climbed. To the south I could see nothing as monsoon clouds hung heavily in the air above India, which lay somewhere at my feet; beyond lay an intermediate range that we were to cross later by the 13,500-foot Rotang pass. But that was the pass of another world, one we would cross on wheels.

Reluctantly leaving the splendid grandeur of the Shingo-la we began the terrible descent. Here again there was no track to guide us as we plodded up and down over the bumpy surface of a glacier whose menacing crevices appeared here and there like death traps. In part the glacier was covered with snow, but most of it was stacked with loose, jingling shale, the spill of avalanches being slowly carted away. This rubble rolled at each of our steps, making progress painful and dangerous, especially when suddenly the glacier began to tumble in a near vertical fall. The horses skidded and fell, pawing at the loose rubble or desperately sliding on their rumps. All we could do was shout to steady them. As a result of these falls the loads kept on slipping and had to be readjusted, an operation that was painful with freezing fingers – none of us had gloves. As we struggled on and on we suddenly saw a trail of blood over the stones which we tracked down to the smallest pony, a little grey mare. In falling she had deeply cut a tendon just above her hoof. This called for urgent repair, using bandages from my first-aid kit. Fortunately the horse did not develop a limp and carried on slithering down the glacier with the others. The snow-line was lower on the south face for it received the monsoon clouds in the shape of snow which only rarely, if ever, reached the dry northern face.

At the bottom of the glacier we found ourselves obliged to clamber up another, surrounded by an indescribable chaos of loose rock and ice. When climbing uphill one always dreams of the moment when one will walk down, but now I began to appreciate how tiring this can be, for at every step the body must strain to hold back its weight while one's toes are rammed against the end of one's shoes. During all this journey I had worn the same pair of walking shoes, which now showed serious signs of collapse. The once well-patterned sole was smooth, the seams split, the soles gaping, and yet they had been new when I had put them on for the first time in Kargil. Their condition reminded me that I had covered perhaps four hundred miles, over sharp rocks, since leaving Rangdum monastery.

The second glacier eventually led us to a rocky ridge and then firm land at last. Two hours after leaving the summit I saw between two wet rocks a little yellow flower; we had found vegetation once again. This flower, Lobsang said, was good medicine for the throat. He said that if he mixed it with a blue poppy brewed with a piece of wolfskin, he could make a cure against lumps in the throat. Intrigued, I asked what he understood by lumps and listened while he described what I thought must be a tumour. I thought that possibly the toxic qualities of the blue poppy, rather than the wolfskin, might have a true medicinal value.

Our track now followed the rocky sides of a very steep, enclosed valley lined by tall, snow-covered peaks. Nordrup told me it was still part of Zanskar, which owned 'both sides of the great mountains' and all of this valley until the stream's confluence with a large river, by the side of which we hoped to camp that night. The ownership of this valley meant a lot for the Zanskaris because of grazing rights. I felt certain that the magistrate in Padum was ignorant of this extension of his district to the southern face of the Himalayas, a territorial claim from the days when Zanskar had controlled a larger empire spreading over most of the south-western Himalayas from Tibet to Kashmir.

Amazingly enough the shepherds of Lahoul and Chamba, who grazed their sheep and goats up this valley, still paid a grazing tax to the Lumbo of Teta, the famous lord of the 'Chronicles'.

Upon a ledge above the roaring stream, which carried down the waters from the melting glacier, we discovered two modern tents. As we approached, several Indians clad in khaki came out. They were geologists working for the Survey of India. I had a chat with the leading geologist, who explained they planned, in conjunction with geographers, to map Zanskar and study the geology of its valleys. Was this, I wondered, the thin edge of a wedge that might lead to massive exploitation of Zanskar's mineral wealth? It was ironical and a telling proof of Zanskar's isolation that it had escaped serious attention from geologists until after samples from the surface of Mars had been examined. But these geologists had yet to cross the Shingo-la to study the minerals of what all knew to be called the 'Land of White Copper', a land where gold is also found.

Carrying on down we reached a point where avalanches of snow had completely filled the valley, yet under which flowed the river. This represented the early stages of the formation of a snow bridge and several miles further down I came upon two great arches of snow, bridging the river. These bridges were the result of avalanches blocking the valley every year along the same path, thus accumulating snow so deep that it never melted during the brief summer.

Late afternoon found us exhausted and still plodding down the same valley. Nordrup complained of a headache, while my feet felt like one raw sore from bumping against the toe of my shoes. It then began to rain and fresh water mingling with sweat made me certain that I would die of pneumonia before I reached my destination. But what destination? Was not my heart behind me in Zanskar? The thought then slowly awoke of my family, my children, my country, the yearning for a glass of wine, a bath, food. So many temptations beckoned that I forgot my other self. From that world of bows and arrows, of kings and knaves, of horses and donkeys, of bridges made of twigs and palaces made of earth, of fortresses in cliffs, of divinities in dark chapels, of wild sheep and wolves, of songs and laughter, of blessings and gongs, of conch shells and little bells, of the flutter of prayer flags.

And thus my mind whirled about, torn between nostalgia and anticipation, exhaustion and exhilaration, until at last we reached Zanskar *Sumdo*. 'The three stones of Zanskar' mark the southern frontier at the meeting point of the rushing stream (the one we had been following since its birthplace under the glacier), with a huge, roaring torrent emerging from a broad valley guarded by majestic sentinels.

Just as we reached the confluence Nordrup pointed to my left.

'Look,' he said, 'it is broken.'

I looked and could see nothing until I realised that between two banks of snow on either side of the torrent, a hundred yards before its waters threw themselves into the bigger stream, there had once been a snow bridge. I now understood why Nordrup and Lobsang had been reticent. The snow bridge had collapsed.

We would have to ford the river, or return all the way back to Kargya. The very thought made me feel slightly ill. In the rain we hurriedly unloaded the horses and I set up my tent. I suggested that Lobsang and Nordrup sleep under it but they refused, preferring to sleep out, apparently oblivious of the rain as they had been of snow and frost. Finding the remnants of a wall and checking that the earth was not too damp, they piled the saddles as usual to form a low windbreak, and then, taking a blanket, they spread it over their meagre shelter.

Too tired to graze, the horses just hung about looking haggard, some lying down and the others panting. At rest I slowly began to take in the implications of our situation. It was nearly six o'clock, and it was raining. As a result the two rivers were totally unfordable. Of course the flow would decrease with the freezing of the water running from under the glaciers, and the rain might stop. But would that be enough?

Nordrup and Lobsang and I looked at the rushing mass of silt-carrying foam bounding and swirling down the two rivers. Even if the flow had decreased considerably by dawn, it would still be a very deadly operation to try and get across.

'Can't we backtrack to the last standing snow bridge?' I suggested hopefully.

'No good,' Lobsang answered. 'There is a cliff the other side and no way down.'

'I once lost two mules here,' Nordrup recalled, 'they fell and were swept away like pieces of wood.'

That night I could not sleep as I listened to the rushing torrents, a constant reminder of our problem. Never before had I understood the true meaning of a bridge. Had I gambled and lost? I could not bear the thought of having to return up and over that pass. I was exhausted. One month spent at altitudes over 12,000 feet in endless effort and alertness, to the point that it seemed I had spent a year in Zanskar. One month only, yet what a month with its incredible succession of festivals, the constantly staggering beauty of so many a different valley and vista of peaks, the incredible backdrop of daily life in that little Kingdom called Zanskar.

Fear, anguish and terror haunted my insomnia. I was up as soon as the flaps of my tent showed signs of going grey. My shoes half on, I tripped over to the smaller of the two torrents. My heart sank. It seemed as great as the day before. The white water spitting, rushing, swirling and pouring between rocks as it bounded down.

I walked over to where Lobsang and Nordrup had slept. Peering under their blanket I noticed that they were reciting prayers. Did they also suffer pangs of fear? Had they too spent a night of worry?

'Yes, of course,' Nordrup answered with a smile. My heart warmed to him and Lobsang as I realised how I had abdicated all responsibility to them on this journey. I had not had to worry about who to see, where to camp and where to arrive. Lobsang and Nordrup had taken care of everything, hardly as servants or companions, but as leaders and good friends. They had hosted me as a guest from another land, directing me in and out of the homes of their people, through and over the tortuous trails of their country, enlightening me on my way about all that was dear to themselves and Zanskar; the merriness of festivals, the sadness of disease and old age, and they had revealed their hearts.

Nordrup, who in his arrogant sort of way had overshadowed Lobsang's milder personality, was now to fade before Lobsang's calm professionalism. Together we approached the small torrent, Lobsang carefully inspecting four possible different approaches, explaining how such and such a rock could be reached by throwing oneself in this or that direction. Taking small rocks Lobsang threw them into the river, listening for the little 'click' which would escape the unknowing ear, but which told him whether or not the stone had hit the bottom and where. In this manner he was able to fathom the stream with precision, detecting unsuspected pools or higher rockbeds.

With Nordrup I looked on. We knew our lives were at stake; to stumble and fall would be to die, either by being bashed against the rocks or by hypothermia from the freezing flow. Again and again Lobsang tossed up rocks, listening for the tell-tale click. It did not always come. Nowhere could we cross on foot. His verdict was final.

'Let's look at the larger river,' I suggested, afraid I would have to accept the bitter need to backtrack up the pass. This gave us new hope and we now walked upstream along the bank of the major river, over eighty feet wide. Its flow was evidently lethal, yet two hundred yards from the camp it fanned out between boulder beds. Maybe here each branch would be shallow enough to ford? Once again Lobsang hurled rocks into the river. This time it required all his strength to lob stones far enough.

As I watched him I remembered all the journeys he had undertaken, travelling to Lhasa and all over the Himalayas. I admired his calm assurance.

'Have you some underpants?' was Lobsang's startling query as he came up to me from the river.

'Why yes,' I replied, going to the camp to fetch him a pair.

In a second Lobsang had shed his red robe and stood in a shirt and my underpants in the cold dawn. At once he began to wade out to the first island of gravel. Slowly the water rose to his knees then up to his thighs but no higher. On the island he began again to toss stones into the water, and then returned.

'No, it's too deep,' he commented, 'there is a channel along the edge in which we would get swept away.' Then he moved upstream to where there was but one rocky island in midstream. Repeating his probing tests he called out:

'We can try here. This may be all right.'

So we set off to get the horses and load them. Lobsang had declared that at ten o'clock the river would be at its lowest; there was no hurry. The horses were found perched upon a rocky ledge far above the river. Apparently they had been too tired to graze during the night.

When they were loaded and saddled we set out to where we would try the crossing. I felt sick at the thought that maybe all this was the prelude to a tragedy.

Nordrup now took off his robe and with Lobsang stood like a strange Oriental swimmer with his shirt on. Nordrup had striped underpants I noted as a piece of useless anthropological observation, for monks do not by custom wear anything under their robes in the Himalayas, although in very cold regions in winter they may wear trousers like the laymen wear under their cloaks.

Presently both Lobsang and Nordrup tied around their waists the sashes that had held their gowns. Then, linking arms, they grabbed each other's belts; this done, Nordrup took the bridle of the strongest horse and the three, thus attached, set out across the river.

Horses are known to be great swimmers, but above all they have an incomparable ability that very few of us suspect; a true gift for crossing the fastest and most dangerous rivers. This I was now to witness and saw again in an even more dramatic fashion before the day was over.

Clinging to the horse's bridle and to each other the two men advanced, linked altogether like some strange eight-legged monster with three heads.

The water slowly rose to their waists as they made it to the central island. In awe I stared, retaining with trouble the three other horses which wanted to follow.

From the central island Lobsang and Nordrup proceeded into the dark, frothing waters of the mainstream; to slip here would be fatal. Rapidly they sank as water rose above their waists, the current piling up against their chests, the horse forming a dam, further raising the water-level. The pressure against them was enormous, or so I guessed as they leant to one side, little dark forms fighting against an angry sea. I suffered for them knowing that the water would be numbing their bodies by now, lancing their bones with the deep pain I had so often suffered when crossing smaller streams. Step by step, fumbling blindly for a foothold, they advanced to the middle of the central channel. Here at any drop of the river they would lose their footing and be swept away. Then they began to emerge; the water fell to their waists, they had made it. In a leap the horse jumped free and Lobsang and Nordrup rushed after it. They were over. My heart beat with excitement and joy that they had made it. For an instant I forgot that it was my turn next.

I could see Lobsang and Nordrup running up and down the beach on the far side howling from the effects of the cold. They moved their limbs violently to warm up and then, losing no time, they grabbed the horse again, our largest, a palomino-coloured stallion, and started out back across the river. Knowing its depth and that no unexpected pothole would swallow them up they were soon back on to the island, and wading towards me.

I patted them on the back in admiration. As they were shivering, their legs blue from the cold, we hurriedly grabbed the horses. I rode the stallion while Nordrup took the small grey horse, and Lobsang grabbed the bridle of one of the black ponies and we set off together. Lobsang was now alone in the water but seemed to manage all right. Clutching the saddle I prayed that my horse would not slip; if he did I knew that it would be the end of me. We made the central island without trouble, then struck out across the wide branch of the river. Slowly my shoes and then my ankles went under water; the freezing flow then reached my calves, although I held my legs as high as I could. The stallion advanced very cautiously, slipping a little in the deepest flow. I could feel him strain and lean against the force that beat his flank. The loose pack horse was in front of me and seemed in difficulty as he had lost his footing and began to be swept down. Swimming and thrashing about with his feet he regained his balance and scrambled up the other side. My horse followed and together we safely reached the other bank. In this dramatic way we left the territory of Zanskar.

It was nearly eleven o'clock and we still had a full day's march ahead, one all the more arduous because we were in fact on the wrong side of the river from the usual track. It took a good half hour for the pain in Lobsang's legs to dissipate, after which we struck out across slopes of mighty boulders that fell from a line of peaks that formed the austere sentinels to the nameless torrent we had forded. The roar of water accompanied us as we headed down towards the Bhaga, one of the principal affluents of the Chenab river that runs into India from the southern slope of the Himalayas. Half a mile from where we had crossed, the sole of my shoe parted company with the tattered top; the pair had failed by about thirteen miles to see me to safety. I now put on a pair of tennis shoes and continued down the valley.

Slowly we began to reach a reasonable altitude and I saw three trees. Three wild trees, the first I had seen since leaving Srinagar and crossing the Zoji-la. I was so delighted I took seven photographs of these banal birches that looked to me as they did to Lobsang and Nordrup, like a real forest.

We did not see a house or human being all day; towards evening we reached a roaring torrent that leapt from rock to rock in a near vertical rush to join the main river. A minute bridge made of two thin tree trunks crossed it. To my surprise I saw Lobsang and Nordrup begin to unload the horses. Would we spend the night here, I wondered?

I was still standing on the far bank when Lobsang threw me a long, yak-wool rope which was attached to the smallest of our horses. Lobsang then pushed him into the foaming water, calling out for me to pull. I pulled with all my strength, while the pony, thrashing about like a seal, somehow recovered its stance, swam and stepped across the fierce current to safety. The three larger horses followed in the most staggering demonstration of equine agility I had ever seen. Certainly it must have been this amazing capability of crossing water that had enabled the great herds of wild horses of Central Asia to survive lengthy migrations.

We pitched our last camp on the other side of this stream in a grassy enclosure between great rocks. Travelling had to me, as to my companions, become second nature. Now we sat relaxed around a great fire, our first in many days. As wood was abundant I decided to bake a loaf. Our goal was now close; the following day we would reach the road.

How bitter-sweet the end of such a journey can be in which the satisfaction of having accomplished one's objective, or having reached one's destination safely, mingles with the sourness of the loss of a familiar world. Would I ever again see Lobsang, Nordrup, or his brother Nawang Trile, or for that matter, the King of Zangla, Lobsang's old aunt, the Lama of Thonde, the King of Padum, not to mention the magistrate, all the monks and abbots. The monastery of Karsha, nobly standing upon its slope, that of Bardhan on its tower-like rock, that of Phugtal in its cave; all those hives of humanity praying. Prayer that all may not end in oblivion, that the things that men do should not only live after them but that our souls should carry forever the bliss of a cold sunny morning, the warmth of friendship and the beauty of love. That night the journey ended for me.

What happened later was beyond the realm of that particular dream; I had, once again, found a lost valley hidden in the folds of the Himalayas. A valley, where time stands still. Zanskar, a land 'revealed by the gods', an example and a hope for our modern world.

Epilogue

The following day we rose early and marched down the valley until, reaching an incredible bridge, we crossed back over the river we had forded with such trouble. This bridge, made up of two planks, crossed a canyon a hundred feet deep, down which roared the river. Upon the other bank we came to the first villages of upper Lahoul. Here we had entered the territories of what had been another Tibetan-speaking realm (Karja), alas long ago annexed to British India and having by now lost most of its ancient customs. *Layul*, literally, 'the villages of the gods', is surrounded by verdant luxury. First we saw scraggly juniper trees but soon gigantic fir trees appeared. It was midday when we saw in the distance something I dreaded, the large modern steel and concrete bridge which announces the military road that rises to the Baralacha pass which leads, via Rupshu, to distant Leh, the capital of Ladakh.

Here civilisation began. Four police officers greeted us and soon established that my permit had just expired and therefore held me until they could escort me to Keylang, the district capital some twenty miles down the road. To my anger they treated Lobsang and Nordrup like beggars, although they produced the necessary permits and I was there to vouch for them. Yet such is the little respect shown to the Buddhist of the Himalayas.

Civilisation at last came in the form of a truck. Lobsang and Nordrup had in the meantime left with the ponies, which I saw go with a twinge of sadness. Although animals, they had become now truly familiar and I was sad to see them go. I was to pick up Lobsang and Nordrup on the truck that was taking me to the police station in Keylang, but the Hindu driver, spitting at the Lamaist priest, refused to allow Lobsang on the truck.

Nordrup had jumped on to the back unnoticed and we called out to Lobsang to join us by bus the next morning. Our organised little party that had travelled so far was now breaking up.

The District Commissioner proved quite understanding and agreed to extend my visa. The next day Lobsang appeared and we were at last together again, three foreigners in India speaking Tibetan, looking with surprised eyes at the oddities of civilisation. Lobsang and Nordrup were sneered at by the half-civilised inhabitants of Keylang and the primitive brow-beaten Indians, the bus drivers and contractors who marched in the valley of the gods like conquerors. For it is the Hindus who have inherited the Indian Empire, and who rule today all those territories that the British once controlled by way of shaky alliances. If today there are two imperialistic powers, they are China and India. It is they who share the spoils of Songsten Gampo's great empire and rule Tibet, Sikkim, Lahoul, Zanskar, Spiti, Kulu, Kangra and Ladakh, the land of the gods, the seat of the only civilisation that has dared, and succeeded, in surviving until the second half of our twentieth century unspoilt by Western technology and its accompanying ideals. Proud dynamic lands run by young people and which may yet have many a lesson to teach us. Today, the last survivor in all its purity of that cultural, social and political system is Zanskar.

How long will Zanskar preserve its unique culture? How long will it take before there, too, children will learn to despise their parents as old-fashioned, and then those traditions which made the 'Land of White Copper' the longest-lived Himalayan state will disappear forever?

In Lahoul I looked sadly at the little school children, with their Mongolian faces and Tibetan names, queueing up to watch a showing of the monthly 'Kung-Fu' film. The local monastery was empty.

Eventually Lobsang, Nordrup and I headed for Manali in the Kulu valley. We arrived there exhausted, covered in dust, and depressed. The next morning at five o'clock I took a bus to Delhi. In the eerie light of dawn two monks helped load my luggage, sadly I said goodbye. When the bus roared off, a young European with long hair turned and gave me a strange look.

'Where did you spend your holidays?' he asked.

'Roaming Zanskar,' I answered in Tibetan.

Acknowledgements

I would like to thank here The Honourable Sheikh Abdullah, Chief Minister of Kashmir, for his kind assistance on my various journeys to his State. I wish also to thank Mr Sonam Norbu, Minister for Ladakh, and Mr M. Ashraf of the Directorate of Tourism for their kind help over the years. To the King of Zangla and the rGyalpo of Padum I am indebted for their warm hospitality in the course of my three visits to their land. I am also particularly indebted to Lesley Powell whose collaboration I will never forget.

M P.

Index

Personal and place names have been phonetically rendered throughout the book. The scholar of the Tibetan language will I hope excuse and understand the reason for this concession to clarity at the expense of precision.

M.P.

Index